Preface

This book is intended primarily as a fieldwork manual for students in the sixth form or in their first year at university. It attempts to cover a wide range of techniques for data measurement and analysis which can be readily understood by students with little or no previous fieldwork experience. The book does not set out to be a text on ecological theory, although the reasoning behind the use of each technique is explained.

An individual ecological project now frequently forms part of the coursework at this level. With this in mind, advice is offered to the student on the choosing, planning and carrying out of a project. An entire chapter is devoted to project examples taken from a range of habitats. These will hopefully assist students in devising and carrying out original projects of their own.

G M Williams

Contents

Introduction

Ecology has become one of the most important components in A-level and undergraduate biology courses. Recent changes at A-level have seen the adoption of an agreed common core syllabus by the different GCE Examination Boards. Ecology has emerged to occupy an important linking position in that core syllabus. Greater emphasis is now placed upon fieldwork and its associated techniques than ever before. Examination papers regularly include compulsory data interpretation questions requiring the candidate to analyse the results of fieldwork exercises. Some examination boards, in common with many undergraduate courses, require the submission of an original project. This book attempts to show that there is great scope and potential in fieldwork projects.

Practical ecology textbooks have often dealt with one particular community and prescribed a number of exercises appropriate to it. Others have sought to combine ecological theory with a review of all the major communities in one volume. This book has a different approach: it can either be used as a field manual covering techniques which can be applied to any habitat or else it can be read and worked through in class.

Many of these techniques have been described before in specialist texts which have sometimes been complicated and difficult to read. In this book the emphasis is upon ease of understanding; every technique is described in a step by step fashion, using simple language, diagrams and worked examples where possible. All the methods outlined can be carried out by students with limited time and resources; the use of expensive pieces of apparatus has been avoided. However, the book does take into account the new techniques available for the electronic measurement of environmental factors and the development of computers for data handling and simulation exercises.

Exercises using structured questions are included in the text to involve the student. Many of these are original whilst others are reproduced from recent A-Level examination papers by permission of the Associated Examining Board, Joint Matriculation Board, Welsh Joint Education Committee and University of London School Examinations Department. The final chapter gives outlines of fieldwork projects that have been carried out in a number of different habitats and which have produced interesting results. It is hoped that these suggestions may give the reader ideas for developing an original fieldwork project.

1 Fieldwork projects

1.1 Choosing a project

Making the choice of exactly what you are going to study is the most important and often the most difficult part of any project work. At this stage it is well worth devoting a lot of thought and preparation in order to minimise the problems that may arise when collecting and processing the information. Choose a project which interests and motivates you but at the same time it must be *ecological* in nature. Soil formation and classification, for instance, may form an interesting topic, but unless related to plants and animals it can not be regarded as ecology. Your topic must also be feasible in terms of time, equipment and location. There is little point in planning a study of the growth and distribution of limpets if you can only visit the coast for two weeks a year.

Some important considerations should be taken into account when selecting your project.

1 **Avoid choosing a project which merely ends up proving the obvious.** Certain types of projects have proved to be successful in the past:

a Those that set out to test a particular hypothesis or theory which you yourself propose, e.g. woodlice congregate in dark, damp places during the day because they are susceptible to water loss.

b Those which compare information collected from two different locations, e.g. a study of the invertebrates inhabiting long and short grass. Diurnal, seasonal or long term changes in any one particular habitat can produce interesting information.

c Those which study the growth and distribution of plants and animals in relation to measureable environmental factors, e.g. the effects of soil temperature and pH on earthworm populations.

d Those which investigate the effects of man-made pressures on a particular ecosystem, e.g. the effect of aerial pollution on lichen growth.

e Those which study biotic effects on a particular population, e.g. parasitism of caterpillars by ichneumon wasps.

2 Try to choose a fairly narrow subject. A detailed study of just one stream community may well produce a better project than one which deals superficially with a number of streams. Also avoid the temptation to extend the project into other areas as you proceed with it.

3 Choose a subject that will enable you to collect most of the information yourself. This will make for an original approach which is far more satisfactory than relying on someone else's data.

4 A number of other considerations may influence your final choice. Which parts of your course have particularly interested you? Would any of the other subjects that you are taking be of help? For instance a knowledge of chemistry may be useful when analysing water pollutants. What sort of habitats are available to you for study around your area? Are any of these subjected to any particular urban pressures?

Chapter 8 gives outlines of a selection of projects carried out in some of the major ecological communities of Britain. These may suggest ideas for similar projects and give you some idea of the planning required.

1.2 Planning a project

Before you start to collect any data try to think your project through and anticipate any problems which might arise:

1 Is the habitat that you have chosen to study easily accessible during the period of your investigation? It is advisable to make an initial site survey before you start; this will enable you to familiarise yourself with the habitat and think up new ideas. Will any apparatus, e.g. Longworth traps or minimum and maximum thermometers, remain unmolested during the course of the project?

2 Do you have available all the apparatus that you will need? This book avoids the use of complicated and expensive pieces of equipment but some simple apparatus may need assembling. Equipment such as portable oxygen meters or collecting nets can probably be loaned by most biology departments.

3 Try to work out in advance what you are going to sample and what your sampling strategy will be. Likewise make a decision as to which environmental factors you wish to measure and how you are to do it. Be careful *not* to attempt to collect too much information and *not* to overestimate what can be achieved in the time available. A short preliminary exercise may help you to predict how long the fieldwork will take as well as bringing to light any problems regarding experimental technique. Further advice on planning how you are going to sample is given at the beginning of Chapter 2.

4 Decide how you intend recording your results. The use of suitable tables makes the recording of data clear and readily available for further analysis. How often does the data need to be collected? What about weekends and holidays? You should also think about how the recorded data should be presented in the project write-up. Are tables appropriate, or may be some graphical method such as histograms or pie charts?

5 Before you start you should also consider how to analyse the data collected, especially if this involves statistical techniques. This may affect the sampling programme since some tests of significance require larger sample sizes than others if they are to be representative.

1.3 Carrying out a project

After the planning stage you can commence the project proper. This can be divided up into three stages:

Stage 1   Collecting the data.
Stage 2   Summarising and analysing the data in the form of tables, graphs or by statistics.
Stage 3   Describing *1* and *2* by a written account.

The chapters that follow deal with techniques which cover *1* and *2*. The written account should be concise and written in a logical sequence. It can usefully be divided up into the following sections:

Aims.
Methods used.
Analysis and results.
Discussion.
Data appendices.
Bibliography (books or articles used).

Another hurdle in project work is the interpretation of the results obtained. Are the results reliable? How do they stand up to a comparison with similar work already documented? It is very unlikely that your fieldwork project could be completely original, so read through some suggested texts to gain a background knowledge of the topic. This may also suggest ideas for further investigation. At the end of the discussion the main deductions should be clearly set out in summary form. Also see Tricker B J K and Dowdeswell W H (1970) *Projects in biological science, Nuffield Advanced Science*, Penguin Education.

Illustrations can add much to the account and should be integrated into the text, labelled, numbered and referred to in the written account.

Safety in fieldwork

All fieldwork holds potential dangers even when carried out in a familiar location. An initial reconnaissance of the area to be studied may well reveal any potential hazards before commencing the project. Commonsense precautions should always be taken, no matter how remote the risks may appear. Reference should be made to the Health and Safety at Work Act, 1974, and essential reading is Nichols D (1983), *Safety in biological fieldwork, Guidance notes for codes of practice*, Institute of Biology, London. Warm waterproof clothing should be worn in anticipation of adverse weather conditions; similarly protective footwear should suit the terrain that is likely to be encountered. Mountain and upland moorland areas present special problems and are often beset with unsuspected hazards. Students working in remote habitats should always group themselves into a party supervised by a person in possession of the Mountain Leadership Certificate (*Safety on Mountains* (British Mountaineering Council) is essential reading). Plan well before attempting any fieldwork in such locations: prepare a checklist of requirements, develop a working knowledge of basic first aid and practice the interpretation and use of Ordinance Survey maps and compasses. Exercise particular care when sampling from coastal or inland waters. This kind of fieldwork is dealt with more specifically on page 80.

1.4 Background

The nature of an ecological project will fall into one of two categories: *autecology* or *synecology*. Autecology involves the study of a single plant or animal species, e.g. the population dynamics of gall midges. This type of investigation will be concerned with population size and growth and may examine the effects of certain factors on these, e.g. food resources, predation, parasitism or competition.

Synecology on the other hand deals with the study of communities, e.g. the plants and animals found in a certain habitat, their interrelationships with each other (*biotic* factors) and with the habitat itself (*abiotic* factors). The study of the trophic structure of a stream community may involve the measurement of various physical and chemical variables which are then correlated with the abundance of the plant and animal species. In such an investigation try to avoid attempting too much identification of species since this can prove to be difficult and time consuming. It is far better to limit your study to the distribution of about six readily identifiable species.

Autecology

An autecological study confines itself to one particular species of animal or plant looking at its distribution and levels of growth. Looking at the effects of various physical factors upon the distribution of a plant or animal species may prove to be a stimulating exercise, e.g. the distribution of the water louse, *Asellus*, in relation to the presence of calcium ions in the water, or the effects of light on the distribution of dog's mercury, *Mercurialis perennis*. Numerous similar projects could be devised measuring the physical factors and estimating the distribution and abundance of the particular species in the field, processing the information and examining any possible correlation.

Methods of estimating population size are dealt with in the next chapter and enable variations in density of the species to be studied seasonally or over a longer duration. Investigations could be carried out into the biotic factors which influence the size of a population, such as food supply, (e.g. the density of symphylids with variation in humus content of the soil). Interaction between species has often been studied in the past, e.g. competition between two barnacle species *Chthalamus montagui* and *Semibalanus balanoides*, the effects of parasitism on the holly leaf miner or predation by the caterpillars of the oak-leaf roller moth, *Tortrix viridana*. Investigations into the causes of variations in the distribution and abundance of a particular species form the basis of many successful projects and allow the student to attempt a detailed study focussing his attention upon a specific problem.

Synecology

Projects investigating communities often attempt a quantitative estimation of the abundance of organisms at each trophic level. Fundamental to *all* communities is the primary production carried out by green plants during photosynthesis.

These *primary producers* provide food for the herbivorous animals (Fig 1.1) or *primary consumers* which in turn are eaten by the carnivores or *secondary consumers*. In some cases tertiary consumers feed upon the secondary consumers. This sort of feeding relationship can be shown by a *food chain*, e.g.

Phytoplankton ⟶ barnacle ⟶ dog-whelk ⟶ gull
(primary   (primary   (secondary   (tertiary
producer)   consumer)   consumer)   consumer)

Fig 1.1 Herbivory on leaves of hazel (*Corylus avellana*)

Decomposers such as bacteria and fungi are responsible for the breakdown of dead and waste organic matter and the consequent re-cycling of nutrients for uptake by plants.

Our food chain oversimplifies things since the relationships between the different trophic levels in a community can be complex. This complexity is more accurately summarised by a food web (Fig 1.2). Observed feeding habits of animals along with an examination of mouth parts and/or gut contents enables us to place them in the correct trophic level in the community. We can represent the relationships between the different trophic levels in a quantitative manner by the use of pyramids. *Pyramids of numbers* reflect the feeding relationships between different individuals within a community (Fig 1.4).

Fig 1.3 Small bumble bee feeding on nectar of yellow archangel (*Galeobdolon luteum*)

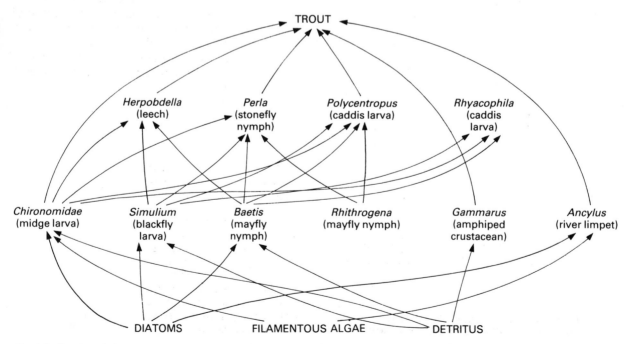

Fig 1.2 Food web for a stream community (after Badcock, from Russell-Hunter 1970)

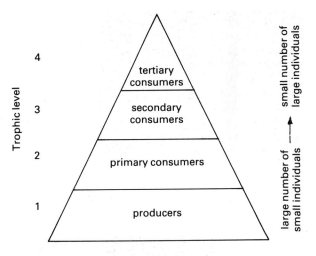

Fig 1.4 Pyramid of numbers

Pyramids of biomass are based upon the total amount of living material at each trophic level at any one time (Fig 1.6). They are often represented by dry weight measurements in g/m² but only reveal the amount of material at a particular time, i.e. the *standing crop*. This gives no indication of the rate at which material is produced and used up, i.e. the *productivity*.

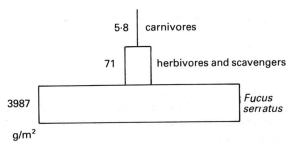

Fig 1.6 Biomass pyramid for a rocky shore community dominated by the saw wrack (*Fucus serratus*)

They are essentially bar charts, the length of each bar proportionate to the numbers of organisms at a particular trophic level. The organisms at the base of the pyramid (primary producers) are relatively abundant and of small size. As we go up the pyramid from one trophic level to the next, the numbers of organisms decrease and their size increases. Pyramids of numbers fail to distinguish between the sizes of different organisms. For instance it is not very informative to equate one oak tree with one grass plant since the tree can obviously support far more primary consumers (Fig 1.5). When primary producers are few and large the pyramid takes on a different form and if parasites are involved the end result may be an inverted pyramid.

For instance the standing crop of phytoplankton in a lake is small but because these plants have a high turnover rate their production is high. A grazed field will also have a low standing crop which underrepresents its high productivity. For this reason *pyramids of energy* are often more useful since they show the rate of energy flow or productivity at successive trophic levels in a given area over a fixed period of time. Energy pyramids reveal the efficiency of energy transfer from one trophic level to the next, and since only a proportion of the energy is passed on, they are never inverted. Estimating productivity is a difficult proposition, however, since one needs to be able to measure the rate of production and consumption of material at each trophic level (Fig 1.7).

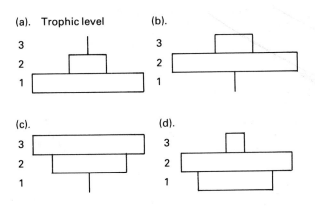

(1 = primary producers, 2 = primary consumers, and 3 = secondary consumers)

Fig 1.5 Some pyramids of numbers

In Figure 1.5, (a) is a pyramid with many small primary producers, e.g. grass, (b) with one large primary producer, e.g. an oak tree, (c) is an inverted pyramid involving parasites, e.g. a rose tree fed upon by aphids which support their own parasites, and (d) is a pyramid where the primary producers are small in number but have a high turn over rate, e.g. phytoplankton, zooplankton, and fish.

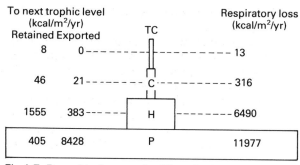

To next trophic level (kcal/m²/yr)			Respiratory loss (kcal/m²/yr)
Retained	Exported	TC	
8	0		13
46	21	C	316
1555	383	H	6490
405	8428	P	11977

Fig 1.7 Pyramid of energy for Silver Springs, Florida, USA (after Odum, 1957, courtesy of Ecol. Monogr.)

Energy flow through a community

As we have seen the dynamic concept of a community involves the transfer of energy from one trophic level to another. The sun is the ultimate source of this energy but very little of this light energy becomes available for photosynthesis and subsequent conversion into plant and animal tissue. About 90% of the energy reaching the earth's surface is reflected or absorbed and radiated as heat. The remaining 10% may be utilised by green plants and converted into food energy. The rate at which photosynthetic products are produced is known as the *gross primary productivity*. However, a large amount of the organic matter fixed as a result of gross primary productivity is used up in plant respiration. The remainder is termed net primary production and the rate at which photosynthetic products accumulate as plant tissue is termed the *net primary productivity*.

Net primary production represents potential food for primary consumers. However, nothing like all of the stored chemical energy becomes available to the primary consumers. Large losses of energy occur at each trophic level as a result of respiration and in the form of faeces and urine, and consequently only a small part (about 10%) of the original plant production ends up in animal tissue (Fig 1.8). The proportion of the available energy passed on to the next level varies: wastage by primary consumers may result from only part of the available plant material being eaten, some may be egested unchanged and, as mentioned, a large proportion goes to energise the herbivores' own metabolic process. Similar wastage occurs between subsequent trophic levels, all energy being eventually dissipated as heat.

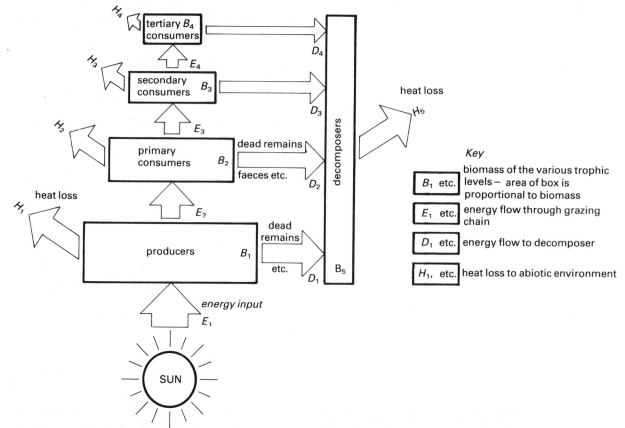

Fig 1.8 Energy flow through an ecosystem (after Jenkins)

Decomposers do not often appear on food chains, webs or ecological pyramids and yet their presence is of vital importance in energy transformation and in the re-cycling of nutrients. Energy is not re-cyclable but organic material is. The activities of decomposers such as bacteria and fungi convert the dead remains of animals and plants and organic waste materials into mineral nutrients which may be absorbed and utilised by green plants. Chapter 4 contains project suggestions for studying the activities of these decomposer organisms.

1.5 Exercises

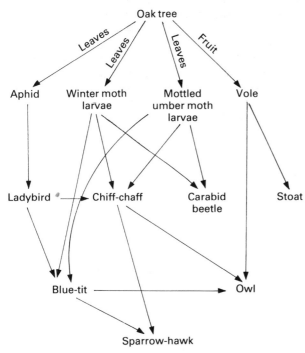

1 The diagram shows some of the feeding relationships in a British oak wood.
a i) Name the source of energy for *all* the organisms in this food web.
   ii) Name *three* substances which the oak tree could obtain from the environment and which would contribute to its structure.
b From the diagram, select
   i) one carnivore,
   ii) one producer, and
   iii) one food chain which includes *four* different organisms.
c Draw a simple diagram to compare the likely numbers of each of the species in the food chain which you have selected in b (iii).

d Explain how energy is lost to the environment from the food web.
e In some years there are exceptionally large numbers of winter moth and mottled umber moth larvae. Describe two probable effects of this on other organisms in the food web.
f Each autumn the oak trees shed their leaves. Explain how the elements contained in the cellulose in the leaves are made available for the growth of trees in subsequent years. (JMB O-level 1982)

2 Table 1 gives data from a simple food chain.

Table 1

	Number of individuals per unit area	Mean dry mass (g) per individual	Energy content (kJ g^{-1} dry mass)
Lettuces	10 m^{-2}	52	18.9
Slugs	24 m^{-2}	0.63	12.6
Thrushes	20 ha^{-1*}	60	23.5

*ha = hectare (10 000 m²)

a i) To which trophic level do slugs belong?
   ii) Outline *briefly* how each of the following might have been obtained.
      A The number of slugs.
      B The number of thrushes.
      C The energy content of the lettuces.
b The relationship between the various trophic levels can be investigated in three ways: by analysing the numbers, biomass and energy content per unit area.
   i) Using the information in Table 1, calculate the missing figures in Table 2 below. These relate the data to one square metre of the lettuce field. Copy the table and write the figures in the spaces provided.

Table 2

	Number per m²	Biomass (g) per m²	Energy content (kJ) per m²
Lettuces	10		
Slugs	24		
Thrushes	0.002		

The values you have calculated in Table 2 can be used to construct ecological pyramids. The pyramids of numbers, biomass and energy constructed from these figures are of different

shapes or proportions. Account for the differences in shape or proportion between
ii) the pyramid of numbers and the pyramid of biomass;
iii) the pyramid of biomass and the pyramid of energy.   (JMB 1984)

3   The energy content of a grassland has been estimated for each trophic level as follows:

	KILO-JOULES* PER SQUARE METRE
primary producers	5033
herbivores	122
omnivores	12
carnivores	10

*1 kilo-calorie is equivalent to 4.2 kilo-joules.

a   Comment on the biological significance of these data.
b   What is meant by 'primary producer' in this habitat?
c   Discuss the factors that would affect the net production of the grassland's primary producers.
d   The table below gives figures for two species of arthropod that live in the same grassland habitat. Plot graphs to show the numbers of each species against time.

| TIME (WEEKS) | NUMBERS OF INDIVIDUALS | |
	Species A	Species B
1	0	50
2	5	100
3	50	500
4	100	1000
5	500	2000
6	2100	1000
7	800	400
8	400	80
9	10	50
10	50	500
11	150	1000
12	500	2000

e   What deductions can be made from the graphs concerning the biological interrelationships of the two species? Outline an experiment which might be carried out to provide further information in support of your deductions.   (London: January 1977)

Part A

Collecting the information

A major portion of the time allocated to an ecology project will be spent on data collection. The information required will depend upon the individual nature of the project in question but it will very likely require estimations of both the biotic and abiotic components of the ecosystem. We may well have to sample the animal and plants in order to gain an estimate of their total population size; likewise the measuring of environmental factors such as temperature, light or oxygen concentration may be relevant. Much thought and planning is required before starting to collect your information: there is no point in assembling masses of data much of which may have no useful application in your particular investigation. Also data collection has to be realistic in terms of time and resources and should not be destructive to the environment.

P C H Rogers

2 Collecting and sampling techniques

2.1 Before you start

Most projects and exercises in practical ecology will involve the collecting of living organisms with a view to their subsequent identification and estimation. For this to be successful the techniques used must be appropriate to the ecological community being studied. You will need to have the most effective apparatus (though not too expensive) and know how to use it properly. You must also work out your sampling strategy beforehand in order to make the best use of the time available to you. Before going into the field it is useful to ask yourself some questions about the collecting and sampling techniques you intend to use:

Will the techniques and apparatus be suitable for the collection of the organisms in question?

Are the techniques to be quantitative and will they be easily repeatable?

Is it possible to complete the work in the time available?

Will the work be needlessly laborious?

Are you aware of the limitations of the apparatus and techniques that you are using?

Will the activity of collecting and sampling cause harm to the environment?

With the latter point in mind it is important in the interests of conservation of the environment that certain commonsense procedures be followed when collecting in the field:

1   **The numbers of individual animals and plants collected should be kept to a minimum.** Depending upon the nature of the exercise one or two specimens may well suffice. Alternatively, if a quantitative study is to be attemped in order to estimate the population of a particular species, then the number of samples taken should be strictly limited.

2   **As far as possible all organisms removed during the exercise should be returned to their original habitat after study.** Even dead organisms can be eaten by others within the ecosystem.

3   **Repeated collecting at the same site can have an adverse effect** upon the density of plant and animal species within the community in question.

4   **Damage to the habitat during the collecting process should be avoided at all costs** as this will inevitably have an adverse effect upon the organisms found there. So when collecting shore animals, upturned rocks should be replaced in their original position. Failure to do so will result in death by desiccation of hydroids, sponges and sea squirts normally found underneath the rock. Perhaps more obvious harm to the environment is the erosion suffered in sand dunes as a direct result of trampling by humans.

In general collecting and sampling plant communities poses few problems for the investigator. They tend to be conspicuous, needing light as they do for photosynthesis. Animals on the other hand are often hidden or camouflaged to avoid detection and many are active only at night. Clearly different sampling techniques will need to be employed for animal populations.

2.2 Problems in identification?

The identification of plants and animals down to species level can be difficult and very time consuming. Tracing the scientific name of one organism may well take the investigator a disproportionate amount of time at the expense of other aspects of the exercise undertaken. It is often more productive to concentrate the project on the distribution of five or six readily identifiable species. 'Species-poor' habitats such as heathlands and salt-marshes have much to recommend them since their low species diversity facilitates ease of identification. Access to a good range of literature is essential when attempting to identify an organism and the bibliography cites many of these. Matching the specimen with illustrations encourages observational skills but has its drawbacks, e.g. colour is often a poor criterion for identifying an organism. The best alternative is to use a diagnostic key, which by a series of stages each requiring observations and decisions, enables the user to arrive at the correct scientific name. Identification aids are common for such groups as trees, wild flowers and birds but sparse for others such as polychaetes, liverworts and nematodes. New material is being produced all the time notably by the AIDGAP Project of the Field Studies Council, the Linnean Society (Synopses of the British Fauna) and the Freshwater Biological Association. A concise and easy to use key takes much of the tedium out of the identification process and releases the investigator to pursue other aspects of the project.

2.3 Why sample?

It is seldom possible to count all the individual animals or plants within a given population ('population' being the total number of a particular species in a definite area, e.g. in the bottom of a pond). This would not only be extremely laborious and time consuming, but would almost certainly involve disturbance and damage to the habitat and population we wish to study. When sampling we aim to select for study a small representation of the total population. In order to sample such a population the area must be divided up into sampling units of equal size. These sampling units must be distinct, must not overlap and together they make up the total population. The sampling unit may be a 0.25m² area of grassland, a core of soil of diameter 6 cm × 8 cm deep, or if sampling for caterpillars, one individual leaf of a certain area. As well as being of an equal size, the units in the sample must be chosen at random from the whole population. Rarely is it possible to remove all the sampling units from a population. Instead a group of units is selected and hopefully they will be representative of the whole population. The number of individuals of a species in each sampling unit is then counted or estimated and from this information is gained about the frequency and distribution of that species in the population as a whole.

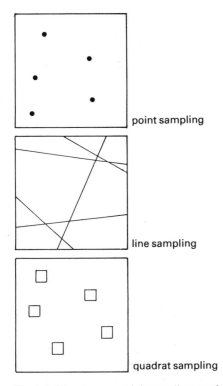

point sampling

line sampling

quadrat sampling

Fig 2.1 The three spatial sampling methods

2.4 Spatial sampling methods

When sampling to discover the diversity and relative abundance of animals and plants in an area three methods are commonly used.

Point sampling Individual points are chosen on a map and the organisms sampled at those points.

Line sampling Lines are drawn across the map and the organisms occuring along the line sampled.

Quadrat sampling Sampling units or quadrats are used to choose squares on the sample area. The occurrence of organisms within these squares is noted.

Random sampling

But how do we decide where to locate our points, lines or quadrats? One way is to throw the quadrat for instance over one's shoulder and collect the information from the place where it lands. But does this achieve randomness or will there be some human bias? Clearly true random selection is difficult to achieve and the most reliable method involves the use of a table of random numbers to select where we sample. There are three commonly used methods and to illustrate these we will use in each case the example of an area composed of two rock types (*A* and *B*) on which we wish to sample the vegetation. We will use the point sampling method but it would have been possible to use the line or quadrat methods instead.

1 Simple random sampling

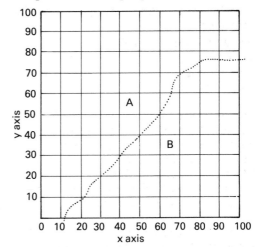

Fig 2.2 An area of land with two rock types, A and B. The map is covered by a grid

a Before sampling, the area to be studied has to be divided up into sampling units of equal area (Fig 2.2). The *x* and *y* axes can be marked out by two 30 m tapes at right angles to each other.

b Decide how many sample points you want.

c Refer to the random number tables (page 146). These are compiled so that the numbers are totally random in their ordering. Read the instructions on how to use them.

d Use the random number tables to give *x* and *y* co-ordinates. When starting off in the top left-hand corner of the table on page 146 the first pair of numbers is 20 17. Thus we take 20 as the *x* coordinate and 17 as the *y* coordinate to plot the point on Figure 2.3. This procedure is repeated to obtain twenty points.

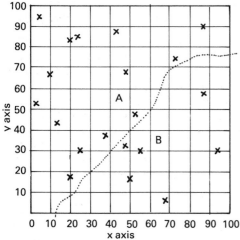

Fig 2.3 Random sampling, points method. 20 points are plotted on the map at random

e Each point on the actual sample area can be located either by pacing or measuring with a tape. When quadrat sampling with this method be consistent by always locating the bottom left-hand corner of the quadrat at the point where the coordinates meet. An estimate of percentage cover of each plant species within the quadrat may then be attempted.

2 Stratified Random Sampling

In this method the area is divided into subsets and the separate random samples are drawn for each subset. Stratified random sampling may well be appropriate to our example since there are two different rock types and the vegetation we wish to sample is very likely influenced by the underlying rock. Using simple random sampling we might be unlucky enough to get all our sample points on just one of the rock types and this would result in bias. It is desirable to get a complete cover of the whole area with a proportionate number of sample points occurring on each rock type. The method is as follows:

a Decide how many subsets you need. In our example there are two rock types and therefore we need two subsets.

b Decide how many sample points you need. In our example we have chosen to sample twenty points.

c Divide the number amongst the strata in proportion to their importance. In our example rock type

A takes up 60% of the area and will thus receive 60% of the sample points, i.e. twelve points (Fig 2.4). The other eight points will be allocated to rock type *B* which takes up 40% of the area.

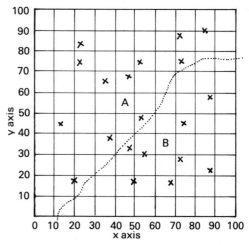

Fig 2.4 Stratified random sampling. 20 points are plotted on the map, 40% (8 points) in area B which is 40% of the total area.

d Proceed as for simple random sampling (stages *b–e*). Do not allow any more than the allocated number of points to fall on each stratum. Ignore any excess points which may arise.

3 Systematic aligned sampling

In this method the sample points are located in a regular or systematic fashion across the map or area. The method is simple:

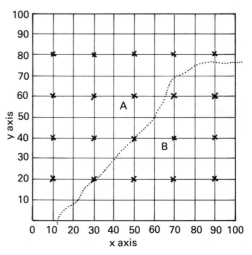

Fig 2.5 Systematic aligned sampling. 20 points are plotted on the map in a regular fashion

a Decide how many sample points you need.

b Place these points regularly over the map (Fig 2.5).

c As in stage *e* in simple random sampling the plants present at each point are identified and in the case of quadrat work their abundance estimated.

The advantages of this method are that it ensures a complete cover of the area (like stratified random sampling) and is simple to do.

2.5 Quadrats

These have been used extensively in determining the distribution of plant communities (Fig 2.6) but can also be used with slow moving invertebrates such as those which occur in leaf litter or in intertidal habitats. Quadrats are sampling units of a known area. They usually take the form of a rectangular frame and come in a variety of dimensions. When using a quadrat it is assumed that its contents will be representative of the whole sampling area.

Fig 2.6 Recording local frequency of plant species in grazed upland grassland, Cwm Idwal

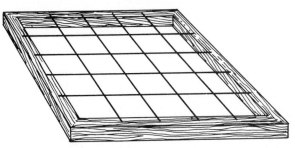

Fig 2.7 A frame quadrat: 0.5 m wooden frame with wires fixed at 10 cm intervals

Large quadrats can be laid out using string and pegs as in the case of sampling grassland and woodland communities. More commonly used are the 1 m² and 0.25 m² frame quadrats. These are easily constructed out of wood with cross wires or strings subdividing them at 10 cm intervals for ease of counting (Fig 2.7). 0.25 m² collapsible quadrats are available commercially and 0.0625m² quadrats are often used in determining the distribution of lichens and mosses on tree trunks and walls. The use of quadrats poses three problems for the ecologist:

What size of quadrat should be used?

How many quadrats in each sampling area?

Where should the quadrats be positioned within the sampling area?

(The location of quadrats was considered on page 11 using random numbers for plotting *x* and *y* coordinates.) Let us consider the other two problems.

What size quadrat?

If the dispersion, (i.e. way in which the individuals are arranged in space) of a population within the sampling area is truly random then all quadrat sizes would be equally efficient in the estimation of that population. However, the spatial dispersal of a population is seldom random or regular. An aggregated distribution (Fig 2.8) is more likely, with individuals found in patches (since many environmental factors will be unevenly distributed within a sampling area).

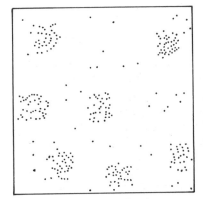

Fig 2.8 An aggregated distribution

A small quadrat has generally been found to be more efficient than a large one when the dispersal of the population is aggregated. The reasons given are:

1 More small samples can be taken for the same amount of labour.

2 Since many small quadrats cover a wider range of habitat than a few large ones, the sample will be more representative.

3 Statistical error will be reduced as a sample of many small units will have more degrees of freedom than a sample of a few large units (see Chapter 7). Although a small quadrat may be theoretically best there are practical considerations which will set a lower limit on the size. Thus when sampling in a wood a small quadrat may undersample the dominant species of tree. In addition, the smaller the quadrat the greater the sampling error at its edges – are the plants on the edges of the quadrat to be included or not?

To determine the optimum quadrat size for a particular type of vegetation, a series of quadrats of increasing size are laid out. The cumulative number of plant species counted after each successive increase in quadrat size is then recorded, e.g.

Quadrat Size	Total number of species
0.25	11
1	15
4	20
8	22
16	24

Eventually a point is reached where a further large increase in quadrat size results in only a few extra species. Since the common species will have already been included the extra time and effort required in recording very large quadrats is unproductive. The optimum quadrat size is reached when a 1% increase in quadrat size produces no more than a 0.5% increase in the number of species present.

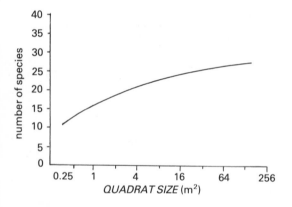

Fig 2.9 Graph to determine the optimum quadrat size (after Hall)

How many quadrats?

As we have seen the dispersal of many species is aggregated so that a large variation can be expected when sampling natural populations. In order to make our results statistically significant a large number of samples should be taken. However, sorting and counting all the species in a very large sample can be tedious and time consuming. A similar exercise enables us to estimate the optimum number of quadrats required when studying the species composition of a particular site. A series of quadrats of satisfactory minimum size are placed randomly across the sampling area. The cumulative number of species is recorded after each increase in quadrat number used, e.g.

Number of Quadrats	Total number of species
1	14
4	34
8	37
16	40

Eventually a point is reached when all the common species have been identified and a further increase in quadrat number will not merit the time and effort required. A satisfactory minimum number of quadrats is reached when a 1% increase in the number of quadrats produces no more than a 0.5% increase in the number of species found.

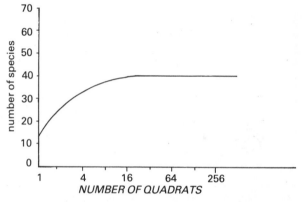

Fig 2.10 Graph to determine the optimum number of quadrats (after Hall)

2.6 Measurements of abundance

Quadrats are useful when attempting to identify the species composition of a particular community and for making a quantitative assessment of the abundance of those species. The four measurements of abundance most often used are **density, frequency, biomass** and **cover**.

Density The mean number of individuals per unit area. Although objective, the assessment of density can be laborious and time consuming if the size or number of sampling units used is large.

Frequency The number or percentage of sampling units in which a particular species occurs. This gives an indication of the dispersion of a species within the sampling area and is rapidly assessed.

Biomass This is a measure of the dry weight of plants and animals in a certain area at a particular time. Since this requires harvesting it is inevitably destructive and the sorting, drying and weighing of individuals can be time consuming.

Cover The percentage of the ground covered by a species within the sampling unit. This overcomes the need to count all the individuals in a certain area as in the case of density estimation. It is particularly useful when estimating the abundance of species which are not easily distinguishable as individuals, e.g. mosses, lichens, sponges.

Abundance scales

A subjective estimate of abundance may be obtained by identifying each species within the sampling area and assessing it on a five point DAFOR scale:

D–Dominant   A–Abundant   F–Frequent
O–Occasional   R–Rare

This method is usually only employed when a large area of vegetation is being studied. It has many drawbacks arising from the subjective nature of the assessment; also a superficial survey may miss out altogether some of the rarer plants.

Other abundance scales make use of percentage cover and are more objective than the DAFOR scale. They are also far quicker and more readily repeatable than direct counts: Figure 2.11 shows two commonly used scales which assign percentage cover to a class for ease of recording.

Class	Domin Scale	Braun–Blanquet Scale
/ +	A single individual	(<1%)
1	Scarce, 1–2 individuals	(1–5%)
2	(<1%)	(6–25%)
3	(1–4%)	(26–50%)
4	(4–10%)	(51–75%)
5	(11–25%)	(76–100%)
6	(26–33%)	
7	(34–50%)	
8	(51–75%)	
9	(76–90%)	
10	(91–100%)	

Fig 2.11 Two abundance scales which make use of percentage cover

Figure 2.12 shows abundance scales for some common intertidal organisms making use of the following categories:

Ex – Extremely abundant F – Frequent
S – Super abundant   O – Occasional
A – Abundant   R – Rare
C – Common

Notice that the symbols need to be redefined for each species depending upon the size of the organism. Thus $10–50\,cm^{-2}$ for dog-whelks would be classed as 'extremely' abundant but for the much smaller barnacles to be 'abundant' they must occur in relatively far greater numbers of $100–299\,cm^{-2}$.

Algae
E	More than 90% cover
S	60–89% cover
A	30–59% cover
C	5–29% cover
F	Less than 5% cover but zone still apparent
O	Scattered plants, zone indistinct
R	Only one or two plants present

Small barnacles and small winkles
E	500 or more $0.01\,m^{-2}$
S	300–499 $0.01\,m^{-2}$
A	100–299 $0.01\,m^{-2}$
C	10–99 $0.01\,m^{-2}$
F	1–9 $0.01\,m^{-2}$
O	1–99 m^{-2}
R	Less than 1 m^{-2}

Large barnacles *Balanus perforatus*
E	300 or more $0.01\,m^{-2}$
S	100–299 $0.01\,m^{-2}$
A	10–99 $0.01\,m^{-2}$
C	1–9 $0.01\,m^{-2}$
F	1–9 $0.1\,m^{-2}$
O	1–9 m^{-2}
R	Less than 1 m^{-2}

Mussels and piddocks (score holes)
E	More than 80% cover
S	50–79% cover
A	20–49% cover
C	5–19% cover
F	Small patches, covering less than 5% of the rock surface
O	1–9 individuals m^{-2}: No patches
R	Less than 1 individual m^{-2}

Lichens and *Lithothamnion*
E	More than 80% cover
S	50–79% cover
A	20–49% cover
C	1–19% cover
F	Large scattered patches
O	Widely scattered patches, all small
R	Only one or two small patches present

Limpets and large winkles
E	20 or more $0.1\,m^{-2}$
S	10–19 $0.1\,m^{-2}$
A	5–9 $0.1\,m^{-2}$
C	1–4 $0.1\,m^{-2}$
F	5–9 m^{-2}
O	1–4 m^{-2}
R	Less than 1 m^{-2}

Dogwhelks, topshells and anemones
E	10 or more $0.1\,m^{-2}$
S	5–9 $0.1\,m^{-2}$
A	1–4 $0.1\,m^{-2}$
C	5–9 m^{-2} locally sometimes more
F	1–4 m^{-2} locally sometimes more
O	Less than 1 m^{-2}, locally sometimes more
R	Always less than 1 m^{-2}

Tube worms such as *Pomatoceros*
A	50 or more tubes $0.01\,m^{-2}$
C	1–49 tubes $0.01\,m^{-2}$
F	1–9 tubes $0.1\,m^{-2}$
O	1–9 tubes m^{-2}
R	Less than 1 tube m^{-2}

Fig 2.12 Abundance scales for some common Littoral organisms (from Chalmers N and Parker P, 1986)

Point quadrats

Estimating percentage cover by means of a frame quadrat has a high subjective element. The point quadrat was developed to give an objective assessment of cover and gives reliable results for low growing vegetation. The apparatus consists of a free standing frame with a row of ten sliding pins, the points of which can be lowered down onto the vegetation (Fig 2.13). As each point is lowered to the ground, a record is kept of the number of times out of ten (there being ten pins) that each species of plant is touched, i.e. the number of *hits*. The number of point quadrats used is dependent upon the same considerations taken into account when using frame quadrats. The most convenient number per sampling area is ten, thus giving the number of units per 100 points.

$$\text{Percentage cover} = \frac{\text{Hits}}{\text{Hits} + \text{misses}} \times 100$$

Let us say that there we use 15 point quadrats per sampling area and that the number of hits for one particular species is 20. The total number of hits and misses will be 150 (since each quadrat has 10 points),

$$\text{therefore percentage cover} = \frac{20}{150} \times 100 = 13.3\%$$

The placing of point quadrats within the sampling area may be done by using random coordinates as for frame quadrats. If the percentage cover values for the different species recorded are added together, the total often exceeds 100%. This is because a pin may well touch more than one species on the way down. If the same species is hit more than once by the same pin it only counts as one hit. As in the case of the frame quadrat, a point quadrat could easily be constructed out of wood. A horizontal bar, drilled with ten equidistant holes through which long knitting needles slide, could be supported by some tripod arrangement.

Permanent quadrats have been used to study the long term changes in the composition of different plant communities. Their size will vary with the nature of investigation, large; quadrats or plots may be marked out with pegs. Permanent quadrats can be visited at regular intervals for seasonal effects, e.g. the appearance and disappearance of annuals within the sample area studied. A point quadrat is the best means of estimating the species composition and distribution on these experimental plots. Records could also be kept of relevant environmental parameters, e.g. soil temperature and pH, water content, light estimation. Plots could be treated in different ways, e.g. different mowing or grazing regimes, different fertiliser applications, treatment with different doses or types of herbicides (see Exercise 5).

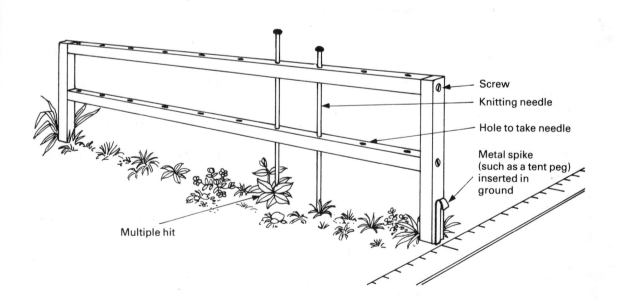

Screw

Knitting needle

Hole to take needle

Metal spike (such as a tent peg) inserted in ground

Multiple hit

Fig 2.13 Home-made point quadrat frame

a Determine the cover value for each of the three species shown in the quadrat in Figure 2.14.
   Do this by counting the number of sample points (*hits*) touching each species, expressed as a percentage.

b When using a point quadrat, explain why the cover values for the different species may exceed 100% when added together.

c Explain why cover values, obtained by using a point quadrat, may well underrepresent tall, erect species such as the moor rush, *Juncus squarrosus*.

d How might cover and biomass estimates differ for a tall, erect species such as *Juncus*?

2.7 Transects

The use of transects constitutes a form of systematic sampling but in this case the samples are arranged in linear fashion. Transects are useful for recording changes in the species composition of plant communities where some sort of transition exists, e.g. from water to land or from one soil type to another. The stages of plant succession are well highlighted by transects. For example,

estuary $\longrightarrow$ salt marsh $\longrightarrow$ land community
   bog $\longrightarrow$ wet heath $\longrightarrow$ heathland
beach $\longrightarrow$ fore dunes $\longrightarrow$ yellow dunes $\longrightarrow$ grey dunes

The succession of plants colonising waste tips makes an interesting exercise involving the use of transects.

Fig 2.14 A quadrat containing plantain (*Plantago lanceolata*), dandelion (*Taraxacum officinale*) and clover (*Trifolium repens*); with a superimposed grid of 100 sample points (from Baker and Sinker)

Two types of transect are commonplace:

1 Belt transect

This is a strip usually 0.5 m in width that is located across the study area in such a way as to highlight any transition. A tape or rope marked off at 0.5 m intervals is laid across the sampling area and a 0.25 m² frame quadrat laid down at 0.5 m intervals by the side of the

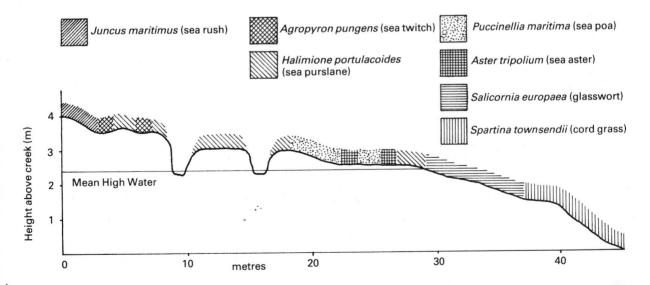

Fig 2.15 Profile across a salt marsh showing main communities in relation to height

tape to give a continuous belt transect. The animals
and plants within each quadrat are identified and
counted and an estimation made of their relative abundance. With a transect over 15 metres long this procedure becomes too time consuming and it is more
usual to carry out quadrat sampling at every metre
interval to give a ladder transect.

Clearly this sort of sampling is quite intensive and
can give an accurate record of the organisms present.
However, the length of the transect will be limited by
the time available and the laborious nature of the technique. Most transect work also requires the recording

of a profile indicating changes in the height of the
ground. The surveying technique used will depend
upon the length of the transect and how steep the
sample area is (see Surveying methods in Chapter 3 for
details). The belt transect has long been used to give
quantitative data about the zonation of intertidal
plants and animals (many shore invertebrates being
sedentary or slow moving). Figure 2.16 shows the
method for presenting the data collected and plotting
the profile. A data sheet for recording the information
in the field is shown in Figure 2.17.

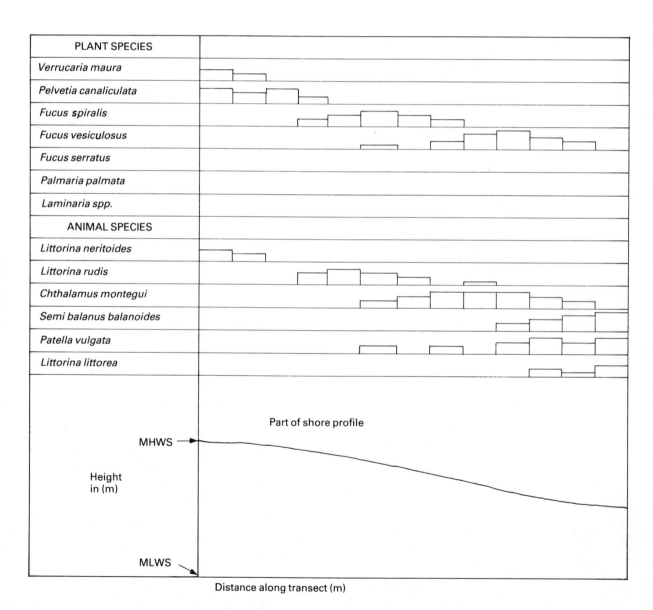

Fig 2.16 Part of a chart showing data collected on a rocky shore belt transect

		Quadrat numbers															
		1	2	3	4	5	6	7	8	9	10	11	12	13	14	15
PLANTS	*Verrucaria maura*															
	Pelvetia canaliculata															
	Fucus spiralis															
	Fucus vesiculosus															
	Ascophyllum nodosom															
	Fucus serratus															
	Laminaria spp.															
	Palmaria palmata															
	Chondrus crispus															
ANIMALS	*Littorina neritoides*															
	Littorina rudis															
	Littorina obtusata															
	Littorina littorea															
	Nucella lapillus															
	Patella vulgata															
	Chthamalus montagui															
	Semibalanus balanoides															
	Mytilus edulis															
	Carcinus maenus															
	Cancer pagurus															

Height of lowest quadrat above chart datum:

Fig 2.17 Data sheet from a belt transect of a sheltered rocky shore

2 Line transect

This is a far quicker though less quantitative and therefore less representative method. Again a tape or rope marked off at 0.5 m intervals is laid along the area of ground to be sampled. The plant species that are touched or covered by the line are then recorded either all the way along or else at regular intervals. Since there may be many species which do not touch the line and are therefore not recorded, the results may give a completely unrealistic sample of the community in question. However, where an impression of the main features of a transition is all that is required, as in Figure 2.15 where the dominant plant species across a saltmarsh are shown, this method has considerable use.

Question 2
The following table shows the data collected from a belt transect of a sheltered rocky shore at the time of a low spring tide. A 0.25 m² quadrat was placed at 1 metre intervals along the tape which stretched from EHWS to MLW. The percentage cover of the plants in each quadrat was converted to a value on a five point abundance scale as were the number of animals:

1 = Rare   2 = Occasional   3 = Frequent
4 = Common   5 = Abundant

At each sampling point the drop in height from 0 was recorded (using one of the surveying techniques described in Chapter 3) so that a shore profile could be drawn.

	STATION NUMBER	0	1	2	3	4	5	6	7	8	9	10	11	12	13	14	15	16	17	18	19	20
PLANTS	*Verrucaria maura* (black lichen)	2	1																			
	Pelvetia canaliculata (channelled wrack)	3	3	2																		
	Fucus spiralis (spiral wrack)		1	3	3	4		2	1													
	Ascophyllum nodosum (knotted wrack)						1	3	5	5	4	5	5	4		3	1	2				
	Fucus vesiculosus (bladder wrack)							4	3	4		3	3	2	2							
	Fucus serratus (saw wrack)												1		5	5	5	5	4	5	5	5
	Laminaria sp (oar weed)																				4	5
ANIMALS	*Littorina neritoides* (nerite winkle)	2	2																			
	Littorina rudis (rough winkle)			1	3	4	3	3														
	Littorina littorea (edible winkle)						2					4	3		5	4	5	5	4		2	
	Littorina obtusata (smooth winkle)												4	2	4	4	1	5		4		
	Nucella lapillus (dog-whelk)							2		1	4		5	4		2	5	4	4			
	Chthamalus montagui (barnacle)			1	2			4	5	5	5	5	5	3		1						
	Semibalanus balanoides (acorn barnacle)											2	2	4	5		5	5	5	4	2	
	Drop in height from Station 0 (cms)	0	19	32	43	60	83	101	139	184	204	225	224	265	286	308	326	343	368	375	384	400

Arrange the data on graph paper drawing histograms to show the distribution and abundance of the species as shown in Figure 2.16. At the bottom of the graph paper plot the profile so that each histogram is located above the part of the profile where it was estimated.

1 From the plotted data, describe any zonation patterns that are evident for a) brown seaweeds, b) periwinkles and c) barnacles.

2 What environmental factors might be expected to give rise to such zonation?

3 Explain how a) brown seaweeds and b) periwinkles inhabiting the upper shore are adapted to withstand the environmental hazards posed by a prolonged period of emersion (exposure to the air).

2.8 Estimating the size of animal populations

The techniques for estimating the abundance and distribution of species mentioned so far were designed for the study of plant communities. Many animals are hidden or difficult to locate whilst those that are visible are often active and highly mobile. Exceptions to the rule are sedentary animals, such as barnacles, or slow moving animals such as the intertidal molluscs. These, along with the invertebrates in leaf litter, can be conveniently estimated by means of quadrats. However, highly mobile animals such as winged insects, birds and mammals, require different techniques, since they may easily enter or leave the sampling area during the period of investigation. *Mark, release* and *recapture* is the basic technique when population estimates of highly mobile animals are attempted.

Mark, release, recapture technique

A large number of animals are collected, marked and released into the population and allowed to remix. A second sample is taken and hopefully the ratio of marked individuals to total number of individuals captured will be the same as the ratio of marked individuals released to the total population. Using this technique estimates of the density of population of animals which are highly mobile, e.g. butterflies, or *cryptozoic* (hidden from view), e.g. woodlice, are possible.

Let us take as an example a study of the population density of a night flying insect, such as a particular species of moth.

1 During the first sampling period (one night) 60 individuals were caught in a light trap.
2 They were each marked with a spot of cellulose paint which was allowed to dry.
3 They were then released and time was allowed (48 hours) for these marked individuals to redistribute themselves within the population.
4 The next night a further sample of 50 moths were caught and of these 15 were individuals marked on the first occasion.
5 The population of moths can now be estimated using the following equation known as the **Lincoln Index**:

$$N = \frac{n_1 \times n_2}{n_3} \text{ where}$$

N = population estimate
n_1 = the number captured, marked and released on the first occasion
n_2 = the number captured on the second occasion
n_3 = the number recaptured, (i.e. the number of marked individuals found during the second capture)

Thus using our results:

$$\text{Estimate of moth population} = \frac{60 \times 50}{15} = 200$$

When using the mark, release and recapture method the following notes should be borne in mind:

1 The population should have a finite boundary.
2 Marking should not affect the behaviour of the animals in any way nor make them more noticeable to predators.
3 Ideally during the period between marking and recapture there should be no immigration or emigration into or out of the population, neither should births or deaths occur in the population. Clearly these conditions cannot be rigidly applied since no population remains static in these terms. However, there should not be a great fluctuation in population density between marking or recapturing.
4 A suitable period must be allowed between marking and recapturing to allow for marked individuals to redistribute themselves at random within the population.
5 The sampling method employed must be random. Captured animals will need to be appropriately marked. Quick drying celluloid paint can be easily applied in a number of different colours; coloured nail varnish and felt-tip pen are other possibilities. The main criteria for use are that:
   a The mark has no toxic effect upon the animal.
   b It does not make the animal more noticeable to predators.
   c It cannot be easily removed (therefore not water soluble).

When carrying out a series of mark, release, recaptures, marks of different colours or marks placed upon different parts of the body can be used to denote each catch. A system of tabulating the marks should be worked out. Clipping a small amount of hair from part of the body is the usual method of marking small mammals.

Bailey's triple catch

This may be used to obtain a more accurate estimate of population numbers and involves taking samples on a number of successive occasions. For example, n_1, n_2 and n_3 are the numbers of individual samples taken on successive occasions 1, 2 and 3. Of n_1 and n_2 the numbers a_1 and a_2 were marked and then released (if none die nor are damaged in the marking process, then $a_1 = n_1$ and $a_2 = n_2$) on occasion 1 and 2. The data can be conveniently summarised by means of a trellis diagram (after Dowdeswell W H).

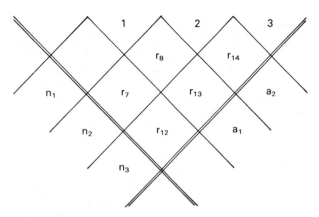

Fig 2.18 Trellis diagram from a mark, release, recapture experiment

From this Figure 2.18 we can see that on occasion 2, n_2 individuals were sampled of which r_8 were marked, and r_7 unmarked. On occasion 3 of the n_3 individuals sampled r_{12} were unmarked, r_{13} were marked on occasion 1, and r_{14} were marked on occasion 2. The size of the population is calculated as:

$$P = \frac{a_2 n_2 r_{13}}{r_8 r_{14}}$$

Using mark, recapture techniques it is possible to study fluctuations in population size of an animal over a prolonged period of time (see Dowdeswell W H).

2.9 Estimating small organisms

Just as it is possible to count the number of red blood cells or yeast cells in a known volume of liquid with the aid of a counting chamber such as a haemocytometer, so it is also the case when it comes to counting both zooplankton and phytoplankton. Phytoplankton are the most important primary producers in many marine and freshwater ecosystems. In turn they support herbivorous zooplankton upon which carnivorous zooplankton depend. A study of the population dynamics of such an ecosystem would require an estimate of these planktonic organisms. As described later, plankton nets can be used to sample though it is difficult to obtain accurate quantitative estimates of the organisms. If a known volume of water is sampled then some method of concentrating the plankton is required such as centrifugation or sedimentation. This will then provide a sample with a suitable concentration of organisms for counting. (These techniques are outlined by Boney AD (1975) *Phytoplankton*, Studies in Biology No. 52, Edward Arnold, but are beyond the scope of this book.)

Counting chambers called 'Rafter cells' may be obtained commercially along with haemocytometers, though the latter are only suitable for the smaller phytoplankton. Alternatively a counting chamber may be made in the laboratory from glass slides, perspex or a combination of a glass slide with two cover slips providing a *trough* (Fig 2.19) for the liquid to be sampled. Whatever the type, a small known volume of liquid is introduced into the chamber and the counting carried out under a low power binocular microscope.

size of counting chamber = 20 × 10 × 1 mm

volume = 0.2 cm³

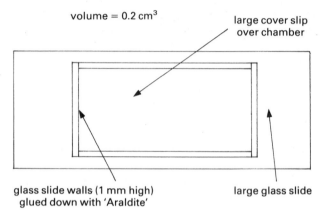

large cover slip over chamber

glass slide walls (1 mm high) glued down with 'Araldite'

large glass slide

Fig 2.19 Home-made counting chamber for estimating small organisms

Two types of counts are usual: absolute abundance or relative abundance. The former involves counting all the individuals of one particular species and obtaining an estimation of numbers per litre. The latter involves identifying and counting all the species in the first 25, 50 or 100 specimens encountered. Clearly it is impractical to try to count all the species and in fact the maximum possible is generally five. The number of each species in a hundred observations gives the percentage frequency of each. A technique for estimating microorganisms in a soil sample is given in Chapter 4. It involves serial dilution of the sample to ensure that its concentration is not too great and can be counted accurately. This, together with a thorough shaking of the sample before counting, may be equally applicable to the quantitative estimation of plankton. In all these methods it is important to make a number of replicate counts and take the mean so as to avoid any local variations in density which would misrepresent the population size.

2.10 Collecting apparatus

Nets

Nets have obvious application in the collecting of small terrestrial and aquatic invertebrates. The particular design of the net will depend upon its specific use but all should be robust enough in their construction to withstand continuous use and have known mesh sizes.

Air nets

The popular **butterfly net** can be used for catching flying insects either in the air or when they have settled. It is light in construction and has:

A relatively wide mouth supported by a flexible frame. A short handle for accurate manipulation. A fine mesh of terylene (preferably black so that the insects can be clearly seen). In some cases the frame is collapsible, folding to fit the pocket.

A **sweep net** is used for brushing through low grass and needs to be of particularly strong construction to withstand rough treatment (Fig 2.20). A fine mesh bag on a heavy duty frame is securely clamped onto a long hardwood handle. As the net is swept through low growing vegetation animals become dislodged and fall into the bag. It is important not to walk over the area to be sampled since some animals respond to footsteps by dropping down deeper into the vegetation.

Water nets

Many commercially available models have attracted criticism in the past due to their failure to withstand the rigours of prolonged use. Figures 2.21 and 2.22 show two general collecting nets that can be recommended, manufactured by G B Nets, Birmingham and S M Davis of Malvern. Both models are realistically priced and combine many useful features which include:

1 A sturdy outer frame of aluminium which resists abrasion to the headband of the net bag.
2 The net bag is supported by an inner hoop of aluminium which is attached by clips to the outer frame. This supports the bag when it is full of water.
3 The net bag is constructed from synthetic rot proof fabrics, usually 1 mm mesh nylon. The net in Figure 2.22 combines a nylon headband with a 1 mm mesh terylene bag strengthened by tapes down the sides.
4 The bag depth should be related to mesh size to prevent back flushing of samples, (e.g. if the mesh size is reduced to 0.3 mm then the bag needs to be deeper).

As with all nets there are practical difficulties inherent in their use. Are the numbers of individuals caught representative of the density of the species in the area under investigation? There may be escapes from the mouth of the net or through the meshes.

J Rowan

Fig 2.20 Sweep net in use

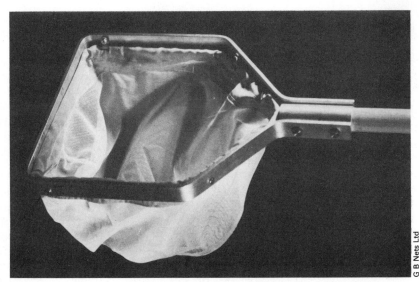

G B Nets Ltd

Fig 2.21 One of the better designs of general collecting nets

Fig 2.22 Sampling freshwater invertebrates.
Note the robust net construction

S M Davis of Malvern

Question 3

From the data in Figure 2.23

a Which size of *Baetis rhodani* nymph was caught in virtually equal numbers in each type of mesh?

b Comment upon the ability of the coarse net to catch smaller nymphs as compared to the fine net.

c Suggest why the larger the nymph the less there are caught in the fine net.

Plankton nets require meshes with a small aperture size: 0.3 mm for collecting zooplankton and 0.075 mm for phytoplankton and protozoa. An extension pole (Fig 2.24) is useful for sampling at different depths in ponds.

Once again the conical bag and supporting frame must be robust enough to stand the pressure of water collecting in the net. At the net apex is tied a transparent plastic collecting jar into which the filtered plankton accumulate as the net is passed through the water.

Larger plankton nets are required when sampling from the sea. Each consists of a long cone of bolting silk (Fig. 2.25) with a mouth 50–100 cm in diameter kept open by a metal hoop. The hoop is attached to a tow rope by three bridles whilst at the other end of the cone is a plastic collecting jar. These plankton nets need to be towed by a boat no faster than at 1–1.5 knots. Towing at a fast speed will result in turbulence and regurgitation of water from the mouth of the net since the fine mesh of the cone presents too high a resistance to the flow of water through it. Operated at the right speed, the net will filter efficiently and the plankton accumulates in the collecting jar (Fig 2.26). The net will need to be washed out into a suitable container after hauling as a lot of material will have collected on its walls. The plankton may be concentrated and examined under the microscope (Fig 2.27) or else preserved for later study.

A dredge net (Fig 2.28) can be a versatile piece of collecting equipment as it has a useful function both in grassland and in freshwater habitats. It is constructed on a D-shaped frame which is supported by steel runners. The net is of coarse mesh and the leading edge is reinforced with canvas where it is attached to the frame. When towed over the bed of a pond it samples benthic invertebrates. Alternatively the dredge net may be hauled over the surface of grassland on its steel runners; dislodged insect larvae will fall into the mouth of the net. Water nets are discussed in greater detail in Chapter 5.

Size in mm	0–1	1–2	2–3	3–4	4–5	5–6	6–7	7–8	8–9	9–10	Over 10
Fine net	19 986	21 872	7730	2657	1244	787	320	174	107	10	17
Coarse net	25	226	252	424	724	761	409	311	152	76	46

Fig 2.23 Numbers of *Baetis rhodani* of various sizes taken with a coarse net and a fine net (from Macan, 1958)

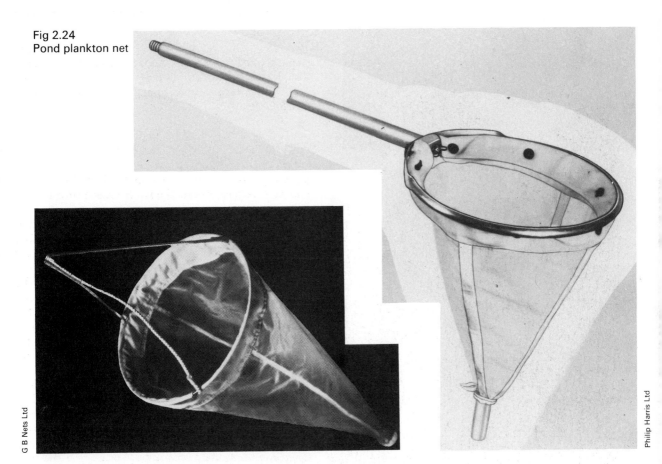

Fig 2.24
Pond plankton net

G B Nets Ltd

Philip Harris Ltd

Fig 2.25 Commercially available plankton net (above) and a simple plankton net drawn below

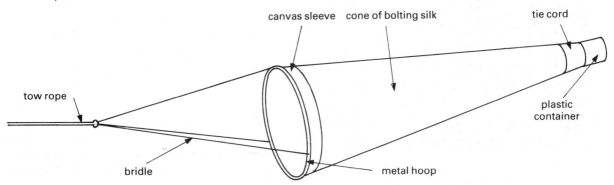

P C H Rogers

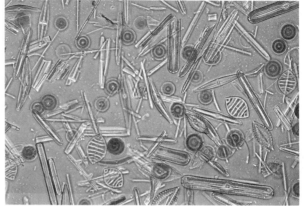

© M Walker/NHPA

Fig 2.27 Phytoplankton

Fig 2.26 Hauling in the catch after a plankton tow

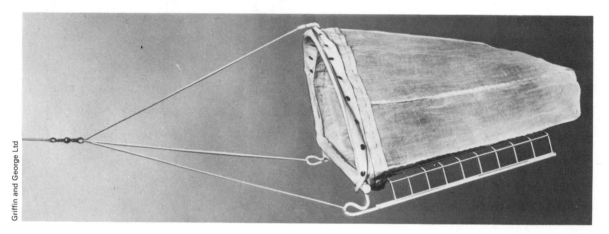

Griffin and George Ltd

Fig 2.28 Dredge net

Beating trays

Nets are difficult to use around bushes and trees but a
suitable alternative could be a **beating tray**. This is
simply a white plastic or linen sheet that is spread out
under the study area. Animals are then dislodged by
beating the branches firmly with a stick. They fall onto
the sheet where they are conspicuous enough to be collected with a **pooter**. The beating tray in Figure 2.30
consists of an elasticated nylon cover fitted over a 0.25
m² quadrat which has a handle for ease of manipulation.

The *pooter* (Fig. 2.31) is especially useful for collecting
small and easily damaged insects inhabiting the bark of

J Rowan

Fig 2.30 Beating tray in use in the field

NET	FUNCTION	NET MATERIAL	FRAME	COMMENTS
AIR NETS				
Butterfly net	Catches flying insects	Fine mesh of black terylene	Wide aperture, flexible frame	Short handle for ease of manipulation
Sweep net	Catches invertebrates in low growing vegetation	Fine mesh nylon securely attached to frame	Rigid and triangular or stirrup shaped	Long handle for brushing through vegetation
WATER NETS				
General collecting net	Sampling fresh water invertebrates, e.g. by "kick sampling" method	Nylon or terylene, 1 mm mesh size (0.3 mm for larval stages)	Sturdy outer aluminium frame protects net from abrasion, bag supported by inner hoop.	Long handle, threaded fitting for extension pole
Plankton net	Collecting phytoplankton and zooplankton	Cone of bolting silk, 0.3 mm mesh for zooplankton, 0.075 mm for phytoplankton	Robust to support the bag full of water	Collecting jar at net apex
Dredge net	Samples benthic invertebrates on pond bed, can also be used on grassland	Coarse mesh, headband reinforced with canvas	D-shaped frame supported on steel runners	Towed by means of a harness and line
Surber sampler	Used to give quantitative samples of benthic invertebrates	1 mm mesh, tapering nylon net bag	Incorporating "quadrat" for sampling 0.1 m² area	See Chapter 5
Drift net	Samples invertebrate drift	1 mm or 250 micron nylon mesh, bag tapers to position where sampling bottle is attached	Rectangular frame secured to river bed by metal rods	See Chapter 5

Fig 2.29 Summary of some features of nets

trees. Animals in cracks and crevices can prove inaccessible but they can be successfully collected in a pooter if suction is applied at the mouth piece. The gauze covering ensures that the insects are retained in the specimen tube and are not drawn into the mouth of the operator! When a sufficient number have been caught the specimen tube can be replaced, the catch being retained by a rubber bung or cork.

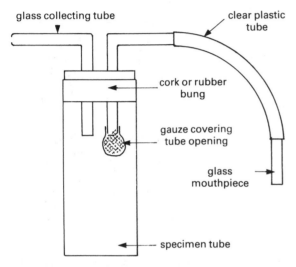

Fig 2.31 The pooter: a useful device for sucking up small insects

Traps

Pitfall traps

These are useful for the collection of animals that are active on the soil surface and amongst leaf litter, such as predatory beetles, spiders, springtails, woodlice, millipedes and centipedes (Fig 2.33). They consist quite simply of a jar or tin sunk into the ground with the soil sloping away from the opening to prevent water draining in (Fig 2.32). They can be thinly camouflaged with sticks and leaves or else a small stone cover can be made to keep out rain and protect the catch from birds.

Pitfalls are extremely cheap and easy to set up so a number can be set up using a sampling grid to investigate the activity of ground living invertebrates in a particular community (see *mark, release, recapture* technique on page 21). They are of little use as a means of estimating population densities since the numbers of individuals caught will reflect the activity of a particular species as well as its abundance. A study could be made of the effects of using different baits in the trap, e.g. meat, fish and over-ripe fruit. Placing 10% meth-

anal (formalin) in pitfall traps kills predators which might otherwise eat other captives.

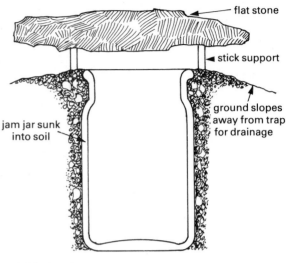

Fig 2.32 A pitfall trap

Question 4
Traps containing methanal have been found to contain much higher catches of some invertebrates such as ground beetles, rove beetles, flies and spiders than do similar water-filled traps. Amongst the reasons for this could be:
a A greater escape of invertebrates, particularly winged ones, from traps filled with water.
b Methanal may act as an attractent/repellent to some invertebrates.
c A certain amount of predation occurs in water-filled traps, either by the animals caught within the traps, or by small mammals or birds which visit them.
Evaluate each of the three reasons in turn, designing experiments to try to validate each one.

Cover traps

These consist of large flat stones or pieces of wood which are placed on soil that has been watered. The traps are then left for a few days before inspection. Cover traps can again be baited with meat, jam and potato and their catch includes slow moving animals, e.g. slugs, earthworms, snails and woodlice as opposed to the fast running animals characteristic of pitfall traps.

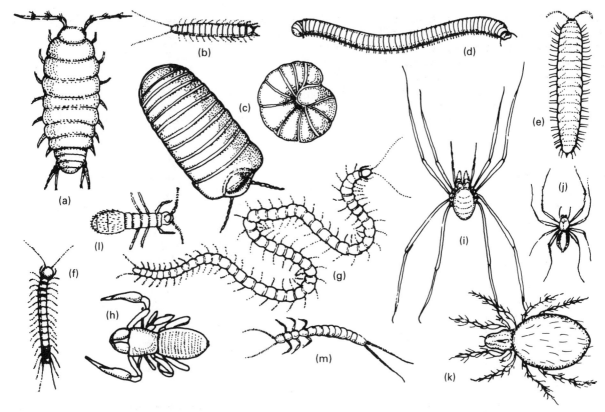

(a) woodlouse (*Isopoda*), (b) symphylid (*Symphyla*), (c) pill-millipede (*Diplopoda*), (d) false wireworm (*Diplopoda*), (e) flat-back millipede (*Diplopoda*), (f) lithobiid centipede (*Chilopoda*), (g) geophilid centipede (*Chilopoda*), (h) false scorpion (*Pseudoscorpiones*), (i) harvest-spider (*Opiliones*), (j) spider (*Araneae*), (k) beetlemite (*Acari*), (l) springtail (*Collembola*), (m) bristle tail (*Diplura*). Drawings not to scale.

Fig 2.33 Animals collected from pitfall traps (from Country-side, 17,460, the Journal of the British Naturalists' Association, after Cloudsley – Thompson)

Water traps

These can be set up using plastic washing up bowls or more cheaply two litre plastic ice cream cartons. They are then half filled with water to which a little detergent and methanal is added. The detergent reduces the surface tension so that any insect landing on the water will tend to sink and the methanal preserves the catch. Water traps can be placed upon stools or cane supports in the open or floated on the surface of ponds provided that they can be suitably anchored. Water traps are cheap enough for a number of them to be used to compare the catch in two locations; they should be positioned at fixed intervals according to a sampling grid. An investigation could be carried out into the effectiveness of different coloured traps: white traps have been found to attract more flies whilst yellow traps are more attractive to aphids.

Question 5

Figure 2.34 shows a comparison of the animals caught in pitfall, cover and water traps over 3 days and 3 nights (after Archer).

a The animals caught in pitfalls tend to be runners and jumpers in contrast to the more slow-moving animals found under cover traps. Explain.

b How do the animals caught in water traps differ from the other two groups?

c Those invertebrates caught in pitfalls were generally carnivores or omnivores in contrast to the vegetarians and scavengers found under cover traps. Try to explain this.

d With reference to Figure 2.35,
   i) Explain the results obtained in water traps and cover traps.

ii) Explain why such a high percentage of winged animals were unable to escape from the pitfall traps (by refering back to the species caught in Figure 2.34).

iii) Many of the greenfly caught in the water traps did not have wings. Account for this fact.

Pitfall Trap		Cover Trap		Water Trap	
Animal	Number	Animal	Number	Animal	Number
Springtails	52	Earthworms	15	Greenflies	85
Ground beetles	40	Woodlice	15	Flies	19
Greenflies	4	Slugs	11	Parasitic wasps	8
Spiders	3	Snails	4	Rove beetles	4
Centipedes	3	Centipedes	2	Bark lice	2
Flies	2	Ground beetles	2	Spiders	2
Harvestmen	2	Ants	2	Sawflies	2
Mite	1	Millepedes	2	Plant bugs	2
Rove beetle larva	1	Rove beetle	1	Other beetles	1
Woodlouse	1	Spider	1	Thrip	1
Ground beetle larva	1	Rove beetle larva	1	Bee	1
Rove beetle	1	Other beetle	1		
Parasitic wasp	1				
Ant	1				

Fig 2.34 A comparison of the animals caught in pitfall, cover and water traps (after Archer)

	Pitfall Trap		Cover Trap		Water Trap	
	Number	Percentage	Number	Percentage	Number	Percentage
Wings present	48	42	4	7	125	98
Wings absent	65	58	53	93	2	2

Fig 2.35 A number and percentage of animals with and without wings, taken in pitfall, cover and water traps (after Archer)

Small mammal traps

Small rodents and insectivores are usually nocturnal and although seldom seen they may be present in great numbers. Amongst the most common rodents are the woodmouse *Apodemus sylvaticus*, the bank vole *Clethrionomys glareolus* and the field vole *Microtus agretis*. Also common is the shrew *Sorex araneus*.

These and other small mammals may be caught in Longworth traps baited with wheat or oats and a piece of potato; dry hay should also be provided for bedding. The trap (Fig 2.36) is made of light alloy and consists of two parts: the tunnel which has a trapdoor at the entrance and the nestbox which is tilted when the trap is set to allow for the drainage of urine and moisture. The trapdoor is released by a treadle wire operated when the animal enters the nestbox from the tunnel. The Longworth trap incorporates a number of useful features:

1   The pressure required to operate the trip mechanism can be adjusted.

2   A locking lever falls across the door as it closes.

3   A pre-bait safety catch can lock the door in the open position.

The last point means that the traps may be left open for several days to allow the animals to become used to their presence before the pre-bait catch is released.

Providing that you have sufficient traps they can be set out using a grid (see Question 6) to determine the ratio of species and also the range of members of that species. (The woodmouse often travels as far as 100 m whereas voles seldom travel more than 20 m from the first trapping site in 24 hours.)

Traps are usually set in the evening and examined the following morning. Voles tend to use well defined runs and traps should not be placed directly on these but to the side of them with some bait on the run itself. If a population study is to be attempted then it will be necessary to mark captured animals: clipping the fur in different parts of the body is preferable to using quick drying paint. A schedule of trapping should be planned out beforehand and a method of recording the data set out (this information could include species, new or recaptured animals, mark, sex, weight, breeding conditions.

Plants provide cover for small mammals and are useful indicators of their presence (see Question 6). A number of distinct habitats could be selected and traps set at regular intervals. Plant cover is then recorded for the four or five dominant plants and correlated with the animals trapped, e.g. *Microtus* is dominant in open country whilst *Clethrionomys* prefers heavy cover.

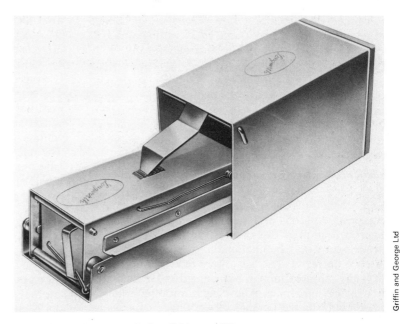

Griffin and George Ltd

Fig 2.36 The Longworth Small Mammal Trap

Date & time	Trap No.	Species	Sex cond.	Alive or dead	Wt g	Mark		Action taken
						old	new	
6/7/80	12	Microtus agrestis	♀	A	32		Red Spot	Released
1900	12	Sorex araneus	♂	A	12		Red Spot	"
	26	Sorex araneus	♀	A	10		2 Red Spots	"
	31	Sorex araneus	♀	A	8		3 Red Spots	"
7/7/80	5	Sorex araneus	♂	D	10		Yellow Spot	―
	10	Microtus agrestis	♀	A	32	Red Spot		"
0900	12	Microtus agrestis	♂	A	31		Yellow Spot	"
	14	Apodemus sylvaticus	♀	A	35		Red Spot	"
	28	Sorex araneus	♂	A	10	2 Red Spots		"
	31	Sorex araneus	♀	D	9		2 Yellow Spots	―

Fig 2.37 Record of catches of small mammals in 40 Longworth traps at the Middlewich Copse site. All releases at trap 1

Precautions

1 If traps are not to be mapped, mark their positions clearly to avoid the risk of mammals dying in a lost trap.

2 Early inspection of traps is advisable since shrews cannot survive long without food.

3 To remove the captured animal from the trap de-

tach the nestbox and gently tip the catch into a polythene bag. Transfer the animal to a more suitable container for observation.

4 Be extremely careful when handling the catch, voles can bite and shrews die of fright if roughly handled. Always use a pair of strong fabric gloves (see notes on *mark, release, recapture* techniques on page 21).

Recommended reading: *Live Trapping of Small Mammals – A Practical Guide* by J Gurnell and J R Flowerdew, published by The Mammal Society.

Commercially available small mammal traps may prove expensive if used in large numbers. Reference should be made to Walsh R (1980), 'An inexpensive small mammal trap', *School Science Review* Vol 61, No 217, 701–702, which shows how a cheap, light and corrosion-resistant trap can be constructed relatively easily.

═══════════════════════════

Question 6

Longworth traps capture small mammals alive and are equipped with food and bedding. The diagram shows the distribution of Longworth traps during a 10-day investigation into the small-mammal population of an area of parkland. The traps were reset at noon each day, any captured animals being noted and immediately released unharmed. Above each trapping point in the diagram is the number of woodmice (*Apodemus sylvaticus*) trapped there and below it is the number of bank voles (*Clethrionomys glareolus*) trapped there. No other small mammals were trapped. The bracken in the parkland was dense; the woodland had a sparse herb-layer.

a i) Construct a table to show the numbers of mice and voles caught in the rough grass, woodland and bracken.

ii) Calculate the percentage of mice and voles in the total catch.

iii) Comment on the relation that appears to exist between the animals caught and the type of vegetation.

b The traps in this investigation were reset at noon each day. The usual procedure is to reset them at sunset and again at sunrise. Comment on the advantages and disadvantages of the two procedures.

c The release of the captured small mammals could have made a reliable estimate of the population impossible. Why is this? Suggest a procedure that would have eliminated this weakness without harming the animals.

d Describe three visible features that identify living mice and voles as mammals.   (AEB 1984)

═══════════════════════════

Light traps

These make use of an ultra-violet light source to catch night flying insects such as moths. The type shown (Fig 2.43) is collapsible for ease of transport and the 6W Actinic 5 lamp operates from a 12 volt accumulator or car battery. Insects attracted to the light become stunned when they hit the baffles and fall into the base of the trap down a funnel. Fragments of egg cartons may be placed around the base of the funnel as these

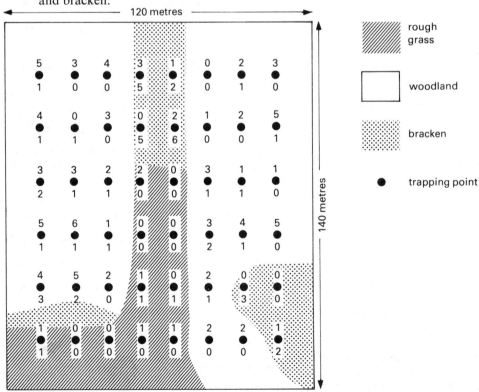

provide the insects with roosting sites and this facilitates easier handling of the catch. A small drainage funnel at the base of the trap prevents the accumulation of rainwater. The ultra-violet light source may produce a spectrum attractive to many nocturnal insects, but it can be harmful to our eyes. The light should therefore be disconnected from the power supply before the catch is inspected.

Question 7
Which collecting technique would you use to sample the following:
a Small arthropod populations e.g. springtails in leaf litter.
b Mayfly nymphs at the bottom of a pond.
c Night flying insects, e.g. moths.
d The standing crop of phytoplankton in a lake.
In each case state how you would attempt to make the sampling technique as quantitative as possibile.

2.11 Exercises

1 An ecologist tried to estimate the population of voles and the population of fleas on the voles in a large area of grassland. He captured 120 voles on one night. He removed (captured) 360 fleas from these voles, marked them by dusting them with a dye powder, and released them by replacing each on its original host. The voles were also marked and released.

Ten nights later 125 voles were captured. Sixty of them had been previously marked. The 60 marked voles had 305 fleas, of which 28 showed traces of dye. The 65 unmarked voles had 327 fleas, of which 8 showed traces of dye.
a Express all the above data clearly in the form of a single table.
b The equation for estimating the size of population is
$$N = \frac{n_1 \times n_2}{n_3} \text{ where}$$
n_1 = the number captured, marked and released on the first occasion.
n_2 = the number captured on the second occasion
n_3 = the number recaptured (i.e. the number of marked ones found during the second capture).
Use this equation to estimate i) the total vole population and ii) the total flea population.
c i) Now estimate the total flea population in a different way. There is an average of 5 fleas per vole (on the second sampling). How many fleas would you expect in the total vole population?

ii) There is a large difference between the size of the flea population estimated in the two ways used in b(ii) and c(i). Suggest **two** biological explanations for this discrepancy.
iii) Say what additional evidence in the data is consistent with one of these explanations.
(JMB 1980)

2 A quadrat frame with 25 divisions, each of 10 cm side, was thrown at random ten times in each of two nearby areas of chalk grassland, one heavily, the other lightly, trampled. A species was awarded one point for each of the smaller divisions of the frame in which it occurred, irrespective of the number of individuals by which it was represented in those divisions. The results obtained for five species are given below. Comment on the results and describe how you would further investigate the differences observed.
(O. and C.)

Species	Trampling Heavy	Trampling Light
Sheep's fescue (*Festuca ovina*)	205	241
Mouse-ear hawkweed (*Hieraceum pilosella*)	2	60
Bulbous buttercup (*Ranunculus bulbosus*)	10	25
Hoary plantain (*Plantago media*)	55	10
Ribwort (*Plantago lanceolata*)	27	29

3 An area of heathland community was studied for some years. Measurements were made of the above-ground standing crop biomass for major components in the community. The dominant species was heather. Data were also collected for other vascular plants and for mosses, as shown in Table 1.

Table 1

| | dry biomass (g m^{-2}) | | | | |
	Year 1	Year 5	Year 15	Year 25	Year 35
Heather	210	1230	1800	1500	830
Other vascular plants	93	52	41	61	75
Ground-cover mosses	320	55	65	90	222
Epiphytic mosses growing on the heather	3	9	20	35	20

a i) Give **one** reason why dry rather than wet mass

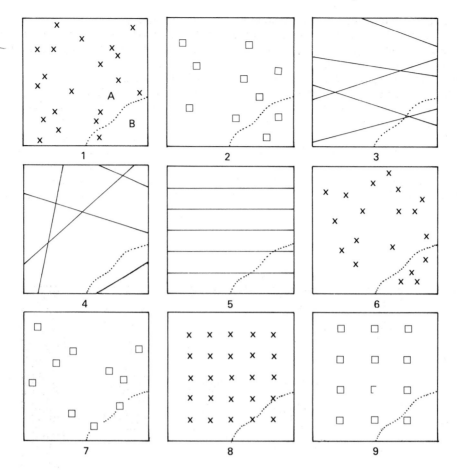

is usually determined in this kind of study.

ii) Describe concisely how you would determine the dry mass of plant material in such an investigation.

b i) Using the data for heather and ground-cover mosses, suggest why the biomass of the ground-cover mosses fluctuated over the period of the investigation.

ii) Suggest why the pattern of change in biomass for the epiphytic mosses differed from that for the ground-cover mosses.

The net primary production of the heather was determined over the same period. In Table 2 the net primary production is given in relative terms for each year as compared with Year 1.

Table 2

	Year 1	Year 5	Year 15	Year 25	Year 35
Relative net primary production	1	2.1	1.9	1.3	1.1

c i) Explain briefly the meaning of the term "net primary production".

ii) What units might be used for net primary production in such a study?

iii) How do you account for the fact that between Years 5 and 15 the net primary productivity decreased although the biomass (Table 1) increased?   (JMB 1982)

4 Nine different spatial sampling methods are shown above. For each map state whether the method used is point, line or quadrat, and random, stratified or systematic (from Lenon & Cleves).

5 The effect of fertilisers and grazing management on the botanical composition of a hill pasture was studied over a period of several years on a hill farm at Llety-ifan-Hen, near Aberystwyth. Fertilisers were applied annually to plots and sheep were given either free access to unfenced plots or were man-

aged in a controlled rotational grazing system on fenced plots where each plot was allowed to recover after an intensive period of grazing. In this manner the latter plots underwent several graze-rest-graze cycles during the year in contrast to the unfenced plots which were continually but less intensively grazed. The histograms below show the species composition of the plots for the various treatments after a 5 year period.

a What was the species composition of the original pasture?

b For the open grazing regime, how is the botanical composition of the pasture altered by the addition of:
   i) fertiliser alone,
   ii) fertiliser plus lime?

c For the rotational grazing regime, how is the botanical composition of the pasture altered by the addition of:
   i) fertiliser alone,
   ii) fertiliser plus lime?

d i) What are the main overall differences between the two grazing regimes?
   ii) Try to explain these differences.

e From the above data it is clear that *Trifolium repens*, a species not originally present in the pasture, can become successfully established within a few years following a change in management. What is the ecological significance of this observation?   (WJEC 1978)

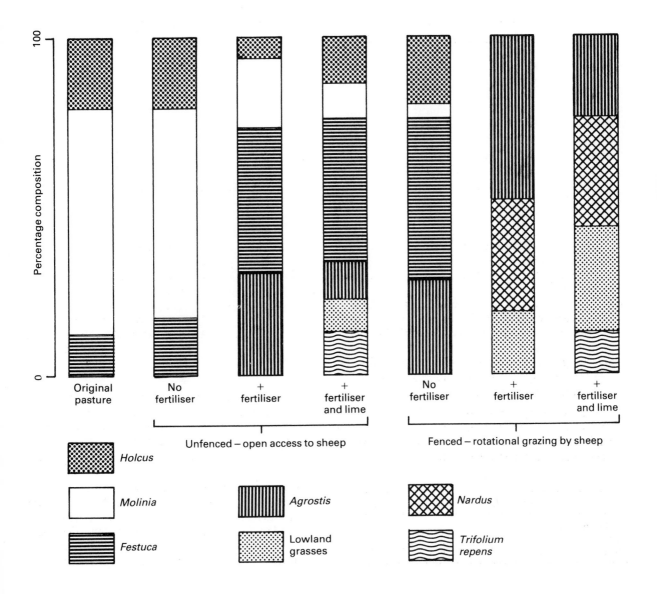

3 Monitoring the environment

Most ecological projects will involve a certain amount of environmental monitoring. The past ten years have seen a response from commercial suppliers to the demand for a range of instruments, designed for field use, which can measure a number of environmental parameters. Portable battery operated meters are now available, capable of measuring light, oxygen concentration, pH, temperature and conductivity. Together with established techniques this new technology has increased the possibilities for project work in a range of habitats.

It is important to decide early on in the planning of a project which environmental measurements are to be made. It is pointless to take a whole variety of different recordings only to find that some have little relevance to the study in question. Clearly the environmental factors that are important are those which are likely to play a part in influencing the distribution and abundance of the plants and animals under study. Figure 3.1 shows the measurements likely to be of relevance in the study of a number of habitats.

	Habitat	Measurement
Water:	Fresh	Temperature, light, oxygen, pH, hardness
	Polluted	Temperature, light, oxygen, pH, specific ions, turbidity
	Sea	Temperature, light, oxygen, pH, conductivity
Field:	Open	Temperature, light, humidity, wind velocity
	Wooded	Temperature, light, humidity
	Soil	Temperature, pH, specific ions
Town:	Outdoors	Temperature, light, sound, SO_2

Fig 3.1 Measurements likely to be of use in the study of various habitats (after Crellin)

Whilst it is important not to attempt to record too much, it is also important to realise that environmental parameters do not act independently. It is difficult to isolate the effects of one factor from that of another and easy to attribute an organism's adaptations to one particular factor when in fact they are due to an interaction of several. Leadley Brown cites the example of the nymphs of the mayfly *Ecdyonurus* (Fig 3.2) which seek shelter on the underside of stones seemingly in

response to the current of a fast flowing stream. On further investigation it may be shown that *Ecdyonurus* positions itself in relation to the amount of light falling on it. During daylight hours it is found beneath the stones on the stream bed but moves round to the top of the stones during hours of darkness. Thus its flattened body form and behaviour are adaptations in response to a number of environmental variables, no one factor being solely responsible. Nevertheless, we may well discover during our investigations that some factors have a greater influence than others on the distribution and abundance of organisms in a particular habitat.

This chapter reviews the methods available for measuring environmental factors in the field. The use of complicated techniques and expensive pieces of apparatus has been avoided. The text on environmental

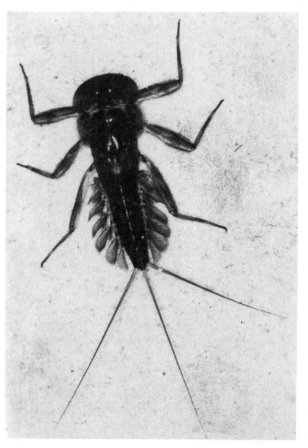

Fig 3.2 Mayfly nymph, *Ecdyonurus*

meters owes much to the work of Crellin in two articles, one with Tranter (see Bibliography). Techniques which are particularly relevant to the analysis of soil and water are dealt with in Chapters 4 and 5 respectively.

3.1 Temperature

Temperature directly affects such metabolic processes as respiration, growth and reproduction. Most living organisms have an optimum temperature range below which these processes tend to slow down. Rapid growth rate often results from an increase in temperature though the optimum for a species will be below the highest tolerable temperature. Lethal effects of temperature are probably rare since organisms take steps where possible to avoid them, e.g. bud and seed dormancy in plants and diapause in insects. The severe winter of 1962–1963 had a devastating effect upon the marine life especially on the southern and western coasts of Britain. During these arctic conditions the sea actually froze on many shores and over 80% mortality was recorded for many species such as limpets.

When recording temperature it is also important to note the time of the day and the location (aspect, altitude, depth or even latitude may be relevant). It may be necessary to record temperature gradients in certain investigations, e.g. stratification of temperature in a sunlit rock pool on a summer's day. Diurnal or even seasonal fluctuations in temperature may need to be measured and this will require careful planning.

The ordinary mercury thermometer is of limited use in fieldwork as it is fragile and often difficult to read when investigating inaccessible locations. Many electronic thermometers are now available commercially. Figure 3.3 shows one which incorporates a semiconductor diode sensor which gives linear responses to temperature changes so calibration is not necessary. The environmental comparator (Fig 3.4) involves the use of thermistors and is a useful instrument when comparing temperatures for two separate situations. (It has an additional facility since it incorporates a photoconductive cadmium sulphide sensor with which light intensities may be compared.) However, if absolute temperature measurements are required calibration is necessary. Many electronic thermometers have an expanded scale range, a useful facility if small changes in temperature are to be monitored. Another significant point to bear in mind when buying a thermometer is that most ecological work is unlikely to require temperatures outside the range of 0°C to

Philip Harris Ltd

Griffin and George Ltd

Fig 3.3 Electronic field thermometer

Fig 3.4 Environmental comparator

SENSOR	THERMISTORS	SILICON DIODE SEMICONDUCTORS	THERMOCOUPLES
Operating principle	Solid state semiconductors, the resistance of which varies non-linearly with temperature.	If a constant current is passed through a silicon diode, the potential difference across it is nearly proportional to the temperature of the diode.	These produce a potential difference directly proportional to the temperature difference between two heat sources. (For absolute readings the cold source is maintained at a constant temperature).
Advantages	Extremely sensitive. Good for comparative purposes.	Reliable absolute measurements. No need for calibration.	Durable. No need for calibration. Good for measuring temperature changes.
Disadvantages	Thermistor thermometers have arbitrary scales and require calibration for absolute measurements. Separate calibration may be necessary for different media.	Response time not as rapid as for thermistors.	Less satisfactory for absolute temperature measurements.

Fig 3.5 Table for comparison of electronic thermometer sensors

$+40°C$. A variety of probes can be chosen from to give a suitable range of temperature measurement. Some can be used with extension poles to reach inaccessible places and many are robust enough to be pushed into the soil. The temperature sensing probes involve the use of thermistors, thermocouples or silicon diode semiconductors (Fig 3.5).

3.2 Light

Light is a vital parameter in the majority of ecosystems. If limited it will reduce the rate of photosynthesis of green plants which, being the producers, harness the solar energy converting it into chemical and heat energy. Measuring light presents many problems to the investigator, not least the fact that the level of illumination fluctuates so much from one moment to the next, e.g. with cloud cover. When using electronic light meters it is important to remember that:

1 Few light sensors give a linear response so that if other than comparative measurements are needed, calibration of the instrument is required.
2 The spectral response of the sensor is unlikely to be the same as that of the organisms under investigation, e.g. in a woodland study the leaves of the tree canopy would be absorbing mainly blue and red light whilst transmitting green, thus a meter might record a higher level of light than that actually available to the plant. Most available light meters

compare relative light intensities and make use of one of two types of sensors:

Photoconductive types which vary in resistance with the level of light falling on them. Cadimium sulphide is commonly used being particularly sensitive to red and infra-red light. Despite the fact that resistance is not linearly related to illumination, with suitable circuitry the response may be made logarithmic as in photographic exposure meters.
Photovoltaic Cells   These generate a potential difference when light falls upon them. The selenium type has a response similar to that of the human eye so is suitable for meters calibrated in lux. The output of the cell may be made linear if the circuitry is adapted.

Measurements of light intensity can be confused by the fact that a number of units may be used.

Illumination is the amount of **visible** radiation falling on an area and is measured in lux (lm m^{-2} or lx).
Irradiance is the **total radiation** falling on an area and is measured in watts per square metre (W m^{-2}). Green plants tend to make use of blue, red and infra-red parts of the spectrum to which the human eye is least sensitive. The use of lux, a unit weighted with reference to colour in the same way as the response of the human eye, may lead to inconsistencies since the greatest emphasis will be placed upon green light. Ecologists therefore tend to use W m^{-2} even though this unit refers to total radiation rather than just the wavelengths of interest.

The proportion of solar radiation falling within the wavelengths 400 to 700 nm may be absorbed by photosynthetic pigments. This irradiance in the visible light range is termed **photosynthetically active radiation** (PAR) and it has obvious importance for ecological studies. Sophisticated instruments can nowadays give direct measurements of PAR in quantum fluxes (μE (microeinsteins) cm^{-2} s^{-1}).

Because of the nature of the sensors used many light meters designed for field use are uncalibrated and have arbitrary scales. However, in many cases only comparative measurements of light intensity are required. Crellin has produced a useful method for the calibration of environmental light meters which do not give direct readings in lux or W m^{-2}:

Distance from 100 Watt, clear 240 VAC single-coil bulb (cm)	Illumination (lx)
10	7500
15	3200
20	2000
30	900
40	550
50	350
60	250
80	150
100	100
150	45
200	25

Values for illumination given in lux can be converted approximately into Wm^{-2} by dividing by 50.

In ecological investigations light intensity alone may not be the most important limiting factor. More crucial may be the *total* amount of light which falls upon the organism during the period of study. Light intensity not only varies diurnally and seasonally, it can also vary momentarily when the sun is covered by cloud. Therefore a single measurement of light intensity is often meaningless and can be misleading. What is needed is a series of measurements of light intensity taken at regular intervals during the period of investigation. From these a mean light intensity can be estimated. In practice the taking of a large number of readings over long periods of time can be tedious. This problem can be overcome by the use of an integrating photometer, which operates continuously and will record the total quantity of light which has fallen on it during the period of use.

Question 1 (Refer to Fig 3.6)
a Explain the differences between the percentage daylight recorded at ground level in summer and in winter i) under oak cover and ii) under pine cover.
b Explain the greater diversity of herb and shrub species found under oak cover compared to that found under silver beech cover.
c Why are mosses the only ground layer plants found under beech?
d Explain why fungi are the only plants found under pine.
e Explain why many plants of the field layer, such as the primrose *Primula vulgaris*, and the celandine *Ranunculus ficaria*, flower in early spring.

Tree cover	Percent daylight penetrating to ground level	Typical species in herb and shrub flora
Oak (*Quercus robur*)	35–52 (summer) 48–63 (winter)	Bramble (*Rubus fruticosus*) Honeysuckle (*Lonicera periclymenum*) Dog rose (*Rosa canina*) Elder (*Sambucus niger*) Willow (*Salix* sp.) Rose bay willow herb (*Chamaenerion angustifolium*) Stinging nettle (*Urtica dioica*) Bracken (*Pteridium aquilinum*)
Silver birch (*Betula pendula*)	30–42 (summer) 41–51 (winter)	Bramble (*Rubus fruticosus*) Rose bay willow herb (*Chamaenerion angustifolium*) Bracken (*Pteridium aquilinum*)
Beech (*Fagus sylvatica*)	20–25 (summer) 28–35 (winter)	Mosses only
Pine (*Pinus sylvestris*)	10–14 (summer) 13–18 (winter)	Fungi only

Fig 3.6 The effect of light intensity on the herb and shrub flora of an oak wood (after Freeland)

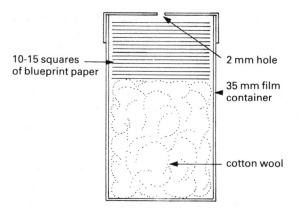

10-15 squares of blueprint paper

2 mm hole

35 mm film container

cotton wool

Fig 3.7 Integrated light measurement (after Atkinson)

Bishop has devised an integrating photometer using relatively cheap integrated circuits: it combines robustness and portability with high sensitivity and the ability to give instantaneous readings.

An alternative method of estimating the average light intensity falling upon a particular site is to use slow response blueprint paper. Atkinson has used a stack of 10–15 small squares of lightweight diazotype paper placed yellow (sensitive) side up in a lightproof container with a single 2 mm aperture in the top (Fig 3.7). As the amount of light increases, so progressively more layers of paper are penetrated. After 24 hours exposure the papers can be developed and fixed by a few minutes exposure to ammonia fumes in a desiccator. Unexposed areas change from yellow to blue and exposed areas stay white. The squares may be stuck onto paper to produce an instant bar chart. This cheap method enables the investigator to compare light intensities at a number of sites simultaneously and involves equipment which can easily be replicated and needs no attention during the period of exposure.

3.3 Hydrogen ion concentration

This is a measure of the degree of acidity or alkalinity of an aqueous solution. pH is a measure of hydrogen ion concentration (since water dissociates: $H_2O \rightleftharpoons H^+ + OH^-$) and this in turn affects the availability of other inorganic ions to plants and animals.

On the pH scale a value of 7 is neutral, above 10 is strongly alkaline and below 4 is strongly acid. Aquatic plants and animals often have differing requirements: some are tolerant to low pH, others pH sensitive, e.g. hill streams with acid water (pH below 5.7) are often completely devoid of invertebrate animals. pH can be affected by a number of factors: precipitation, type of bedrock and consequently soil type and also the activ-

ities of living organisms. When plants photosynthesise during daylight hours they use up carbon dioxide, so increasing the pH of the water. At night the carbon dioxide produced during respiration accumulates since it is no longer being used up in photosynthesis. pH as an important environmental parameter is also examined in the chapters on soil and water analysis.

There are two methods for the determination of pH in the field: the use of multiple indicators, e.g. BDH soil indicator or a battery operated pH meter (Fig 3.8). A wide range of meters is available commercially giving quick and accurate estimations. The electrodes are usually sold separately allowing the user to choose a particular model to suit his or her requirements. Electrodes require calibration before use using a standard buffer solution and generally have a range of pH 0–14. Most models now have gel-filled electrodes that require little maintenance (older versions had to be kept topped up with saturated potassium chloride solution). There are certain precautions that need to be taken efore the electrodes are used in the field:

1 A protective plastic guard should always be fitted around the glass bulb at the electrode tip. (Special spear electrodes are available for pH measurements of soil. These have a spear point of tough glass which resists abrasion when pushed into the soil.)

2 Handling of the glass membrane of the electrode should be avoided as abrasion of its surface will result in inaccuracies.

3 The electrode should be standardised in a buffer solution of known pH value just prior to its use in the field.

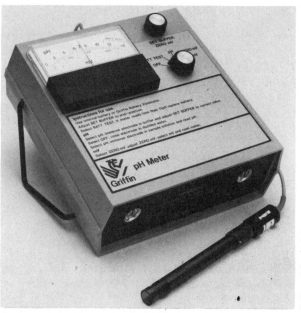

Fig 3.8 Battery operated pH meter

4 When not in use the electrode should be stored in distilled water.

Question 2
Results of stream survey:

Site No.	Altitude (m)	Depth (cm)	Flow speed (cm/s)	Temp. °C	% O² Sat.	pH
1	300	10	26	7	108	4.7
2	250	12	40	7	95	5.1
3	170	10	30	7	100	6.0
4	100	14	90	8	90	8.0
5	80	10	27	9	95	7.2
6	65	36	24	12	70	7.5

a Account for the differences recorded in speed of flow of the stream between the following sites:
   i) 2 & 3   ii) 3 & 4   iii) 4 & 5
b Comment upon the increase in temperature of the water between Site 1 and Site 6.
c Discuss the effects of i) depth ii) temperature and iii) speed of flow on the % oxygen concentration.
d Suggest reasons for the originally low pH and the subsequent increase.

3.4 Oxygen

Very few living organisms are able to tolerate anaerobic conditions for long. Therefore the level of oxygen is often of paramount importance especially to those plants and animals found in aquatic habitats. The photosynthetic activities of plants increase the amount of oxygen dissolved at the air-water interface so that on a sunny day a pond may become supersaturated with oxygen at its surface. Oxygen will also be plentiful where water movement is rapid, e.g. in fast flowing hill streams or where wave action is prominent.

In conditions of poor water circulation oxygen shortage can arise primarily because it is being used up in the decomposition of decaying plant and animal matter. In stagnant pools certain insect larvae, e.g. *Chironomus*, have developed respiratory pigments such as haemoglobin to cope with oxygen deficiency. In fine grained muds deoxygenated conditions may arise because considerable oxygen demand (resulting from high bacterial populations and plentiful organic matter) exceeds the rate at which oxygen can be supplied from above.

The amount of oxygen dissolved in water is usually expressed either as mg/l (equivalent to parts per million) or as a percentage of air saturation (the oxygen present expressed as a fraction of the amount dissolved in water at equilibrium with air at the same temperature). Electronic meters are also available commercially for the estimation of dissolved oxygen in water. These enable measurements to be made quickly in the field but are far less straightforward to use than a pH meter.

There are two main types of sensors for the electronic measurement of oxygen:

1 **Galvanic probes** consist of a pair of dissimilar metals arranged behind a membrane to form a cell. The flow of current between these two electrodes is controlled by the rate at which oxygen diffuses in destroying the hydrogen layer before it builds up on the cathode. The most common types make use of a lead anode and silver cathode in an alkaline electrolyte.

2 **Polarographic probes** do not form a cell. In this case a polarizing voltage is applied between a platinum or silver cathode and a silver anode in a neutral electrolyte, usually potassium chloride. The current which flows as in 1 depends upon the rate at which oxygen reaches the cathode.

A thin plastic membrane covers the cathodes of both types of probe and since the porosity of this plastic will vary with temperature, this in turn will affect the rate at which oxygen diffuses through the membrane. Apart from temperature the sensitivity of these probes is also affected by cleanliness of the cathode surface and composition of electrolyte, amongst other variables. Thus the instrument will require calibration just before use and at the temperature of the sample. Calibration for measurements to be taken in water can most easily be carried out by setting the instrument to read 100% in a saturated water sample (made by shaking a stoppered flask half filled with water for a minute).

Chemical determination of oxygen
An alternative to the oxygen electrode method of dissolved oxygen estimation is the classic Winkler technique. Given its ease of use in field locations, the oxygen electrode does require maintenance and calibration as described and can be expensive. The Winkler method is simple and inexpensive and makes use of the following reagents:

A 45 g manganese (II) chloride in 100 cm³ distilled water.
B 70 g potassium hydroxide and 15 g potassium iodide in 100 cm³ distilled water.
C 50% v/v sulphuric acid (exact concentration is not critical).
D 1.55 g sodium thiosulphate (IV) dissolved in distilled water and made up to 1 dm³.

E 0.25% w/v starch in saturated sodium chloride solution.

Method in the field

1 Obtain carefully and without air bubbles a 250 cm³ sample of water (see Chapter 5 for methods of water sampling).
2 Add 1 cm³ manganese (II) chloride (A) which sinks to the bottom of the bottle.
3 Immediately add 1 cm³ Winkler's reagent (B) and close the bottle without air bubbles.
4 Mix the contents for one minute and allow the precipitate to settle.

The oxygen in the water will now have become 'fixed' since the manganese (II) salt will have been oxidised to manganese (III). The sample can now be taken back to the laboratory.

Method in the laboratory

1 Using a safety bulb pipette carefully add 2 cm³ concentrated sulphuric acid (C) down the inside wall of the bottle.
2 Close the bottle and mix the contents.
3 Titrate 100 cm³ of the sample against standardised sodium thiosulphate (D) until pale yellow.
4 Add 0.5 cm³ starch solution (E) and continue adding thiosulphate drop by drop until the blue colour disappears.

$$\text{Dissolved oxygen in mg per litre} = \frac{1000}{V_1} \times \frac{V_2}{10}$$

Where V_1 = sample volume
       V_2 = volume of 0.0125 mol dm^{-3} sodium thiosulphate solution used.

A variation of the Winkler technique has been outlined by Gill, B F (1977). This makes use of plastic syringes and is therefore particularly suitable for oxygen estimation in field situations.

Question 3
Explain how the level of oxygen in a small pool might be affected by the following:
a The amounts and relative proportions of animals and plants present.
b Temperature and illumination.
c Depth and surface area of the pool.
d The amount of decaying organic material present.

3.5 Humidity

Atmospheric humidity is a major factor influencing the microclimate in which terrestrial plants and animals live. Since it directly affects the transpiration of plants and the water loss from an animal's body surface, it is clearly important in determining plant and animal distribution. Relative humidity is the most frequently

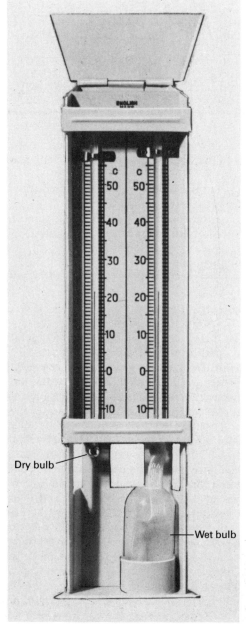

Fig 3.9 Wet and dry bulb hygrometer for measurement of relative humidity

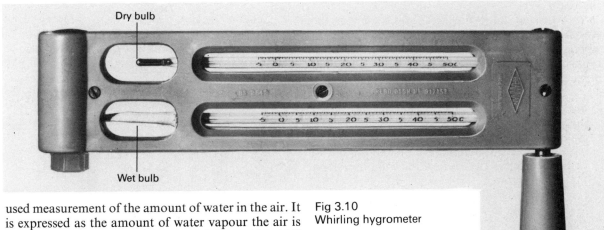

Dry bulb

Wet bulb

Philip Harris Ltd

used measurement of the amount of water in the air. It is expressed as the amount of water vapour the air is holding as a percentage of that which it would hold if the air was completely saturated. Relative humidity can be measured as follows:

Fig 3.10
Whirling hygrometer

1 Wet and dry bulb hygrometer
Two ordinary thermometers are mounted on a stand (Fig 3.9). The bulb of one is wrapped in muslin, the end of which is dipped into a small container of water. The muslin around this 'wet bulb' is thus kept damp. The temperatures of the wet and dry bulbs are recorded and the relative humidity calculated either by using a special slide rule supplied with the instrument or by consulting hygrometric tables.

2 Whirling hygrometer
This comprises wet and dry bulb thermometers mounted on a frame which can be swung round like a football rattle (Fig 3.10). This rotating causes air to circulate rapidly around the wet bulb so accelerating the rate of evaporation. When the two thermometers give constant readings these can be converted into relative humidity from tables or a slide rule.

The previous two methods are of little use when attempting to measure the humidity of microclimates, e.g. at the base of a grassland sward. The animals inhabiting such a microhabitat are particularly sensitive to fluctuations in humidity. Unwin has constructed a miniature electric psychrometer (wet and dry bulb hygrometer) but to date there has been no portable humidity probe and meter developed for the commercial market. In such monitoring of microclimates possible alternatives could be:

3 Cobalt chloride paper
made by dipping filter paper in 25% cobalt chloride solution, allowing it to dry and cutting it up into conveniently sized strips. The paper changes from blue in low humidity to pink in high humidities. Strips of anhydrous cobalt chloride paper can be left in the microhabitat and the time taken for them

to go pink recorded. This technique is fairly subjective depending as it does on the judgement of the investigator. Cobalt thiocyanate paper also gives only a rough indication of humidity though a kit is commercially available which makes use of coloured standards for comparison.

4 Piche evaporimeters can be used to compare the humidity of different microhabitats. They are easily constructed (Fig 3.11) but can produce useful results, e.g. when comparing the humidity of north and south facing roofs during the study of moss and lichen colonisers. Evaporimeters may be located at a number of different sites and the volume of water which evaporates per unit time recorded.

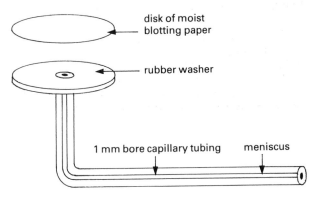

disk of moist blotting paper

rubber washer

1 mm bore capillary tubing   meniscus

Fig 3.11 Piche evaporimeter

Question 4

Green lichens of the *Pleurococcus* group grow on the bark of many tree trunks. The growth is patchy and uneven and presumably this is due to some environmental variable. The lichens tend to be most abundant on bark facing a northerly direction and least abundant on bark facing south.

a Suggest a procedure for estimating the lichen population.

b Name two environmental conditions which could have caused the difference in distribution and in each case explain the effect of the condition upon the lichen's growth.

c Explain ways in which you would measure the following conditions around the circumference of the tree:
   i) humidity   ii) illumination   iii) temperature.

3.6 Wind

Wind has a number of effects notably upon the vegetation of coastal and upland areas. It influences the circulation of water vapour, and therefore transpiration, aids seed and fruit dispersal and can cause mechanical damage. Drying and freezing are accelerated by wind so that buds on the windward side of trees may die as a result. A hand held wind meter (Fig 3.12) can be used to give a direct indication of wind speed. It is held facing the wind and the movement of the small sphere in the vertical tube recorded. The faster the wind, the greater the reduction in pressure in the tube and the higher the sphere rises.

Wind also creates waves which are independent of the tides. The size of waves depends upon the strength of the wind and the distance it has been blowing over the sea – 'the fetch'. In Britain the shores most exposed to wave action tend to be those facing the prevailing south-west winds. Wave action has a major effect upon the distribution of animals and plants on rocky shores. Direct measurement of the amounts of exposure to wave action of a particular shore is a difficult proposition though attempts have been made (Jones and Demetropoulos (1968) have devised a simple dynamometer which enables wave force to be investigated as an ecological parameter). A scale correlating the amount of wave action to biological measurements of the abundance and levels of growth of the common intertidal organisms would be useful when comparing different shores. Some rocky shore organisms are far more tolerant to wave exposure than others so that the distribution and abundance of animals and plants on an exposed shore will be very different from that on a sheltered shore.

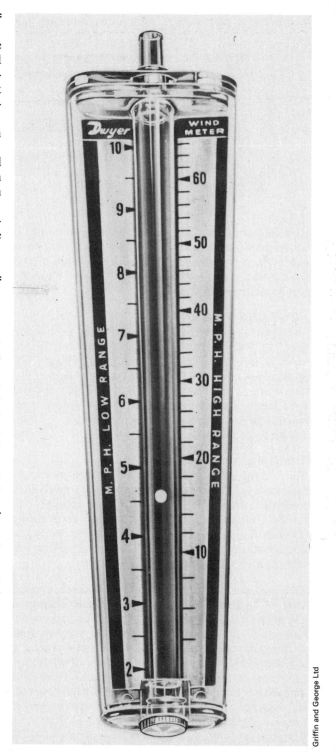

Fig 3.12 Hand held wind meter

Griffin and George Ltd

A summary of species which indicate degrees of exposure

Extremely exposed	Very exposed	Exposed	Semi-exposed	Fairly sheltered	Sheltered	Very sheltered	Extremely sheltered	Indicator species
+ + +	+ +	−	−	−	−	−	−	*Alaria esculenta* (marlins)
+ + +	+	−	−	−	−	−	−	*Himanthalia elongata* (thong weed)
+ + +	+	−	−	−	−	−	−	*Porphyra umbilicalis* (laver)
+ + +	+ +	+	−	−	−	−	−	*Gigartina stellata*
+ + +	+ +	+	−	−	−	−	−	*Fucus vesiculosus linearis**
+ + +	+ +	+ +	+	+	−	−	−	*Lichina pygmaea* (black lichen)
+ + +	+ + +	+ +	+	+	−	−	−	*Patella aspera* (limpet)
+	+	+	+	+	+	−	−	*P. depressa* (limpet)
+ + +	+ + +	+ + +	+ + +	+ +	+	−	−	*Chthamalus montagui* (southern barnacle)
+ + +	+ +	+ +	+ +	+	+	−	−	*Littorina neritoides* (nerite winkle)
+ + +	+ + +	+ +	+ +	+	+	+	−	Supra-littoral lichens
+ + +	+ +	+	+	+	+	+	−	*Lithothamnion-Corallina* (coral weed)
+	+ +	+ + +	+ + +	+ + +	+ + +	+ +	+	*Semibalanus balanoides* (acorn barnacle)
+ +	+ + +	+ + +	+ + +	+ + +	+ + +	+ +	+	*Patella vulgata* (common limpet)
+ + +	+ +	+ +	+ +	+ +	+ +	+ +	+ +	*Littorina saxatilis* (rough winkle)
+ +	+ +	+ +	+ + +	+ +	+ +	+	+	*Nucella lapillus* (dog-whelk)
+ +	+ +	+ +	+	+	+	+	+	*Mytilus edulis* (mussel)
−	+ + +	+ + +	+ + +	+ + +	+ +	+	+	*Laminaria digitata* (kelp)
−	+	+	+ +	+ +	+ + +	+ + +	+ + +	*Fucus serratus* (serrated wrack)
−	+	+	+ +	+ +	+ + +	+ + +	+ + +	*Pelvetia canaliculata* (channelled wrack)
−	−	+	+	+ +	+ + +	+ + +	+ +	*Gibbula umbilicalis* (purple top shell)
−	−	−	+	+	+ +	+ + +	+ + +	*Fucus vesiculosus* (bladder wrack)
−	−	−	−	+	+ +	+ +	+ + +	*F. spiralis* (spiral wrack)
−	−	−	−	+	+ +	+ + +	+ + +	*Ascophyllum nodosum* (knotted wrack)
−	−	−	−	+	+ +	+ +	+	*Laminaria saccharina* (kelp)
−	−	−	−	+	+ +	+ + +	+ + +	*Littorina littorea* (edible winkle)
−	−	−	−	+ +	+ +	+ + +	+ + +	*Littorina obtusata* (flat winkle)
−	−	−	−	+	+ +	+ +	+	*Monodonta lineata* (toothed top shell)

Key: + + + abundant + + common + present − absent.   *This is bladder wrack without bladders.

Barnacles		Mussels	
+ + +	= more than 1 per cm²; rocks well covered.	+ + +	= more than 20% cover.
+ +	= 0.1 to 1 per cm²; up to $\frac{1}{3}$ of the rock covered.	+ +	= large patches up to 20% cover.
+	= 10 to 100 per m²; few within 10 cm of each other.	+	= scattered individuals.

Limpets		Nerite winkles and rough winkles		Lichens	
+ + +	= more than 50 per m².	+ + +	= more than 1 per cm².	+ + +	= more than 20% cover.
+ +	= 10 to 50 per m².	+ +	= 0.1 to 1 per cm².	+ +	= up to 20% cover.
+	= less than 10 per m².	+	= very few in crevices.	+	= widely scattered patches.

Top shells and the dog-whelk		Flat winkles and edible winkles		Algae	
+ + +	= more than 10 per m².	+ + +	= more than 50 per m².	+ + +	= more than 20% cover.
+ +	= 1 to 10 per m².	+ +	= up to 50 per m².	+ +	= less than 20% cover.
+	= less than 1 per m².	+	= less than 1 per m².	+	= scattered individuals.

Fig 3.13 A biologically defined exposure scale (from Jenkins)

Ballantine (1961) and Lewis (1964) attempted to produce a biologically defined exposure scale for the comparison of rocky shores making use of the abundance of certain indicator species and reference should be made to these for more detailed information. Figure 3.13 shows an excellent summary of these wave exposure indicator species by Jenkins (1983).

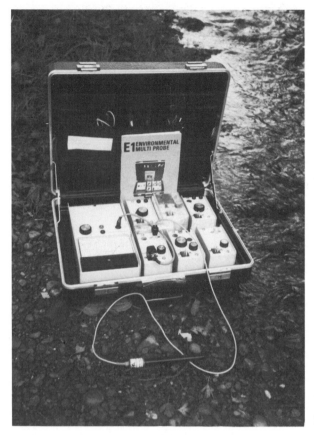

J Rowan

Fig 3.14 The WPA Environmental Multi-Probe

Question 5

With reference to Fig 3.13

a In what ways would a very exposed shore differ in appearance from a very sheltered shore?

b Suggest reasons why large seaweeds such as *Ascophyllum nodosum* and *Fucus vesiculosus* are often absent from exposed shores.

c Suggest why i) powers of attachment and ii) an encrusting body form may be adaptations of species found on exposed shores.

d The diversity of animals and especially of plants is usually greatest in the lower shore on exposed coasts. Suggest possible reasons for this.

e *Fucus vesiculosus linearis* has no air bladders. Explain its distribution and contrast this with the distribution of the variety possessing bladders.

3.7 Multi-purpose environmental meters

As well as manufacturing separate electronic meters for the measurement of some of the environmental parameters so far discussed, commercial firms have also produced **environmental meters**, the first available being the WPA Environmental Multi-Probe (Fig 3.14). The kit consists of a meter/power unit which may be used with a variety of modules and probes to measure temperature, light, oxygen concentration, pH, conductivity and sound level. Other firms have since produced competing sets of instruments, some self-contained enabling a number of separate measurements to be made at the same time.

Before buying a multi-purpose environmental meter a decision should be made as to how many of the six parameters mentioned above you need to measure. If all six are required then such a kit is certainly cheaper. (It must be emphasised, however, that it may not be possible to measure all six environmental parameters at the same time).

If only three or four are required it may well be cheaper to buy four self-contained meters each of which could be used at the same time and independently of one another.

3.8 Multi-channel data memory systems

When investigating the measurement of light the problem arose of recording results over a long period. This could prove to be tedious and also require measurements to be taken at inconvenient times. Multichannel data recorders (Fig 3.15) are now commercially available which will allow simultaneous monitoring from light, temperature, oxygen and pH sensors. Back in the laboratory the recorded data may be transferred to a microcomputer for display, statistical analysis or permanent storage on disc. Stored results may also be printed out, replayed on a chart recorder or displayed on an oscilloscope. The system shown has four input channels allowing the same variable to be monitored at four different places. This facility is of obvious use as it would allow simultaneous measurement of say light or temperature of different levels in the same location, e.g. in tall grass, rock pools, soil etc.

Fig 3.15 The Vela multi-channel data memory system, measuring temperature at four different points simultaneously

Educational Electronics Ltd

traditional method makes use of an **Abney level** and two levelling staffs and is outlined in Figure 3.16.

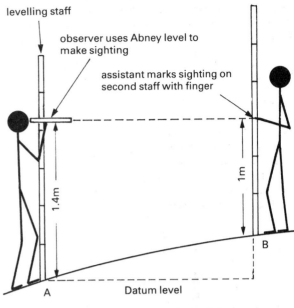

Height of B above A = 1.4 − 1 = 0.4 m

Fig 3.16 Method for measuring vertical distance along a slope

---

Question 6

Copy and complete the following table to show which environmental measurements you think would be relevant in a study of the habitats listed.

Measure-ment	Woodland leaf litter	Estuarine mud	Diurnal changes in a small pond	Peat bog
Temperature				
Light				
pH				
Oxygen con-centration				

Consider in each case the techniques and equipment which would be most likely to give you the most satisfactory results.

3.9 Surveying techniques

Belt and line transects are often carried out to investigate changes in the species composition of a particular habitat, e.g. a hedgebank, pond margin, peat bog or rocky shore. As well as compiling records of the animals and plants present it is also important to record the differences in height along the transect which influence the succession and zonation. The method of measuring vertical distance along any sloping area is known as surveying. It involves measuring the distance between successive points along a transect line together with the vertical distance between them. The

The level incorporates a sighting device and a spirit level to ensure that it is kept horizontal when measurements are being taken. The observer holds the level against one staff (preferably at one of the black and white junctions) and making sure that it is horizontal, he sights onto the second staff, the assistant moving his finger up or down the staff until it is judged to be in line with the sights of the level. The relative heights of the Abney level on the one staff and the finger on the other staff are recorded and the rise and fall in the ground calculated. The method is then repeated at the next station and when all the heights have been recorded a profile can be constructed. This method is very accurate though Abney levels can be expensive. It is probably the only satisfactory method for surveying an area with a gentle even gradient such as a sandy beach, where the distance between each station may be many metres. Figure 3.17 shows a commonly used alternative which is simple and cheap. Commencing at the top of the transect line one end of a metre rule is placed upon station 0 and kept horizontal by means of a spirit level. Against the other end of this another metre rule is placed vertically. The difference in height between station 0 and station 1 is now measured on the vertical metre rule. The procedure is repeated at 1 metre intervals along the transect line and the profile data recorded in the field as in Figure 3.18.

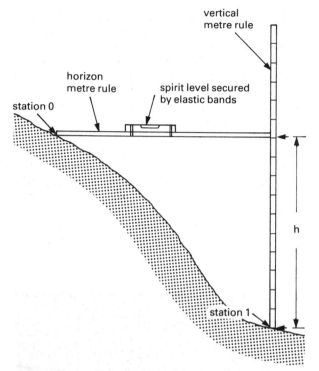

Station	Level below previous station (cm)	Total drop (cm)	Substrate
0	0	0	Bed rock
1	19	19	Bed rock
2	13	32	Pebbles
3	11	43	Pebbles
4	17	60	Bed rock

Fig 3.18 Method for recording profile data

The method is most useful on steeply sloping profiles, e.g. some rocky shores. It can, with practice, be carried out single-handedly but is less accurate than the previous method; errors are also cumulative. Points on the survey can be no more than 1 metre apart. As with all surveying, profiles must be related to a known datum level. This can be an O.S. bench mark (BM) or a temporary bench mark (TBM) which can be related to ordinance or chart datum later. When shore profiling it is usual to arrive at the lowest station on the transect at exactly the predicted time of low tide; this level can then be related to chart datum by reference to Admiralty Tide Tables and calculations.

The Cross staff (Fig 3.19) is reasonably simple to construct in wood, the height (h) being 0.5 m or 1 m. In use the point is placed upon the lowest station of the transect and the operator sights along the cross bar keeping it level by observing the spirit level in the inclined mirror. He observes a point along the transect line which is at a height (h) above the base of the instrument; this

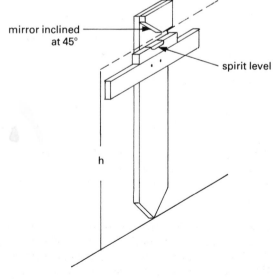

Fig 3.19 The Cross staff level

Fig 3.17 Meter rule and spirit level method of surveying and the technique in use

point is marked by the assistant and used as the next station. The horizontal distance between the two stations on the transect line is measured with a tape. This method is very quick, can be used single-handedly and over relatively long distances.

An alternative method for surveying is the **Debenham water level** which makes use of a siphoning technique. This has been described by Wood-Robinson and makes use of cheap and easily assembled equipment. The method utilises a large plastic can (about 5 litres capacity) and about ten metres of clear plastic tubing of say, 1 cm internal diameter.

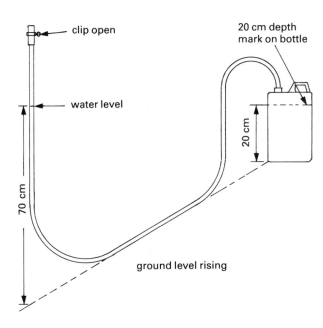

Fig 3.20 The Debenham water level (after Wood-Robinson)

The method is as follows:

Preparing the apparatus
1 Fill the can with water, remove the pinch clip and start a siphon by suction.
2 Allow the water to run to about 50 cm from the end of the tubing. Close the pinch clip.
3 Adjust the water level in the can to a previously made 20 cm mark.

To measure the vertical distance between two stations
1 Place the plastic can on the upper station and take the clipped end of the tubing to the lower station.
2 Hold the end of the tubing slightly higher than the can and open the clip.

3 Allow the water in the tubing to come to the same level as that in the can and measure its height above the lower station with a metre rule.
4 Deduct from this height 20 cm (the constant depth of water in the plastic can) to obtain the vertical distance between the two stations.

This method is intrinsically very accurate and makes use of cheap, robust equipment.

The profile along the transect is usually recorded before it is sampled to determine the frequency and distribution of species. Details of the sampling techniques used when investigating a belt or line transect are given in Chapter 2.

When the height of a tree needs to be estimated a clinometer (Fig 3.21) can be used to measure the angle of elevation.

Fig 3.21 A clinometer for measuring the angle of elevation

Method
1 The instrument is held like a target pistol with the arm outstretched and forefinger on the trigger. It is then pointed at the top of the tree to be sighted and the trigger pressed until the graduated disc becomes stationary. The trigger is then released and the clinometer brought down from the aim position and the angle of elevation read.
2 The distance y from the foot of the tree to the operator must be measured accurately together with the height z of the operator to eye-level (Fig 3.22).

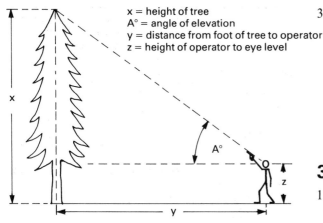

x = height of tree
A° = angle of elevation
y = distance from foot of tree to operator
z = height of operator to eye level

Fig 3.22 Angle of elevation method for determining the
height of a tree

3 Use tables to look up the value of the tangent of the
   angle of elevation = *tan A⁰*
Height of the tree $x = y \times tan\ A^0 + z$
For example:
Distance of operator from tree $y = 60$ m
Height of operator to eye-level $z = 1.52$ m
Reading on clinometer (angle of elevation A) = 17°
               Therefore $x = 60$ m × 0.3057 + 1.52 m
                             = 19.86 m

3.10 Exercises

1 The following figure is a diagrammatic representation of the differences in daily mean values of some
   environmental factors between the two sides of a
   valley in Central Europe (average inclination 20°)
   in midsummer.

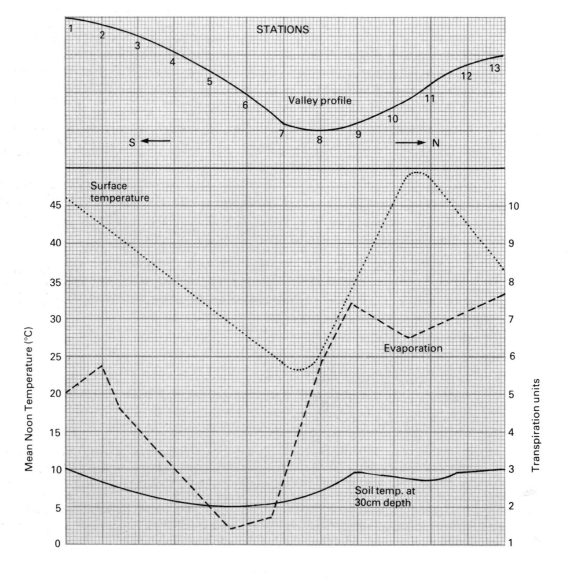

a Explain the contrast in the values of the surface temperature and rate of evaporation at stations 6 and 11.

b State the range of temperature in soil at 30 cm depth.

c Explain the reasons for the differing temperature ranges on the soil surface compared with 30 cm below the soil surface across the valley profile.

d Describe how you would quantitatively measure the
i)   soil temperature,
ii)   water content of the soil,
iii) solar radiation.

e What simple experiment would you conduct to investigate the hypothesis that plants at different stations were adapted to their particular habitat?
(WJEC 1981)

2 Water samples containing aquatic organisms from a pond are placed in sealed bottles. The bottles are suspended in the pond at the depth at which each sample was taken. At each depth, transparent and opaque bottles are used to provide data for samples kept in the light and in the dark. The oxygen concentration of the water in each sample is determined initially and after a period of twenty-four hours.

The table shows the changes in oxygen concentration in relation to depth for a pond four metres deep.

Depth of sample	Changes in oxygen concentration in bottles over 24 hours (arbitrary units)	
	Light	Dark
Top metre	+3	−1
Second metre	+2	−1
Third metre	0	−1
Bottom metre	−3	−3

a What metabolic processes of the community are being measured in
i)   the bottles kept in the light?
ii   the bottles kept in the dark?

b i)   What is meant by the ecological term "gross production"?
ii)   Give the figure for gross production (as indicated by changes in oxygen concentration) in the sample taken at the second metre.

c Account for the changes with depth in the bottles kept in the light.

d i)   Where in a pond would you expect saprobionts to be concentrated, and why?
ii)   Explain whether or not your answer to d (i) is supported by the data in the table.

e Would you say that this pond was polluted by organic matter? Explain your answer.
(JMB 1978)

3 Measured changes in some climatic factors caused by the presence of a hedge are given in the figure below. The values for each factor are as compared with the values obtained in an open field.

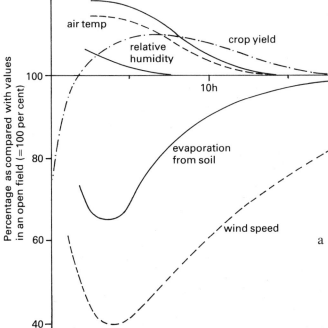

a i)   Which two environmental factors are affected the most by the presence of the hedge?
ii)   At what distance from a 2 metre high hedge would these factors be most marked?
iii) Why is the relative humidity increased near the hedge although evaporation from the soil is reduced?

b The figure shows the changes in yield of crop plants near to the hedge. Account for
  i) the decreased yield close to the hedge.
  ii) the increased yield between 2 h and 18 h from the hedge.
c i) From the information given what would be the likely effect on the total crop yield of removing the hedge?
     State one piece of evidence to support your answer.
  ii) Suggest two reasons why farmers may wish to remove hedges. (JMB 1983)

4 Llyn Peris and Llyn Padarn are two adjacent lakes in Snowdonia and both contain phytoplankton (suspended algae). On a clear sunny day during August 1975 the following measurements were taken.
Light penetration with depth This was measured with an underwater light-meter and the results are expressed as percentages of the light at the surface of the lake, with the latter given a value of 100%.
Phytoplankton biomass (total amount of phytoplankton) with depth This was determined by collecting algae at different depths and extracting their chlorophyll. The results for total biomass are pre-

sented as mg chlorophyll per m³ of water.
The above parameters were measured simultaneously at the surface, and at depths of 5, 10 and 15 metres in both lakes and the results are presented graphically below.
a How does light intensity vary with depth in Llyn Padarn?
b How does the biomass vary with depth in Llyn Padarn?
c What are the general differences in biomass between Llyn Padarn and Llyn Peris
  i) at the surface,
  ii) at 5 metres depth,
  iii) at 15 metres depth?
d What is the relationship between biomass distribution and the penetration of light in
  i) Llyn Peris,
  ii) Llyn Padarn?
e Suggest two factors which might account for the far greater productivity of phytoplankton in Llyn Padarn.
f How could you investigate whether one of these factors has a significant effect on productivity
  i) in the 'field',
  ii) in the laboratory? (WJEC 1977)

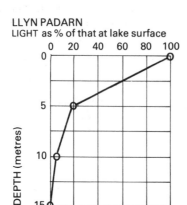
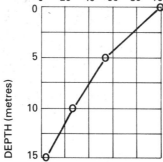
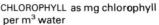
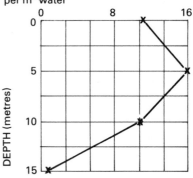
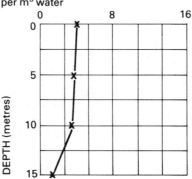

4 Soil analysis

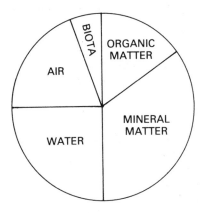

Fig 4.1 Soil constituents

Soils are complex mixtures of different sized rock particles, humus (organic debris), air, water and dissolved minerals (Fig 4.1). They represent a fundamental component of terrestrial ecosystems and as such have a major role in determining the plant and animal communities that inhabit them. Conversely the biota, plants especially, will have an influence upon the soil: root penetration into clay soils improves drainage and aeration, whilst the roots of sand dune vegetation prevent erosion and aid water retention by binding the soil together.

Soils are formed by a combination of physical and chemical processes on the one hand and biological decomposition on the other (Fig 4.2). Physical weathering makes use of climatic factors such as ice, water, wind and gravity to fragment the parent rock into increasingly smaller particles. Chemical weathering involves the action of water, especially if it contains dissolved carbon dioxide. As a result soluble minerals are released from the parent material to form new compounds and become either absorbed onto the surface of colloidal particles or leached out of the soil. The end product is a combination of various particle sizes which in turn determines the characteristics of the soil. A soil with a high percentage of large particles like sand will be light and have good drainage and aeration. Associated with rapid drainage, however, is the leaching out of important minerals often leaving an acid soil. Alternatively if particle size is small then aeration and drainage will be poor, which will result in little mineral loss so the soil will be fertile. Fertile soils are termed *loams* and are composed of various mixtures of

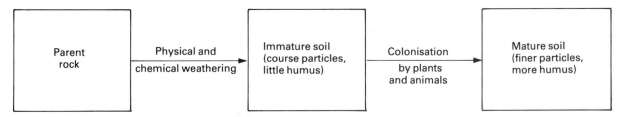

Fig 4.2 Stages in soil formation

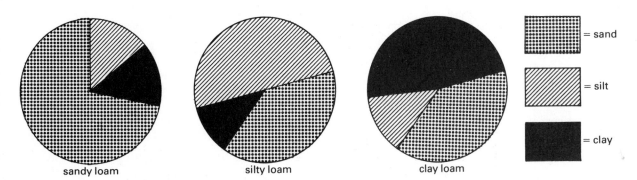

Fig 4.3 Proportions of different types of particle in loams

different sized particles. (Figure 4.3). Soil characteristics are fundamentally affected by the nature of the parent rock: chalk and limestone will break up to form alkaline soils whereas rocks such as sandstones give rise to acid soils.

Biological decomposition results in the production of humus mainly through the action of fungi and bacteria on dead plant material. The amount of decomposition is affected by the physical characteristics of the soil already described. Good aeration will encourage the activity of decomposers, decay will be rapid and little humus will form. However, in conditions of poor aeration the activity of decomposers will be inhibited so that the dead plant material accumulates as peat. Humus forms under conditions intermediate between those two just described, and is a vital constituent of the soil having many important functions. When added to sandy soils it improves the water retaining properties whilst in clay soils it produces a more open and workable structure, therefore improving drainage. It provides an important food source for soil animals and as it is broken down it makes available valuable nutrients for plant growth.

4.1 Soil sampling

Before an analysis of soil constituents can be made a number of carefully collected samples must be taken. In order to obtain samples at different depths a pit is dug preferably down to the bedrock to reveal the soil profile. This consists of a series of layers each of which is referred to as an 'horizon' characterised by differences in colour, composition and texture. A soil with a well developed profile is known as a zonal soil: it has distinct horizons each of which can be conventionally designated by certain letters (Fig 4.4), the main ones being:

A –Topsoil
B –Subsoil
C –Parent material

Investigating a soil profile

1   In a typical area of the study site dig a pit down to the bedrock if possible, leaving one side vertical and clean.
2   Make a sketch or photograph the profile.
3   Measure the depth of the different horizons.
4   Record the characteristics of the different horizons: colour, composition, texture and distribution of organic matter.

Samples can be taken for laboratory analysis if accurate estimations of water content and organic matter are required.

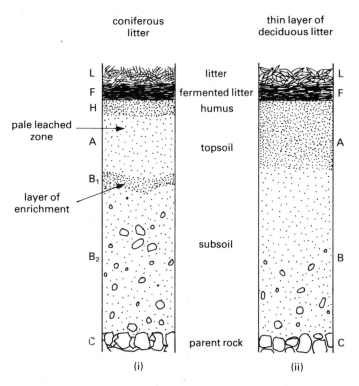

Fig 4.4 Soil profiles of i) a podzol and (ii) a brown earth

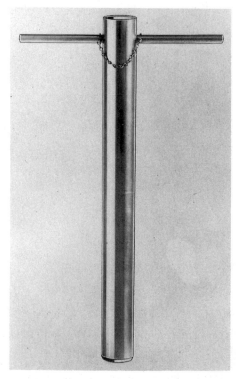

Fig 4.5 Soil augers a) cover type

Where it is not possible to dig a soil pit a soil auger may be used to accurately extract smaller samples from a known depth. These are of two main types (Fig 4.5).

1 A metal cylinder which works on the principle of an apple corer. The steel tube is 500 mm long with an internal diameter of 47 mm. The lower end has a sharp cutting edge and at the opposite end there are two holes through which a tommy bar is inserted.

2 A corkscrew model for sampling harder soils to greater depths. This consists of a stout metal bar 650 mm long incorporating a large screw 200 mm long and 38 mm in diameter. At the opposite end is an eye for the insertion of a tommy bar.

In each case the auger is thrust into the soil to a depth of 150 mm by turning the tommy bar and is then withdrawn by pulling directly upwards. The core sample is removed from the corer by using a piece of wood as a ram-rod; in the case of the corkscrew auger it is carefully removed from the thread. The sample is laid on a plastic sheet and placed in labelled polythene bags for subsequent laboratory analysis.

When samples of topsoil or leaf litter are required a large soil sampler can easily be made from an old biscuit tin about 25 cm square. The bottom needs to be cut out and it may be painted to protect it from rusting. It is then used like a quadrat and is useful in determining the numbers of soil animals per unit area to a given depth of soil. If smaller samples are required then tins of diameters from 8 cm to 15 cm can be used in a similar manner.

b) corkscrew type

4.2 Mechanical analysis

This is the method by which the constituent soil particles are separated by sieving (Fig 4.6). Categorising the various soil components by their size is an arbitrary affair but the following size fractions are recognised by the International Society of Soil Science.

Fig 4.6 Nest of sieves for mechanical analysis of soil

Fraction	Particle diameter (mm)
Gravel	> 2.0
Coarse sand	2.0 – 0.2
Fine Sand	0.2 – 0.02
Silt	0.02 – 0.002
Clay	< 0.002

The sieves are usually stacked together with the larger meshes above the smaller meshes. A suitable size soil sample is first dried in an oven at 105°C and then broken up in a pestle and mortar to disperse the soil particles. The prepared sample is then poured in the top sieve and the whole stack is shaken vigorously. The particles larger than any particular sieve mesh will be retained upon that sieve (Fig 4.7).

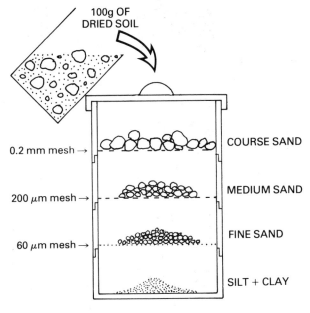

Fig 4.7 Separating soil components by sieving (from Courtney and Trudgill)

The contents of each sieve are then carefully turned out onto a separate sheet of paper and weighed and can then be expressed as a percentage of the whole soil. Figure 4.8 shows some typical results.

Sieve mesh	Texture class (International scale)	Weight retained on sieve (g)	%
0.2 mm	Coarse sand	80	53.3
200 μm	Medium sand	40	26.6
60 μm	Fine sand	10	6.6
PAN	Silt + Clay	20	13.3
	total	150	99.8

Fig 4.8   Results after sieving a 150 g soil sample (after Courtney and Trudgill)

Question 1

The pie graphs (Fig 4.9) show the compositions of four different soils. Which one of these soil samples would:
a Retain most water?
b Be most permeable to water?
c Provide the best agricultural land?

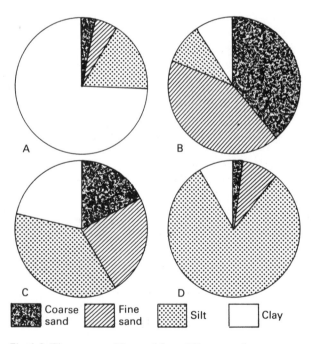

Coarse sand   Fine sand   Silt   Clay

Fig 4.9 The compositions of four different soils

In the light of your answer for *c* what characteristics does a soil require in order to sustain plant growth?

The following method can be used for calculating the percentage by weight of the different fractions.
1   Weigh a sample of oven-dried soil and pass it through coarse and fine seives to separate out the gravel and sand fractions.
2   Weigh each of these fractions and express it as a percentage of the total soil weight:

e.g. $\dfrac{\text{Weight of gravel}}{\text{Weight of soil}} \times 100 = \%$ gravel fraction in the soil

3   The particles that have passed through the fine sieves will be composed of silt and clay and these can be separated by differential settlement in water. The silt and clay fractions are put in a weighed evaporating basin and re-weighed.
4   30 cm of distilled water is now added and the contents thoroughly stirred and left to stand for 3–4 hours.
5   The cloudy supernatant liquid containing the clay particles is now decanted off and the process repeated until the supernatant remains clear.
6   The silt remaining in the evaporating basin is then evaporated to dryness and weighed.
7   Subtracting the weight of silt from the original weight of the evaporating basin contents gives the weight of the clay fraction.

$\dfrac{\text{Weight of clay} + \text{silt} - \text{weight of silt}}{\text{Weight of whole soil}} \times 100 = \%$ of clay in the soil

A rough analysis of the components in any given soil can be made by allowing it to settle out after shaking in a measuring cylinder (Fig 4.10) in water. The larger and more dense particles sediment out most quickly whereas the smallest and least dense remain in suspension. The particles separate out in order of decreasing particle size, i.e.

gravel → coarse sand → fine sand → silt

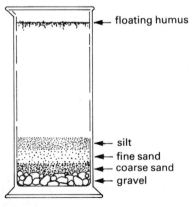

floating humus

silt
fine sand
coarse sand
gravel

Fig 4.10 Separation of soil constituents by shaking with water

Often the small clay fraction remains in suspension causing the water to appear murky. Sedimentation of clay can be brought about by adding calcium hydroxide in proportions of 10:1. The lime causes the clay particles to aggregate into clumps or flocculate so that they become large enough to settle out under gravity. This characteristic is used to improve the drainage qualities of a clay soil. Adding the lime causes the clay particles to clump together so making the soil more porous and consequently improving drainage. The organic component in the soil sample is known as humus and constitutes partially decomposed plant material. This will be seen to float on the surface of the water; an accurate estimation of the humus content of a soil is outlined later in the chapter.

Question 2
a Why is lime sometimes applied to soils?
b Explain fully both the direct and indirect effects of liming agricultural land.
c Suggest two ways in which you could improve the water retaining qualities of a sandy soil.
d Why is a sandy soil often i) acidic and ii) depleted of nutrients?

4.3 Soil texture

The relative proportions of the different sized particles present in a soil will also determine its texture. It is often a useful exercise to assess soil texture in the field as a prologue to more detailed analysis in the laboratory. Broad categories of soil such as sand, loam, silt and clay are fairly easy to distinguish although a number of intermediate soil classifications exist, such as sandy loams and clay loams. Figure 4.11 details this classification. Soil texture can be quickly assessed in the field by rubbing a moist sample of soil between the fingers to determine the degree of coarseness. Figure 4.12 shows a key for the finger assessment of soil texture devised by Burnham.

Pore space

Particle size and shape will in turn determine the percentage pore space in a soil. This is filled with water and/or air and provides living space for soil organisms and room for plant roots to grow. Clay soils have a large pore space but often have a low air capacity. This is because the pores are often so small that they hold water by capillary action even after drainage has occurred. In sandy soils the percentage pore space is

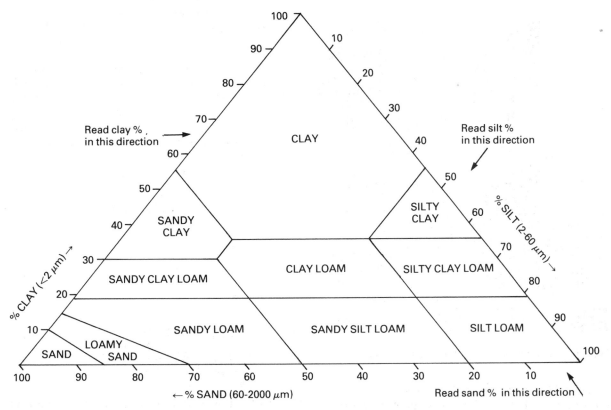

Fig 4.11 Soil texture (UK classification, 1976 system), (after Courtney and Trudgill)

1 Does the moist soil form a coherent ball?
   Easily.   **2**
   With great care   **loamy sand**
                            (but check using tests **2** and **3**)
   No.   **sand**
2 What happens when the ball is pressed between
   thumb and forefinger?
   Flattens coherently.   **3**
   Tends to break up.   **sandy loam**
                            (but check using tests **3** and **4**)
3 On slight further moistening can the ball be rolled
   into a thick cylinder (about 5 mm thick)?
   Yes.   **4**
   No, collapses.   **loamy sand**
4 On slight further moistening can the ball be rolled
   into a thin thread (about 2 mm thick)?
   Yes.   **5**
   No.   **sandy loam**
5 Can the thread be bent into a horseshoe without
   cracking, e.g. around the side of the hand?
   Yes.   **7**
   No.   **6**
6 On remoulding with further moisture what is the
   general 'feel' of the soil?
   Smooth and pasty.   **silt loam**
   Rough and abrasive.   **sandy silt loam**
7 Can a ring of about 25 mm diameter be formed by
   joining the two ends of the thread without cracking?
   (If necessary remould with more moisture and begin
   again.)
   Yes.   **9**
   No.   **8**
8 On remoulding with further moisture what is the
   general 'feel' of the soil?
   Very gritty.   **sandy clay loam**
   Moderately rough.   **clay loam**
   Doughy.   **silty clay loam**
9 On remoulding without rewetting can the surface be
   polished with the thumb?
   Yes, a high polish like wax with few noticeable
   particles.   **10**
   Yes, but gritty particles are very noticeable.
                                            sandy clay
   No.   **8**
10 On wetting thoroughly, how strongly does the soil
   stick one's fingers together?
   Very strongly.   **clay**
   Moderately strongly.   **silty clay**

Fig 4.12 Scheme for finger assessment of soil texture
          (from Burnham CP, 1980, 'The soils of
          England and Wales', *Field Studies*, **5(2)**,
          349–63)

smaller than in clay soils but they will tend to retain
more air as air replaces the water which drains away
through the larger size pores. Irregular particle size
tends to increase the percentage pore space. A collection of particles of different sizes will tend to reduce the
pore space. In a good pasture soil the pore space will be
about 50% of the total volume and the relative vol-

umes of air and water will be about 10% and 40%
respectively, this depending upon environmental factors such as temperature and rainfall.

Question 3
The table shows two soils A and B, which form
permanent pasture (grassland) in areas of the United
Kingdom similar in climate. For some years they have
been spread at the same times with the same amounts
of cattle dung and inorganic fertiliser.

	Soil A %	Soil B %
Particle diameters greater than 0.02 mm (as percentage of soil-particle volume)	83	13
Particle diameters less than 0.002 mm (as percentage of soil-particle volume)	2	47
Pore spaces (as percentage of total soil volume)	32	51

a What type of soil is A? What type of soil is B?
b How would you expect soils A and B to compare in
   their mean annual contents of i) inorganic fertiliser
   and ii) humus? Give one reason for each answer.
c Soil B may be described as 'cold and heavy'. Suggest
   an explanation for each of these characteristics.
                                              (AEB 1983)

4.4 Method for investigating soil air

Air in the pore space is continuous with atmospheric
air and exchange of gases will occur between the two.
Surface soil tends to have a gas composition similar to
that of the atmosphere but with increasing depth, soil
air generally contains less oxygen and more carbon
dioxide. An oxygen meter may be used to examine the
aeration of different soils at varying depth:

Method
1 Obtain a dry porous pot (about 200 cm³ capacity)
   with a split rubber bung suitable for the insertion of
   an oxygen electrode.
2 Set up the oxygen meter and electrode for use with
   gases.
3 Bury the porous pot containing the oxygen
   electrode in the soil to the required depth (20–50
   cm) in the soil with the lead reaching the surface.

Cover the apparatus with soil, if possible to the same degree of compactness as before it was disturbed.

4   Check the reading on the meter. Disconnect the electrode lead but do not alter the calibration control.

5   Leave the apparatus for at least 12 hours to allow the soil atmosphere to stabilise and to equilibrate with the air inside the pot.

6   Take the meter reading, dig up the apparatus carefully and take a reading of atmospheric air for comparison.

The method may be used in a number of habitats though great care is needed to avoid loss of the costly electrode. Marine deposits such as sand and mud may be sampled as well as waterlogged soils such as a marsh or peat bog.

4.5 Soil water

Water is a vital soil component for it not only ensures chemical weathering and the release of nutrients but also critically affects the organisms inhabiting the soil.

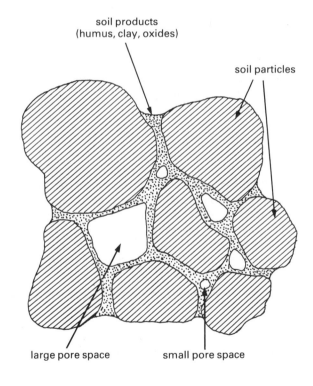

soil products
(humus, clay, oxides)

soil particles

large pore space   small pore space

|———| 100 μm

Fig 4.13 Diagram to show relationship between particle size and pore space

The amount of water in a soil fluctuates but the ability of a soil to retain water is largely determined by the pore space size and organic content. Soil water may be classified as follows:

1   **Gravitational water** found in the large pores (Fig 4.13) with only weak attraction to the solid particles. It drains away through the soil due to gravity, taking with it valuable minerals in solution.

2   **Capillary water** is held in the medium sized pores by capillary action. Together with gravitational water this is available to soil organisms and can be absorbed by plant roots.

3   **Hygroscopic water** forms a very thin film around soil particles and is strongly adsorbed onto their surfaces. Very little of this water is available to soil organisms.

Coarse, porous sandy soils are well drained so that little water is retained and much of the pore space is occupied by air. The water holding capacity of this sort of soil can be improved by adding organic matter such as peat or compost which holds water like a sponge. Conversely, in clay soils all the pore space may become filled with water to the exclusion of air. Such a soil is said to be *water-logged* and with time lack of oxygen may affect the respiration of plant roots and micro-organisms. This adverse affect upon micro-organisms may reduce the release of nutrients which results from their activities. Anaerobic conditions may encourage denitrifying and sulphate reducing bacteria which will further affect the nutrient status of the soil.

Question 4
Soil water content will vary from day to day with climate: the amount of rainfall and evaporation at the surface. Absorption by plant roots and topography (is the soil located on a slope?) will also play a part. The table shows the water content of two experimental plots with similar soils after a long dry period.

Depth	Percentage of water in soil (by volume)	
	Bare soil	Soil under grass
Upper 25 cm	27	18
25 to 50 cm	46	30
Below 50 cm	53	37

a   Comment upon the reasons for the differing results.
b   Describe two other features of a soil which affect its water content.

The water content of a soil can be measured by drying the sample to constant weight but it should be remembered that this does not indicate the amount of soil water available to plants and soil animals.

Method for measuring soil water content
1   Place about 10 g of fresh soil into a pre-weighed crucible and accurately weigh crucible plus soil.
2   Put the sample in an oven at 110°C overnight to drive off the water.
3   Re-weigh the crucible with the now dry soil sample.
4   Subtract the weight of the crucible to give the dry soil weight.
5   Subtract the weight of the dry soil from the weight of the fresh soil to give the weight loss on drying (total weight of water evaporated from the soil).
6   Substitute your figures in the following equation:

$$\frac{\text{Weight loss on drying}}{\text{Weight of fresh soil}} \times 100 = \% \text{ of water (by weight) contained in the soil}$$

The calculated figure above will include all the hygroscopic and some of the capillary water. Providing that heavy rainfall has not occurred in the previous 24 hours then it should not account for gravitational water. Despite the inaccuracies in this method it can be used successfully for comparing different soils.

	Sand soil	Clay soil
Particle size	Large: >0.2 mm diameter	Small: <0.002 mm diameter
Air space	Large	Small
Drainage	Rapid leaving a dry soil	Slow leaving a wet soil
Capillarity	Low	High
Water retention	Low (as a result of 3 & 4)	High (as a result of 3 & Easily waterlogged
Mineral content	Mineral salts leached out by rain	Mineral salts attracted colloidal particles and retained
Specific heat	Low – shows fluctuations of temperature	High – more constant temperature though we clays tend to be cold
Consistency	Very loose – easily eroded	Surface tension of wate surrounding particles holds them together

Fig 4.14 Generalised comparison of sand and clay soils

4.6 Soil organic content

Humus is the main organic constituent of soil and consists mainly of decomposing plant material. It is produced through the action of bacteria and fungi which depend upon aeration and the presence of moisture. Humus is important in improving the texture of the soil: in heavy clay soil it separates the particles into larger aggregates and so improves drainage and aeration. In light sandy soils it absorbs water reducing the rapid drainage associated with these soils and retaining dissolved mineral salts. Humus at the soil surface will also retain water and prevents excessive evaporation from the underlying soil in dry weather. As well as being an essential food for detritivores, humus is decomposed by soil bacteria to release mineral salts for absorption by plants. Different types of humus form depending upon location and the nature of the soil forming environment. In **mor** soils decomposition is slow producing a peaty soil with a fibrous, acid humus poor in nutrients. These form in association with conifers and on heathland where the acid nature of the soil affects bacterial activity. In contrast, in **mull** soils the decomposition of humus is relatively rapid, incorporating its products into the surface soil. Mull humus is blackish, crumbly and rich in nutrients. It is associated with deciduous woodland and fertile grassland and is the most common form in Britain where precipitation almost balances evaporation. Mull humus develops on soil with a high calcium content in which earthworms abound. The worms pull dead leaves into their burrows so that the resulting humus is well mixed into the topsoil.

Question 5
Figure 4.15 shows an analysis of the constituents of five common soils.
a   Comment on the relative percentage of humus in each soil.
b   Explain the conditions which would have lead to the humus percentage i) in peaty soil and ii) in sandy loam.
c   What type of humus is likely to be present i) in peaty soil ii) in the loam?

	Sandy loam	Clay loam	Loam	Chalky	Peaty
Water	2.4	4.4	2.4	2.4	8.4
Humus	4.0	6.4	14.3	6.9	32.8
Coarse sand	10.3	3.9	0.1	20.2	26.6
Fine sand	67.0	30.1	53.3	21.9	14.2
Clay and silt	16.3	55.2	29.7	9.6	18.0

Fig 4.15
Approximate analysis (%) of
five common soils (after Hall)

To determine the percentage humus content of a soil:
1 Take the dry soil from the previous experiment and grind it in a pestle and mortar.
2 Return the dry soil sample to the pre-weighed crucible and weigh it.
3 Heat the soil sample to red heat in the crucible over a bunsen flame for 15 minutes in order to incinerate all the organic material.
4 Wipe off any carbon deposited on the underneath of the crucible after it has cooled for 10 minutes and re-weigh the burnt soil. Subtract the known weight of the crucible.
5 Subtract the weight of the burnt soil from the weight of the soil before burning to give the weight of the organic material.
6 Substitute your figures in the following equation:

$$\frac{\text{weight loss on burning}}{\text{weight of dry soil}} \times 100 = \% \text{ of humus in dry soil}$$

A possible source of error in this method will be due to the decomposition of carbonates and the loss of carbon dioxide (especially in alkaline soils on limestone or chalk). This carbon dioxide can be regained by adding a small amount of ammonium carbonate solution to the cooled soil and then heating in an oven at 110°C to remove excess liquid.

4.7 Soil temperature

This varies with depth and with soil type. The greatest fluctuations in soil temperature are at the surface and dry sandy soils have a more variable temperature than wet clay soils. The amount of vegetation at the soil surface will also influence temperature at deeper levels, since it will affect the amount of solar radiation reaching the soil surface. Temperatures of wet clay soils will fluctuate less than dry, sandy soils because the water they contain has a high specific heat capacity. Soil temperatures will not only fluctuate diurnally but also from season to season. This will have an important influence upon soil inhabitants. With decrease in temperature the activities of many soil animals, e.g. earthworms, are reduced, seeds fail to germinate and absorption of water and mineral salts by plant roots is retarded. The activities of soil micro-organisms is so reduced in winter that the decomposition of organic matter virtually ceases.

Soil temperature may be measured at a number of depths or in different types of soil and compared with the temperature taken at ground level at the same time. An electronic thermometer with a special spear electrode (see page 37) may be used or else a soil thermometer. Possible projects could include a compa-

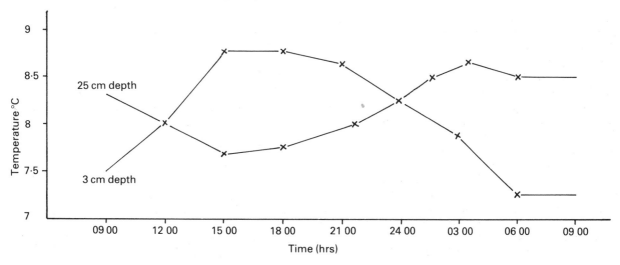

Fig 4.16 Graphs to show diurnal fluctuations in soil temperature with depth

rison of the temperatures of clay soil and sandy soil at different depths, comparing the soil temperature from three plots, one with long grass, one with short grass and one bare soil. Seasonal fluctuations could also be studied or the soil temperature measured over a 24 hour cycle continuously recorded by using a chart recorder (Fig 4.16).

4.8 Soil chemistry

In studying the soil the assessment of nutrient status is one of the most important activities since the nature and amount of the nutrients will affect plant growth. The solubility of nutrient ions is affected by the degree of acidity or alkalinity as assessed on the pH scale (an expression of hydrogen ion concentration). In British soils pH values range from 4.0 (very acid) to 8.0 (slightly alkaline), 7.0 being neutral. Acid soils often result

from the effects of high rainfall leaching out salts and leaving a high concentration of hydrogen ions (Fig 4.17). Alkaline soils result from the weathering of a bedrock rich in magnesium, calcium or sodium carbonate, so naturally soils on limestone or chalk will have a relatively high pH. Only extreme cases of soil acidity or alkalinity directly affect plant growth. Usually pH has a more indirect effect in that it controls the release of plant nutrients. Many of these are most soluble in acid conditions, for example aluminium and manganese compounds are mobilised in acid soils and many reach levels toxic to plants. *Calcifuges* are plants that thrive in acid, calcium deficient soil, e.g. heathers, whilst *calcicoles* prefer alkaline soils with plenty of calcium, e.g. dog's mercury, *Mercurialis perennis*. Many plants are intolerant of alkaline soil due to the deficiency of certain trace elements.

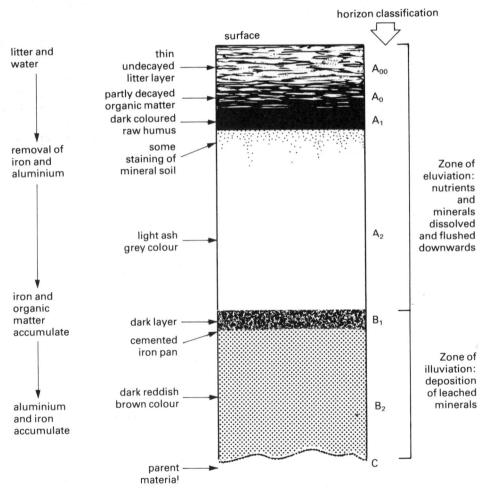

Fig 4.17 Development of a typical UK soil profile (a podzol) (from Lenon and Cleves). This occurs where there is a net downward movement of water: precipitation is greater than evaporation and soil texture allows free drainage

Question 6

Figure 4.18 shows the relationship between pH and the availability to plants of inorganic ions in soils.

a Which nutrients become less freely available in alkaline soils?

b At which of the following pH ranges are the majority of nutrients most freely available?
4.5–5.0, 5.5–6.0, 6.0–6.5, 7.0–7.5, 7.5–8.0

c The presence of calcium ions in soils makes potassium and phosphorus ions less soluble. Heather (*Calluna vulgaris*) has high demands for both potassium and phosphorus ions. In what soil conditions would you expect to find this plant growing and why?

d Why do some plants growing on limestone or chalk show chlorosis?

e Why are acid peat moorland soils considered poor agriculturally?

f Why do many soils in conditions of high rainfall become more acid?

g i) How does clay contribute to the fertility of a soil?
   ii) Why does pure sand have poor fertility?

h Sulphur is said to be seldom deficient in soils in industrial areas. In some places, although not added as fertiliser, it is increasing in quantity in the soil. What may be the explanation for this?

(London Jan. 1984)

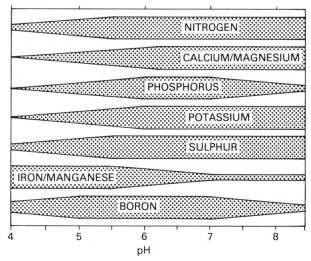

Fig 4.18 Relationship between pH and inorganic nutrients in soil (after D Briggs)

Soil pH will also effect soil-living animals like earthworms which tend to prefer neutral or alkaline soils (Fig 4.19).

Measurement of soil pH makes use of colour changes to indicator solutions. Universal indicator (marketed by British Drug Houses) will test the pH of a soil between 4.0 and 11.0. The method is as follows:

1 Take a small soil sample from a known depth on the soil profile.

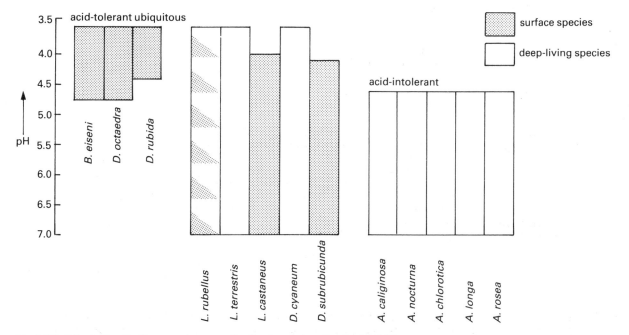

Fig 4.19 Effect of soil pH on earthworm distribution (after Satchell 1955)

2 Place about 1–2 cm of soil in the bottom of a test tube.
3 Add 1–2 cm barium sulphate (this flocculates the clay fraction leaving a clear solution, without affecting the pH of the sample).
4 The tube is now topped up with distilled water and thoroughly shaken.
5 Add a few drops of universal indicator to the clear solution and against a white background compare the colour of the liquid with the colour chart provided. The pH value equivalent to the colour obtained can now be read off to the nearest 0.5 of a unit.

There are various methods of assessing the levels of nutrients in a soil sample. Many of these are very complicated. However, there are test kits available commercially which measure the essential mineral salt levels. (This has obvious application in horticulture and agriculture in assessing soil nutrient deficiency and determining the amount of fertiliser that must be added to correct it.) The self-contained kits involve testing the soil with a particular reagent and comparing the colour with the standard colour charts. Measurements may be made of the level of lime (pH), nitrate, phosphate and potassium salts.

4.9 Extracting soil organisms

The soil provides micro-habitats for numerous animals: some will form burrows, e.g. earthworms, others live in the air spaces, e.g. springtails, or in the water film around the soil particles, e.g. nematodes. Many of these are detritivores and will decompose humus, returning nutrients and affecting soil structure, which will in turn affect the plants growing there (Fig 4.21).

The study of these soil organisms presents problems not experienced when investigating other terrestrial animals and plants. Many are microscopic and spend most of their lives hidden from view. The density of a particular species will also depend upon environmental variables such as pH, temperature, humidity and humus content of the soil. Special methods of extraction have been devised and it is important that these be made quantitative so that numbers per unit area of a given depth of soil may be estimated. Different groups of soil organisms require different techniques to extract them. None of these can be expected to be totally successful so that an accurate assessment of the efficiency of each extraction method is not always easy to make.

1 Hand sorting can be used for material collected from the large soil or litter sampler described earlier (page 55). Some of the sample is placed in a large white enamel bowl and a lamp placed over it. The steep sides of the bowl prevent fast moving animals from escaping and many of these can be collected in a pooter. The same sample can now be spread over an illuminated white plastic sheet and any other animals removed by means of a small moistened paintbrush or picked up with forceps.
2 Smaller soil cores of uniform size can be taken to a depth of 8 cm with the hand held sampler (Fig 4.20). Smaller soil organisms can be extracted by dry and wet funnel techniques.

Tullgren funnel

Soil animals naturally show an aversion to light and to hot dry conditions. This is the principal upon which the Tullgren funnel operates (Fig 4.22). A single core sample is carefully broken up and placed on the metal gauze under a 25 watt bulb. A combination of the light and the heat drying the sample from the top causes the animals to move downwards eventually to fall into the beaker of preservative. The apparatus should be left for 4/5 days before the organisms are identified and counted. The home-made version of this apparatus makes use of a mesh 16 flour sieve and is so cheap to assemble that a battery of funnels may be used to compare the extraction of organisms from a number of replicate samples taken from the same site. There are a number of commercial models of the Tullgren funnel available (Fig 4.23) and these are efficient if used properly.

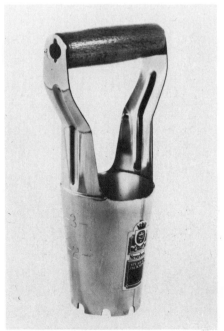

Philip Harris Ltd

Fig 4.20 Hand held soil sampler

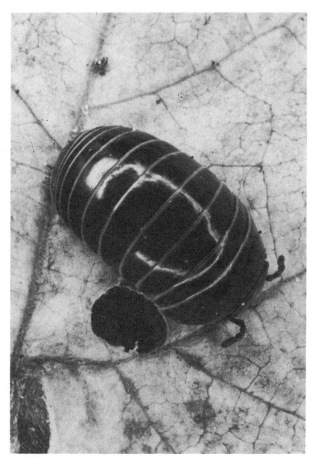

Millipede, *Glomeris marginata*

Isopoda, *Oniscus asellus*

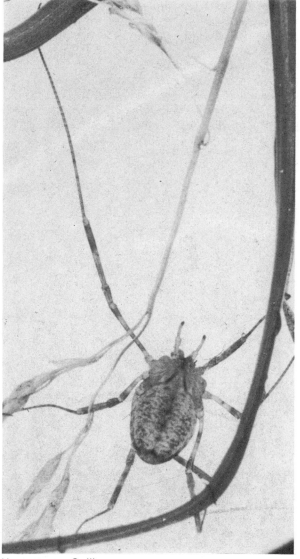

Pseudoscorpion, *Neobisium muscosum*

Fig 4.21 Soil mesofauna

Harvestman, *Opiliones* sp.

J A Wallwork

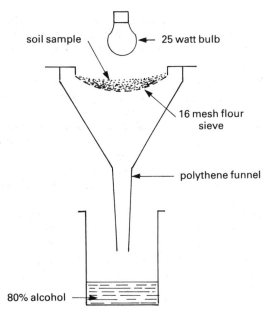

Fig 4.22 Home-made Tullgren funnel (after Archer)

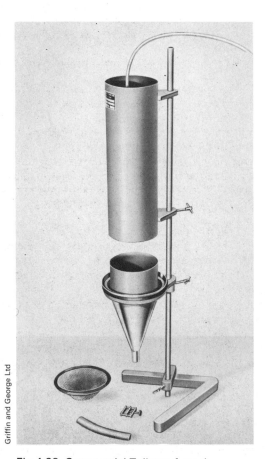

Fig 4.23 Commercial Tullgren funnel

Question 7

The following questions refer to possible sources of error in the use of this equipment:

a Why should the sample layer of soil on the sieve not be too thick?

b Why might a sieve with a convex mesh prove more efficient than a flat one?

c How might the following adversely affect the extraction process:

    i)   using too high powered an electric light bulb?

    ii) placing the electric light bulb too close to the surface of the soil sample?

d The gap between the sieve and funnel prevents moisture forming on the funnel wall. Why is this important?

Baermann funnel

The Tullgren funnel can be used to extract small soil organisms that live in the air spaces between soil particles and that can tolerate lack of water. This technique is unsuitable for animals inhabiting the film of water around the soil particles or those that are easily susceptible to desiccation. For these organisms, which include nematodes, rotifers and enchytraeids (pot worms), a wet funnel technique is required such as the

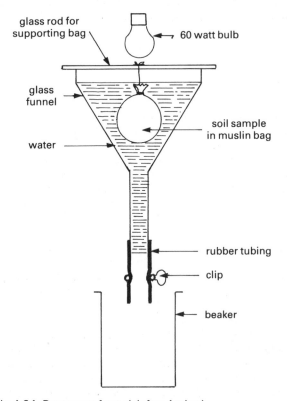

Fig 4.24 Baermann funnel (after Archer)

Baermann funnel (Fig 4.24). In this case the small soil sample is contained in a bag of muslin and suspended in a funnel which is completely filled with water. Since there is no danger of the animals drying up and since there is a relatively large volume of water to heat up, a more powerful 60 W electric light bulb is used. As the water is heated by the lamp a temperature gradient is set up and the animals pass out of the muslin bag, down the stem of the funnel from which they can be collected at intervals by releasing the spring clip.

Flotation

Dry and wet funnel techniques depend upon the ability of the soil animals to escape from the soil sample as a result of stimulation. The ability to do this varies greatly from one species to another and of course resting stages, such as cocoons, pupae and eggs, can not be extracted at all. These along with slower moving forms can be successfully extracted from the soil by flotation on a liquid with a slightly higher specific gravity than water. This method is notably successful in the separation of smaller arthropods, such as mites, using a 25% zinc sulphate or magnesium sulphate solution. Small amounts of soil are gradually stirred into the solution and as the animals float to the surface they can be removed with a small paint brush. This method is not suitable for soils with a high humus content as much of the organic material will also float to the surface and interfere with the separation process. This method of extraction can be rather laborious and it is difficult to make the estimation quantitive due to its relative inefficiency.

Extracting earthworms

Earthworms are common and extremely important members of the soil community. They are detritivores, feeding upon partially decayed leaves which they drag into their burrows and in this way they help to incorporate organic matter into the soil. Any indigestible material is ejected either at the surface as worm casts or underground. Not only do the activities of earthworms improve soil fertility, but their burrows also serve to aerate and drain the soil.

Of the twenty five species of earthworms in Britain ten are common in gardens and on agricultural land. They avoid sandy soils which are prone to frost and drought but are equally intolerant of poorly drained clay soils where aeration may be poor. Many avoid acid soils (Fig 4.19) due to the scarcity of calcium, a vital dietary requirement.

Obtaining a quantitative estimate of an earthworm population has its problems, not least because they display differing vertical distributions. Some species such as *Lumbricus terrestris* and *Allolobophora nocturna* are able to burrow down several feet making normal soil sampling methods impracticable. One method of ex-

traction is to apply a solution, such as 2% methanal (formaldehyde) which will penetrate the earthworm burrows and stimulate them to come to the surface.

Method
1 Make up an approximately 2% solution by placing 25 cm³ of 40% methanal into a garden watering can and filling it to the gallon mark.
2 Mark out a square metre quadrat on the sample area with string and pegs and apply the solution evenly using a sprinkler attachment.
3 Wait five minutes, by which time the more active surface-living species such as *L. castaneus* will begin to emerge.
4 Count the extracted worms and immediately rinse off the methanal with fresh water. They may be weighed if an estimate of biomass is required.

The method can only be regarded as partially successful and the most reliable quantitative technique remains hand sorting. However, for comparing populations from two different sites it is satisfactory and certainly less laborious.

Methanal (formaldehyde) is a 'cancer suspect agent' and great care must be exercised when using it. It may well be that the use of a dilute aqueous solution of potassium permanganate, which yields similar results, is preferable.

Question 8
a With reference to Figure 4.19 outline the effects of soil pH upon the depth distribution of earthworms.
b Try to explain this distribution.
c What other edaphic (soil) factors could affect the density of an earthworm population?
d Devise experiments to test the effects of i) soil temperature and ii) soil water upon earthworm activity.

4.10 Estimating soil micro-organisms

In order to count micro-organisms, such as bacteria, fungi and actinomycetes in a soil sample, a culture technique such as the dilution plate method is widely used:
1 Weigh out 10 g of the soil sample and place it in a conical flask with 100 cm³ of sterile water.
2 Shake the flask vigorously for several minutes to ensure an even disposal of the soil particles.
3 The suspension is now diluted in order to obtain a convenient concentration of the micro-organisms (Fig 4.25).
4 1 cm of appropriately diluted suspension is then pipetted onto a nutrient medium in a sterile petri dish.
5 The plate is then incubated and the colonies counted after 1 or 2 days.

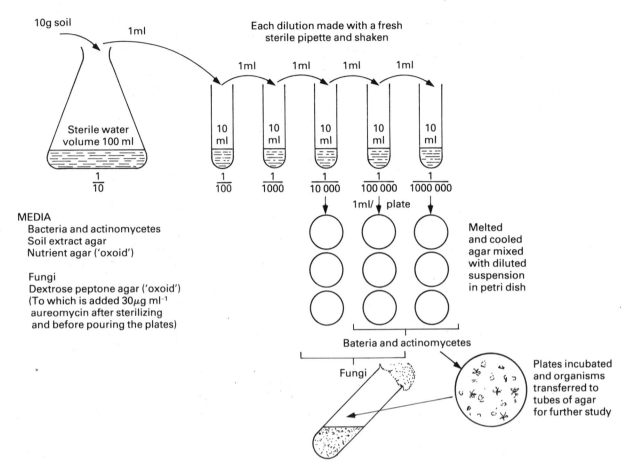

Fig 4.25 Dilution plate method (from Jackson and Raw 1966)

The use of different media means that certain micro-organisms can be selected. The method assesses fairly successfully the numbers of those bacterial species capable of developing on the media used, but is less meaningful for counting fungi. One sporing mycelium will result in hundreds of colonies on the dilution plates whilst one non-sporing mycelium may not be represented at all.

4.11 Extraction of meiofauna of sand and mud

Previously in this chapter a number of techniques were described for the extraction of soil-living organisms. It is convenient to include here techniques for the extraction of microscopic, though not planktonic, animals which are present in marine deposits (Fig 4.26). Few text books of a non-specialist nature have attempted to describe the animals that inhabit the *interstices* (spaces) between the grains of sand or mud. Here there are representatives of most of the invertebrate classes and convergent evolution between phyla is a feature of

this unique microfauna. Certain shapes of body dominate the interstitial fauna: these tend to be worm-like or flattened varying in size from 0.5 mm to 3 mm; mechanical protection of the toughened body wall often involves the possession of scales and spines, others are able to contract their body wall and avoid injury between the constantly moving sand grains. Adhesive organs are present in most species enabling them to stick firmly to sand surfaces and they are negatively phototactic. They are tolerant of a wide range of salinity and temperature and migrate vertically into the sediment in adverse conditions. Figure 4.27 illustrates two methods for the extraction of meiofauna from sand and mud.

1 Take a quantitative sample from a known depth with a 2.5 cm diameter corer.
2 Place some of the sediment in a beaker and add an equal volume of 6% magnesium chloride, (i.e. 73.2 g/litre which is isotonic to 34 ppt seawater).
3 Swirl the mixture and allow 10–15 minutes for anaesthetisation.
4 The sediment is thoroughly stirred and the superna-

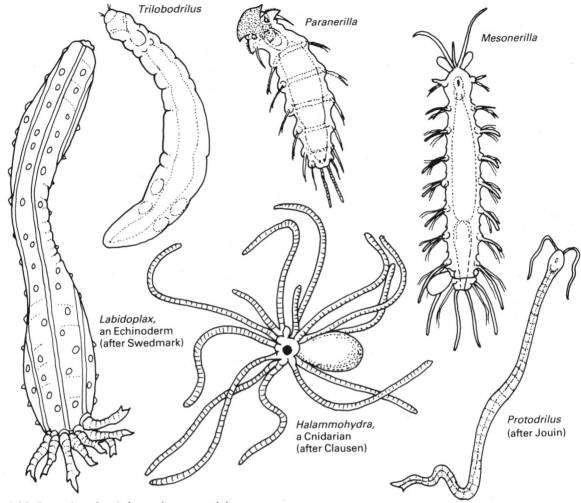

Trilobodrilus

Paranerilla

Mesonerilla

Labidoplax,
an Echinoderm
(after Swedmark)

Halammohydra,
a Cnidarian
(after Clausen)

Protodrilus
(after Jouin)

Fig 4.26 Examples of meiofauna (not to scale)

tant poured through a fine mesh gauze or plankton net (62 µm pore diameter).

5 Invert the gauze in a petri dish and wash the animals off with a jet of filtered seawater from a wash bottle.

6 Remove the organisms with a fine pipette (warning: non-narcotized animals stick to the glass – silicon coated pipettes are preferred!)

7 Place the animals on a slide and examine under the microscope.

An alternative technique not involving the use of a narcotic is the **Uhlig Seawater Ice Technique** which has a greater extraction efficiency of up to 90%:

1 Seawater from the vicinity of the sediment sample is frozen.

2 The sediment sample is placed in a coarse nylon gauze (140 µ pore diameter) at the bottom of a tube (an 8 cm diameter plastic drain-pipe cut to a 12 cm length is ideal).

3 A thin layer of cotton wool is placed on top of the sediment followed by the crushed seawater ice.

4 The ice melts and the small motile organisms are carried through the gauze and collected in a petri dish.

The animals extracted by either of these methods may be preserved in 4% formalin for future examination. Little in the way of identification is readily available on these fascinating and much neglected inhabitants of the interstices. A systematic survey is included in 'The interstitial fauna of marine sand' by Swedmark (*Biol Rev* 1968, 39 pp 1–42). A more extensive treatment appears in two Smithsonian contributions to zoology: *A Manual for the study of Meiofauna*, N Hulings and J S Gray (1971) and *Proceedings of the first International Conference on Meiofauna*, edited by N Hulings (1971), both published by Smithsonian Institution Press.

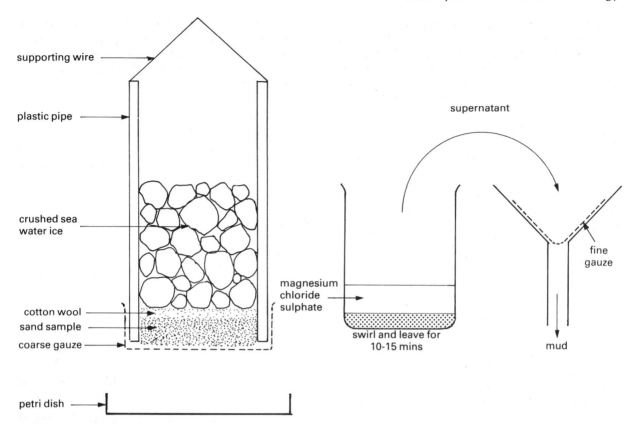

Fig 4.27 Techniques for extracting meiofauna from sand and mud

4.12 Project suggestions

1 Comparing the properties of different soil types

Choose two or more different soils, e.g. under deciduous woodland and coniferous plantation, or cultivated and uncultivated. For each examine the soil profile and make estimations of some of the following properties a) texture b) water content c) organic content d) pH. Try to account for any differences in these properties for each soil type.

2 Soils and associated vegetation

In a similar exercise attempt to classify a particular soil on the basis of its profile and the aforementioned properties. Also take into consideration the geology of the parent rock and the prevailing climate. Subjectively access the associated vegetation and attempt to relate it to the soil type, e.g. calcicole plants on chalk and limestone soils or calcifuges inhabiting acid heathland.

3 Soil formation and colonisation

Mountain screes are slopes of rock fragments (*talus*) which are found below steep rock faces (*crags*).

Examine the physical properties of the scree: aspect, altitude, rock type, 'angle of rest' of scree slope, presence of humus, variation in rock size along slope and pH. Examine the pioneer species of plant on the newest part of the scree. How do they colonise this 'young' soil and how do they modify it? Record later stages of colonisation by carrying out a line transect down the slope. Try to recognise different stages in the succession.

4 The colonisation of newly cultivated soil

Experimental plots can be cleared of vegetation, dug over and then left in order to investigate the process of colonisation over several months. At weekly intervals they should be examined for new species and percentage cover of the vegetation. The changes in the organic content of the soil can also be monitored as colonisation occurs. As some species become established competition between plants may increase with a resultant decrease in the diversity of species present.

5 The effect of insecticides upon soil populations

Establish four experimental plots (2 m × 2 m) removing the vegetation and digging each plot over to a depth of about 15 cm. Take three core samples from each plot and extract any soil animals by means of the Tullgren funnel method. Make a total count for the springtails (*Collembola*) and mites (*Acari*). To two of the plots apply a commercial pesticide leaving the other two as controls. Take further soil samples after 4, 8 and 12 weeks and analyse each by Tullgren funnel extraction. Some pesticides have been found to have less effect upon springtails than they do on their predators the mites. As a result the springtail population may explode when their normal predators are suppressed.

6 The abundance and distribution of earthworms

Earthworms can be extracted from a known area of soil by the methanal technique described earlier. Various studies can be made comparing two sites, e.g. heathland soil and deciduous woodland soil. The pH and humus content of each soil could be determined and the relative abundance of worms related to soil conditions. Other exercises could be devised to study the density of earthworms in cultivated and uncultivated soil, or the depth distribution of different species. Seasonal variations in the numbers of earthworms in the superficial layers of the soil could be related to temperature and soil water recorded. Cages constructed of 1 m² wooden frames covered with chicken wire could be used to study the rate of leaf burial by earthworms.

7 The colonisation and decomposition of cellophane

Pieces of cellophane are boiled in distilled water to sterilise them and remove plasticisers. The cellophane is then cut into 1 × 1 cm squares whilst it is still soft, and four squares are stuck onto one side of a glass slide. A number of slides prepared in this way are buried vertically in topsoil and their position marked. Each week a slide is removed from the soil and examined microscopically after staining with cotton blue in lactophenol. From these observations the patterns of colonisation and succession on the cellulose film can be studied.

8 The colonisation and decomposition of leaf litter

Obtain nets of varying mesh size, e.g. 10 mm, (e.g. a hair net), 1 mm, (e.g. a net curtain) and 0.05 mm, (e.g. nylon tights). Prepare four bags of each of these mesh sizes and into each bag place 10 freshly cut leaf squares of a standard size, e.g. 20 × 20 mm. Tie the opening of each bag. Bury the bags of each mesh type in the soil at a different marked location in the study area. After one month remove one bag of each mesh size from the soil and carefully remove the leaf squares. Use graph paper to estimate the percentage area of decomposition of

the leaf squares from each bag. How does mesh size correlate with the rate of decomposition of the leaf squares? A microscopic examination of the leaf squares will give information about the sequence of colonisation.

4.13 Exercises

1 The diagram shows a profile of a chalk hillside and the tables which follow contain data obtained at various sites on the hillside.

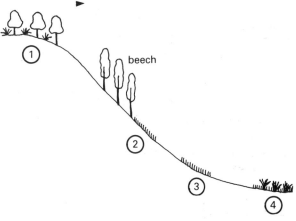

Table 1 Measurements of carbonates (mainly calcium) and pH of soil samples taken from four sites on the hillside

Site	Main vegetation	Carbonates (mainly calcium) in arbitrary units	pH
1	oak and bracken	0.02	5.3
2	grassland	1.50	7.3
3	grassland	28.05	7.6
4	grassland and scrub	16.55	7.5

Table II Calcium content of leaf litter expressed as a percentage of the dry mass

Beech	Oak	Bracken
2.46	1.70	0.83

a Discuss possible reasons for the differences in carbonate content and pH value of the soil at each of the four sites and relate these differences to the vegetation indicated on the profile and in Table 1.

b Suggest a reason for the different values of calcium content of leaf litter.

c If grassland is farmed it becomes deficient in minerals, and artificial fertilisers have to be added. Explain two possible disadvantages of the large-scale use of artificial fertilisers.

d i) State four soil characteristics, other than mineral content and pH, which might differ at the four sites.

ii) Describe how you would carry out a field investigation of any one of the characteristics stated in (i). (AEB 1982)

2 A plastic tube, about 100 cm long was plugged at one end with glass wool and filled with dry clay. A similar tube was set up containing dry sand. Each tube was then stood in water in a beaker. In each tube, as the water rose, its surface was marked at intervals and its depth measured. These results were plotted in the form of a graph to show the water level at intervals over a period of four days:

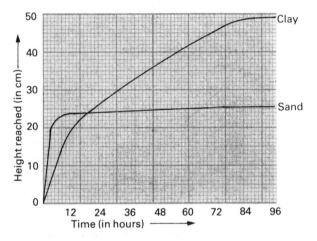

a How long does it take the water to reach the 40 cm mark in clay?

b In which tube did water initially rise more quickly?

c After how long is the water in the two tubes at the same height?

d Suggest a reason for the initial part of the sand graph.

e Suggest a reason for the greater rise in the tube with clay. (WJEC O-level 1971)

3 20 g of garden soil were heated in an oven at 100°C until, on weighing at hourly intervals, the weight remained constant at 18.5 g. The soil was then rubbed and shaken through a sieve with a 2 mm mesh. The part not passing through the sieve was now discarded and the retained portion weighed and found to be 17.2 g. This portion was then placed in an oven and heated at 600°C until there was no further change in weight. It then weighed 14.5 g.

a What was the percentage of water present in the sample of soil?

b How was the water removed?

c What constitutes the 1.3 g of the sample that failed to pass through the 2 mm mesh sieve?

d What percentage of the original sample of soil is composed of humus?

e What percentage of rock particles are present in the soil sample? How are these particles important to the soil? (WJEC O-level 1974)

4 The mites and the *Collembola* together form the most common multicellular invertebrates in the soil, both in numbers of individuals and numbers of species, although in terms of biomass they are generally of less significance than the earthworms. This wide range of species of mites and collembolans plays a variety of roles in the soil community. The majority are saprophagous detritivores, but several are microphytic feeders and a number of the mite species are predatory. Neither group of animals is able to burrow; they penetrate through the soil by utilising existing soil spaces. The porosity of the soil is therefore an important factor in determining both their vertical and horizontal distribution. This was demonstrated by the following experiment in which the soil porosity was deliberately reduced.

An area of grassland was divided into two 30 square metre plots. One plot was compacted by driving a tractor over its entire area ten times, while the other plot was left untouched as a control.

Twelve soil samples were taken from each plot immediately before treatment in December and this sampling procedure was repeated at intervals of two weeks, one month, three months, six months and nine months after treatment.

The table below shows the mean number of mites

Plots	December pre-treatment		December 2 weeks after treatment		January		March		June		September	
	M	C	M	C	M	C	M	C	M	C	M	C
Compacted	89.3	139.9	24.2	5.3	44.0	52.4	39.4	28.9	314.0	64.2	132.4	72.7
Control	83.5	132.2	109.8	163.9	103.9	60.7	98.2	23.5	298.1	58.3	150.7	60.2

(M) and collembolans (C) per sample, from the 12 samples taken on each occasion.

a Explain what you understand by the terms:
 i) biomass ii) saprophagous detritivores iii) microphytic iv) porosity.

b Suggest a possible food supply for the predatory mites.

c Enter the data required to complete the following table:

	Approximate initial % reduction in population caused by compaction	Time after which recovery from compaction is complete
Mites		
Collembola		

d On graph paper plot the seasonal changes in i) mite and ii) Collembola numbers in the undisturbed grassland.

e Does an examination of your graph suggest one possible reason for the recovery period of the mites which you have calculated in *c*? Explain.

f Suggest one other possible reason for a recovery in the mean number of animals in the samples.

g If similar data were required from the earthworm population, outline the sampling method you would use.

h In the control plot, the mean values two weeks after treatment are higher than the corresponding pre-treatment means. How would you decide whether these differences were likely to be due to genuine changes in the population or simply to variation in the numbers of animals in each sample?
(WJEC 1981)

5 In an investigation of soil ecology, discs of oak leaves were buried during July in a loamy soil. Discs were enclosed in nylon bags of three different mesh sizes, 7.0 mm, 0.5 mm and 0.003 mm. The bags were removed from the soil at intervals and the rate of disappearance of the leaf discs was estimated by measuring the area of leaf tissue which remained and expressing the area which had disappeared as a percentage of the original area. The results of the investigation are given in the table.

Date	% disappearance of leaf discs in nylon bags of mesh size:		
	7 mm	0.5 mm	0.003 mm
1979 July	0	0	0
August	20	5	0.5
September	35	10	1
October	50	15	1.5
November	55	19	2
December	56	23	2
1980 January	57	26	2
February	58	27	2
March	60	28	2.5
April	63	30	3
May	70	31	4
June	77	33	6
July	85	36	8
August	95	40	10

a Plot the data given in the table on a single set of axes and use your graph to answer questions *b* to *e*.

b Name **three** types of soil-living organism which are likely to feed upon the leaf discs in the bags with the 7 mm mesh.

c Comment on the data obtained for each mesh size.

d Carefully explain how you would have obtained a figure for inclusion in the table for September 1980 if you had been responsible for recording the data from a nylon bag of mesh 7 mm.

e Suggest with reasons how these data might differ if the site under investigation was the acid soil of a moorland.
(AEB 1982)

5 Water analysis

Fig 5.1 A rapid flowing upper stream at Embercombe, Somerset after heavy rain

J H Oldham

5.1 Properties of water

The physical and chemical characteristics of water have a fundamental influence upon aquatic plants and animals. Water is a far denser medium than air, providing substantial support to the animals and plants which inhabit it (aquatic plants have far less mechanical tissue than do their terrestrial counterparts and many large marine animals, e.g. seals, find movement far more laborious on land). Its high relative density also means that water has high viscosity and provides resistance to anything moving through it (hence streamlining in many larger aquatic animals and the ability of many small animals to reduce the rate at

which they sink).

Water has a very high heat capacity so can absorb a large amount of heat for a small rise in temperature. Therefore life in water does not suffer from wide and sudden fluctuations in temperature. Warm water is also less dense that cold (water is densest at 4°C). In autumn the upper layers of water in a lake will cool and sink to be replaced with warmer less dense water from below. This cyclical water movement is important in replenishing surface waters with nutrients which have accumulated in deeper water, an important factor in the growth of phytoplankton. Water colder than 4°C is less dense which explains why ice will form at the surface of a lake leaving the organisms beneath it protected from freezing.

Surface tension enables many aquatic insects, e.g. water measurers and water crickets, to support themselves on the water surface. Many other aquatic organisms can cling to the underside of the surface water film. Much of the light that falls upon the water surface is reflected and light intensity diminishes with depth until, usually between 4 and 10 metres, there is insufficient light for plants to photosynthesise properly. Light quality also changes with depth, green and blue parts of the spectrum tending to penetrate further into water than do red and orange. Red seaweeds are most abundant on the lower shore and the sub-littoral fringe since, unlike green and brown algae, they contain photosynthetic pigments, such as phycoerythrin, able to absorb blue and green light.

Water is an excellent solvent for solutes such as chlorides, carbonates, sulphates nitrates and phosphates usually in combination with sodium, potassium, calcium and magnesium. The presence of such ions in the water is dependent upon the nature of the land over which it has flowed. The amount of oxygen dissolved in water will depend upon temperature (oxygen is less soluble in water the higher the temperature), the amount of mixing that has occurred with air (fast flowing steams are usually well oxygenated, Fig 5.1) and the photosynthetic activities of green plants. Carbon dioxide combines chemically with water to form carbonic acid (H_2CO_3) which dissociates to produce hydrogen (H^+) and bicarbonate (HCO_3^-) ions. The latter may further dissociate forming more hydrogen (H^+) and carbonate (CO_3^{2-}). These bicarbonate and carbonate ions account for most of the carbon dioxide dissolved in water which originates from the respiration of animals and plants and the decomposition of organic matter.

74

Question 1

Some properties of water and air are given in the table below (the lowest figure for each property is given the value one).

Property	Water	Air
Density	800	1
Viscosity	50	1
Heat capacity (per unit volume)	4200	1
Conductance of heat	23	1
Latent heat of vaporisation	Highest of all substances	—
Concentration of oxygen at saturation	1	33
Oxygen diffusion rate	1	300 000
Concentration of carbon dioxide at saturation	1	1.2

a By reference to the table assess the advantages and disadvantages of life in water for aquatic animals using the following headings:

      Movement

      Gas exchange

      Thermoregulation

b By means of three named examples show how aquatic animals have developed adaptations to enable gas exchange to occur.

5.2 The hydrological cycle

Water vapour is present in the atmosphere as a result of evaporation from streams, rivers and lakes. Loss of water from the soil surface and transpiration by plants also contributes, but by far the biggest source of water vapour is the sea, not surprisingly since it covers 71% of the earth's surface. Where there is a change in temperature, over high ground for example, clouds condense and rain results. Some of the rain flows over the ground as surface run-off into streams and rivers, or percolates through the soil into the groundwater. Either way it inevitably finds its way back to the sea to continue the cycle (Fig 5.2).

5.3 Rivers and streams

These are referred to as the **lotic** environment and serve to convey rainwater from land to sea. At their sources they are fast flowing and cool, with high levels of dissolved oxygen and low concentrations of nutrients. Animals living in these harsh conditions have to be well adapted and species diversity is usually low. At lower altitude the flow of water decreases, areas of fast flowing water (*riffles*) alternating with slower reaches where deposition of sediments may occur. Concentrations of nutrients rise (derived from the watershed) and levels of temperature and oxygen can be more variable. With these conditions the abundance and diversity of aquatic forms increases.

Eroding river beds

In rapid flowing streams the current erodes the finer

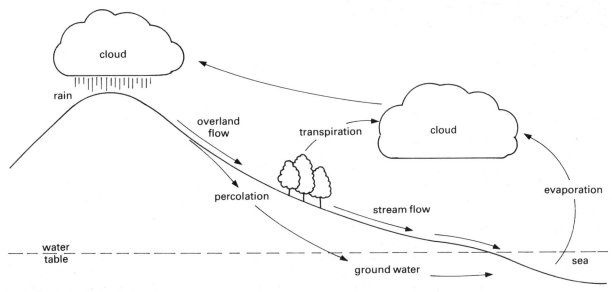

Fig 5.2 The hydrological cycle

particles leaving a rocky bed in which a great diversity and high density of invertebrates are found. In order to survive the force of the current these animals have become adapted in a number of ways. Some, such as the river limpet, *Ancylus* (Fig 5.3), leeches and flatworms, attach themselves to rocks by suctorial action; others become anchored by spinning silken webs, e.g. caseless caddis larvae of *Hydropsyche* and the blackfly larvae of *Simulium*, or cling firmly by means of grasping claws, e.g. nymphal stages of mayflies and stone flies (Fig 5.4). Many invertebrates develop streamlined bodies, e.g. mayfly nymphs of *Baetis*; others have very flattened bodies, e.g. mayfly nymphs of *Ecdyonurus* (Fig 3.2). *Gammarus*, the freshwater shrimp, lives in crevices amongst the stones relying upon this pattern of behaviour and swimming ability to prevent itself being washed away by the current. Most animals

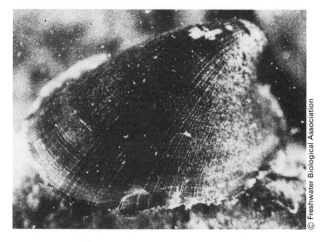

Fig 5.3 The river limpet, *Ancylus*

Fig 5.4 The stonefly larva, *Dinocras*. Note grasping hooks

The mayfly *Baetis*. Note streamlined body, grasping claws and external gills

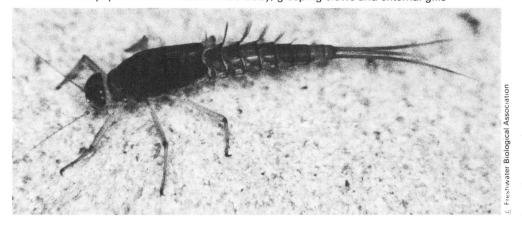

found here require high concentration of dissolved oxygen and consequently have developed conspicuous respiratory apparatus such as external gills.

Question 2
By referring to the invertebrates illustrated in Figure 5.5 decide how each has become adapted to living in conditions of high current velocity.

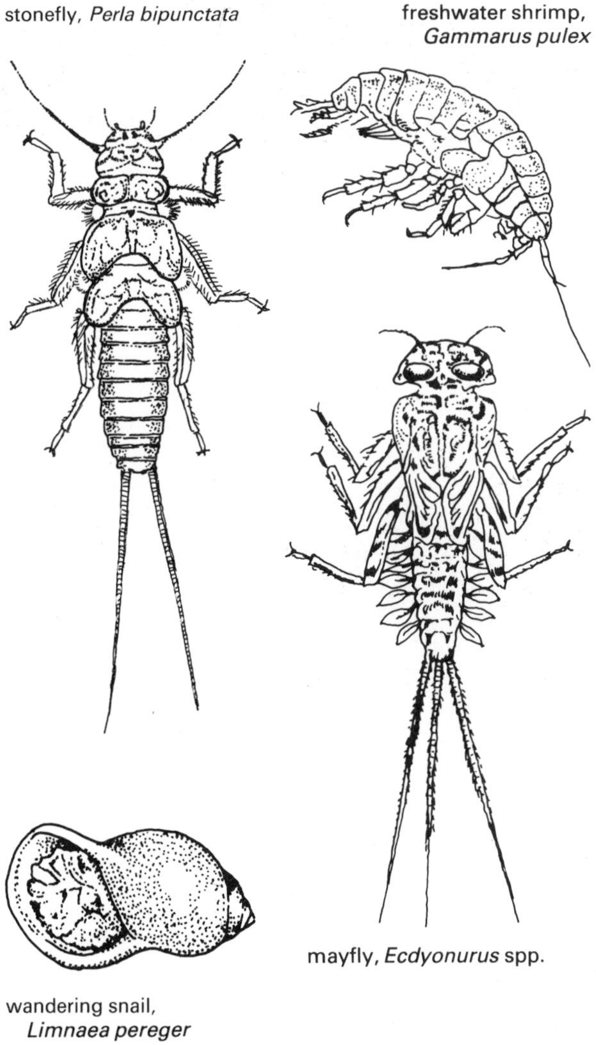

need to be tolerated here are low dissolved oxygen and high turbidity. The mud surface is often inhabited by the water louse, *Asellus*, the larvae of the alder fly, *Sialis* sp. and a variety of snails, e.g. *Bithynia* and *Valvata*. Burrowing in the mud are bivalves such as the pea mussel *Pisidium* and the freshwater mussel, *Anodonta*. The low oxygen concentrations in the mud means that many invertebrates such as the small annelid *Tubifex* and the midge larva *Chironomus* have

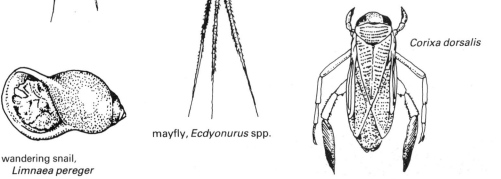

stonefly, *Perla bipunctata*

freshwater shrimp, *Gammarus pulex*

caddis fly larva in case, *Limnephilus* spp.

great diving beetle, *Dytiscus marginalis*

mayfly, *Ecdyonurus* spp.

wandering snail, *Limnaea pereger*

Corixa dorsalis

Fig 5.5 Invertebrates of eroding substrata

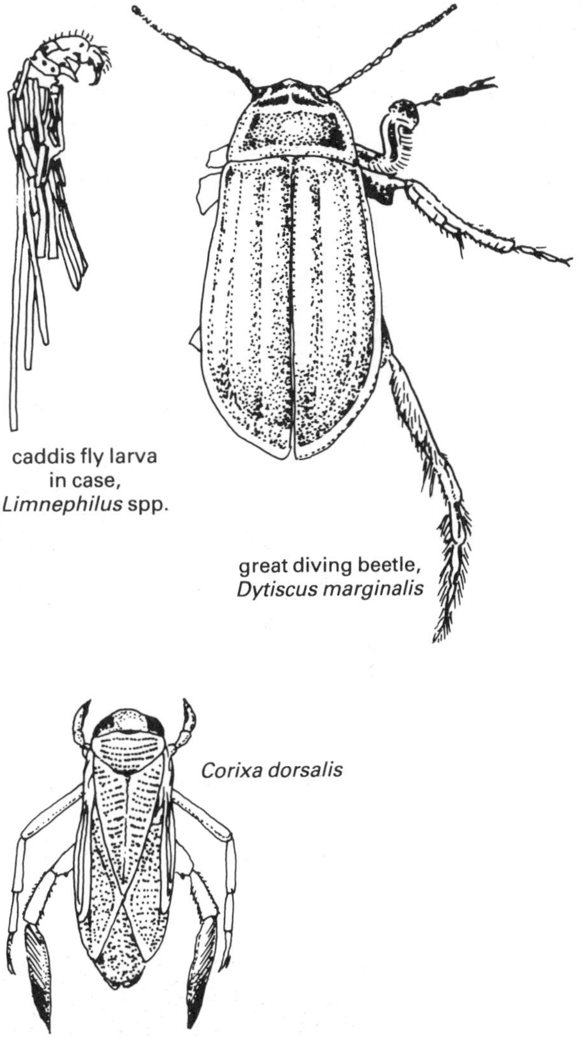

Fig 5.6 Invertebrates of depositing substrata

Depositing river beds

Where the current is slow the deposition of mud and silt may occur producing bodies of water which are less favourable for animals and plants and which consequently show a reduced density of individuals and low diversity of species. Amongst the conditions which

developed haemoglobin in order to extract oxygen under conditions of low concentation. The weedbeds provide shelter for a great variety of animals (Fig 5.6), such as water boatmen (*Corixa* and *Notonecta*), dragonfly nymphs (*Ishnura*), water scorpions (*Nepa*) and some mayfly nymphs (*Leptophlebia*).

D E Rees

Fig 5.7 A pond with good access for study

5.4 Lakes and ponds

Standing water such as lakes and ponds is known as the **lentic** environment (Fig 5.7). Where there is strong wave action, the animals inhabiting the stony shore of a lake may be similar to those inhabiting eroding river beds since they will have to be adapted to cope with a lot of water movement. Others will not be present especially if they require a consistently strong water current to bring them enough oxygen or to carry food to them. Where lakes have sandy, silty or muddy shores, the fauna is often identical to that found in depositing river beds where current is slack. In these lakes water boatmen, chironomids, snails and water beetles will be abundant. Whatever the nature of the substratum, the shore of the lake will contain the richest fauna and flora, for it is here that water plants are able to root and so provide shelter for animals, protecting them from wave action in much the same way as the brown seaweeds protect many invertebrates on a sheltered rocky seashore. An offshore zone devoid of rooted plants gradually gives way to deep water in many lakes to which light does not penetrate so that life is less rich. Lakes with a low nutrient level are termed *oligotrophic*: these are usually deep, low in dissolved minerals and are commonest at high altitude. *Eutrophic* lakes on the other hand are shallow in comparison, lie on rich mineral rock, e.g. limestone, and are found at lower levels. Their comparatively high nutrient status means that they support a rich flora and fauna.

5.5 The marine environment

The analysis of water samples may well be necessary in certain projects on seashores and estuaries. It is unlikely that work in deeper water could or should be attempted since this would involve the use of complex equipment and necessitate experienced boat handling.

Salt water contains a complex mixture of various ions the most common being chloride, sulphate, sodium and magnesium. Despite changes in salinity there is in fact very little fluctuation in the proportion of these major constituents of seawater; greatest fluctuations in such parameters as temperature, salinity and the proportion of dissolved gases occur when small bodies of water such as rock pools become isolated from the sea for a period of time. Diurnal changes of temperature, the effects of hot sun causing evaporation from the pool and so increasing salinity, and the relative proportions of animals and plants in the pool affecting the amounts of dissolved oxygen and carbon dioxide, all produce stressful conditions for pool inhabitants. In estuaries the same can be said since the variation in salinity as a result of freshwater mixing with seawater results in a low diversity of species. Changes in temperature, salinity and dissolved gases in the oceans are minute so it is not surprising that the many marine species found there fail to survive when faced with the hardships that intertidal species have to cope with (see Question 7). The pounding action of waves also affects the distribution of shore populations as was mentioned in Chapter 3.

The seashore is delineated by the tidal cycles (Fig 5.8), being that region between extreme high tide and extreme low tide. Tides are a result of the gravitational attraction of the moon (and to a lesser extent the sun) acting upon the waters. The highest and lowest tides occur about two days after new and full moon when the moon, earth and sun are all in a line and maximum gravitational force is exerted. These tides are called *spring tides*.

In Figure 5.8 the shore levels are shown vertically for different stages of high spring tide, low neap tide and average tidal range. The letters refer to:
E = extreme   M = mean   H = high
N = neap   L = low (or level if last letter)
S = spring   T = tide   W = water
The middle shore is shaded grey; above it is the upper shore, below it the lower shore.

Exercise
Using these letters, write the abbreviations for:
1   The mean lowest level to which spring tides fall
2   The mean highest level to which neap tides rise
3   The highest level that is ever covered by water (a spring tide at the equinox)
4   The mean level when the neap tide is fully out
5   The lowest level that is left exposed when the neap tide is in
6   The mean level of the sea during the year

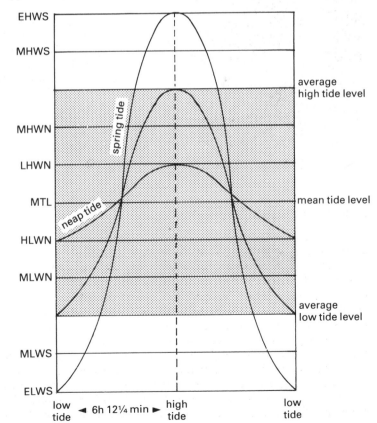

Fig 5.8 The tidal cycles (from Open University S202 Biology: Form and Function)

Slack tides known as *neap tides* occur at the first and last quarters of the moon when the gravitational forces of the sun and moon are acting at right angles to each other. Neap tides have the smallest tidal range represented by the lowest high tides and the highest low tides. Tides of exceptional range occur in March and September around the 'equinoxes' when the effects of the moon and the sun are at a maximum.

Around our coast there are two tides each day, the interval between successive high tides being about 12 hours 25 minutes. So each day the time of high tide will be approximately 50 minutes later than on the previous day. Before working on the shore or estuary consult Admiralty Tide Tables for the area in order to obtain the predicted time of low tide.

5.6 Safety during fieldwork

Many aquatic habitats, whether they be marine or freshwater, are fragile and prone to damage under the pressures of exhaustive fieldwork (see Chapter 2). Working in the vicinity of water also holds many potential hazards for the student carrying out a project. Reference should be made to the publication *Safety in Biological Fieldwork – Guidance Notes for Codes of Practice* produced by the Institute of Biology. A number of points are worth presenting here.

1 **Don't work on your own.** Even if you are pursuing an individual project, work in groups in the field.

2 **Obtain advice about the area you are about to study before going into the field.** Identify any hazards such as eroding riverbanks, tides or sediments.

3 **When working on the shore or estuary refer to Admiralty Tide Tables, adjusting them to local shores.** Don't get caught by an incoming tide, it is best to work following the tide out. On a shallow sandy shore, mud flat or estuary the tide can return surprisingly quickly. Obtain a weather forecast prior to leaving.

4 **Do not attempt to work on very exposed coasts** where the unpredictable wave action can easily sweep a person off the rocks. A life line or even a life belt are advisable equipment in conditions approaching these.

5 **Do not work from a boat unless you are supervised by a person experienced in its use.**

6 **Take great care when working in the vicinity of polluted water.** Seal all samples tightly and wash hands thoroughly in clean water if they come into contact with a polluted water sample.

5.7 Water samplers

A number of methods are available for collecting samples of water for chemical analysis. Sampling in shallow water can be carried out by simply allowing a half or one litre plastic lemonade bottle to fill with water. It is then stoppered whilst still immersed to prevent the entry of air bubbles. Another simple device for sampling from a greater depth is shown in Figure 5.9. This consists of a weighted bottle which can be lowered to the required depth on a line secured to the neck. A pull on the second line removes the stopper and allows the bottle to fill via the plastic tube so preventing the incoming water mixing with the air originally in the bottle. This method is unsuitable for use in deep water and there will be some contamination of the sample as the bottle is drawn back up to the surface.

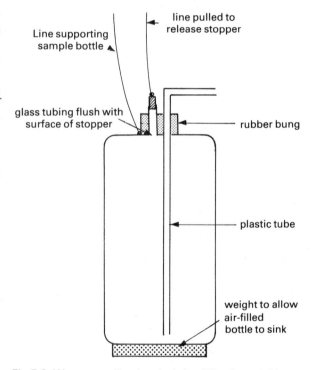

Fig 5.9 Water sampling bottle (after Wigglesworth)

Flexible plastic tubing may also be used to obtain a representative sample of the upper five or ten metres of water in a lake or deep river. In order to trap the water column a 2 cm diameter plastic tube, weighted at its free end is lowered to the required depth. The other end is then closed by means of a rubber bung, the lower end raised by means of a line and the sample run off into a bottle. This method provides an integrated sample and therefore gives no indication of any vertical gradient in environmental factors.

A number of samplers are available commercially for collecting a standard volume of water from a known depth. These basically consist of wide diameter tubes open at both ends which can be lowered to the required depth on a line. A messenger is then sent down the line which triggers off the closure mechanism and the trapped sample raised to the surface. Although expensive, these samplers provide a fixed volume of water from a known depth and will therefore also have application in the quantitative sampling of plankton. For our purposes the type of water sampler shown in Figure 5.10 is probably adequate and less costly. Again it is lowered to the required depth, being weighted by the shot ballasted lower section. The sample is then taken by giving a sharp tug on the line to remove the two polypropylene plugs from the ports in the top of the sampler allowing it to fill with water. After being drawn to the surface the sampler is emptied by removing the screw cap.

Philip Harris Ltd

Fig 5.10
The Philip Harris water sampler

5.8 Sampling aquatic organisms

A quick survey of the sampling site will probably show that it is composed of a number of microhabitats. Different animals congregate in different regions of the river, pond or lake: some are surface dwellers, such as pond skaters, others will live amongst the weeds around the pond margins, on or under stones or in the mud at the bottom. It is probably best to take a representative sample from each of these microhabitats as each will require a different collecting technique (Fig 5.11).

J H Oldham

Fig 5.11 Sampling in a stony hill stream, Chetsford Water, Exmoor

Water nets were mentioned in Chapter 2 and they can be used in a number of ways. Net sampling amongst the weeds at the pond margins can be carried out from the banks to avoid trampling. Collecting the bottom fauna requires different techniques. In fast streams a stone may be lifted with one hand whilst the net is positioned downstream of it with the other (Fig 5.12). The dislodged organisms are swept into the net by the current. In addition the stone can be lifted into the net without being taken out of the water and any animals clinging to it brushed off into the net by hand.

As with all these techniques the animals collected are then washed out into a white enamel or plastic tray and sorted. It is probably better to carry out identification and estimation on site so that the organisms can then be returned to the water. Avoid the needless removal of animals: a subsample is often more manageable when carrying out a total count to estimate percentage frequency. Kick sampling is often used to sample benthic invertebrates. The net is held on the downstream side of the area to be sampled. The substrate in front of the net is then disturbed by 3 or 4 kicks with the collector's

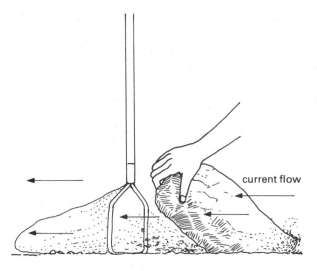

Fig 5.12 Technique for sampling stream invertebrates in rapid flowing water and below, the kick sampling technique

Fig 5.13 The Surber sampler

cleaned of animals and finally the substratum is stirred up so that any remaining animals are carried into the net.

Various other defined area samplers may be constructed, such as large open cylinders which can be forced into the stream bed. Two apertures are positioned on opposite sides of the sampler, one covered by a mesh screen to enable water to flow through the cylinder whilst preventing the entry of drift. Animals within the enclosed area are then dislodged and carried out through the other aperture by the current to be caught in a net.

For sampling invertebrates in fast or slow flowing waters **colonisation samplers** such as that shown in Figure 5.14 may be used.

boot in an upstream direction. Again dislodged animals are washed into the net by the current. These simple techniques can be made semi-quantitative providing the collector is able to repeat them consistently. Collecting should be carried out for a 5 or 10 minute period at each site working slowly up or down the sampling area.

If a standard area of substrate is to be sampled a half metre quadrat may be placed in front of the net and the material within this lifted into the net or else cleaned in front of it so that the current washes the animals into the net. A more refined version of this is the **Surber sampler** (Fig 5.13) which consists of two square frames hinged together. A fine mesh net is attached to the vertical frame and positioned to fill out downstream of the other frame which delineates the sample area. The stones in the horizontal frame are removed and

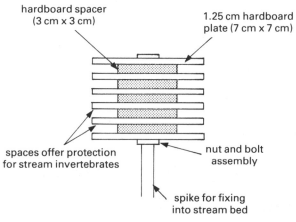

hardboard spacer (3 cm x 3 cm)

1.25 cm hardboard plate (7 cm x 7 cm)

spaces offer protection for stream invertebrates

nut and bolt assembly

spike for fixing into stream bed

Fig 5.14 Multi-plate sampler for aquatic macroinvertebrates (after Gregson)

A great deal of research has gone into the phenomenon of invertebrate drift. Many aquatic invertebrates are present in the surface drift of most streams and rivers. The amount of drift varies considerably depending upon the time of day and the season. There appears to be a marked variation in the numbers of

---

Question 3

Stoneflies of the genera *Protonemura* and *Amphinemura* have aquatic nymphs which are found in freshwater streams. In a survey carried out in 1963–64 the lengths and the densities of nymphs in or on the river bed during daylight, drifting in the water during darkness and drifting in the water during daylight were recorded from samples.

These survey results are shown in the graphs below. Note also that the periods when emerging adults were taken in drift samples (E) and the periods when flying adults could be caught (F) are indicated at the top of each set of graphs.

a Using the information in the graphs construct a scientific description of the life cycle of *Amphinemura*.

b Describe the extent to which the life cycle of *Protonemura* appears to differ from that of *Amphinemura*.

c Discuss variations which are apparent between river-bed and drift samples and between day and night samples. (AEB Nov 1982)

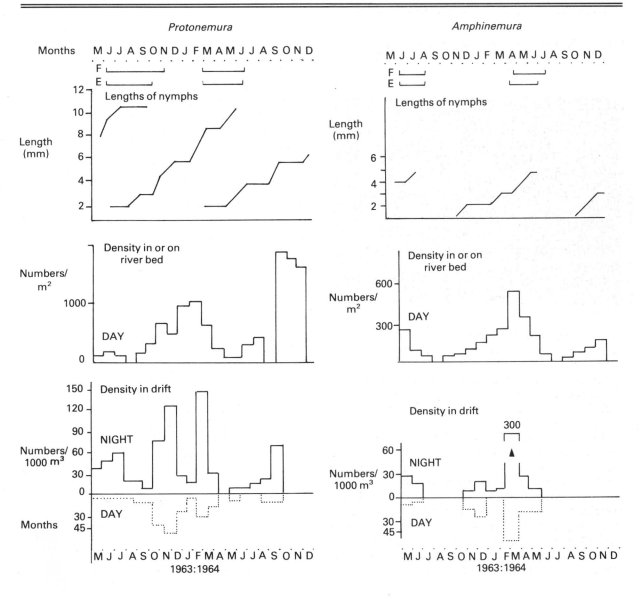

drifting invertebrates present over a 24 hour period, there being far more at night and especially just after sunset. We will see that many environmental variables such as light, temperature, pH and levels of dissolved oxygen and carbon dioxide show diurnal fluctuations. These experiments have suggested that light is the most likely of these variables to be the governing factor af-

fecting the amount of drift. Seasonal variation in drift is also apparent, there being far more in spring and summer. The **invertebrate drift sampler** in Figure 5.15 consists of a rectangular metal frame secured to the river bed by stakes or weighted down. The open end of the tapering net bag (250 μm mesh) is attached to the frame whilst the drift animals are collected in the sampling bottle at the closed end.

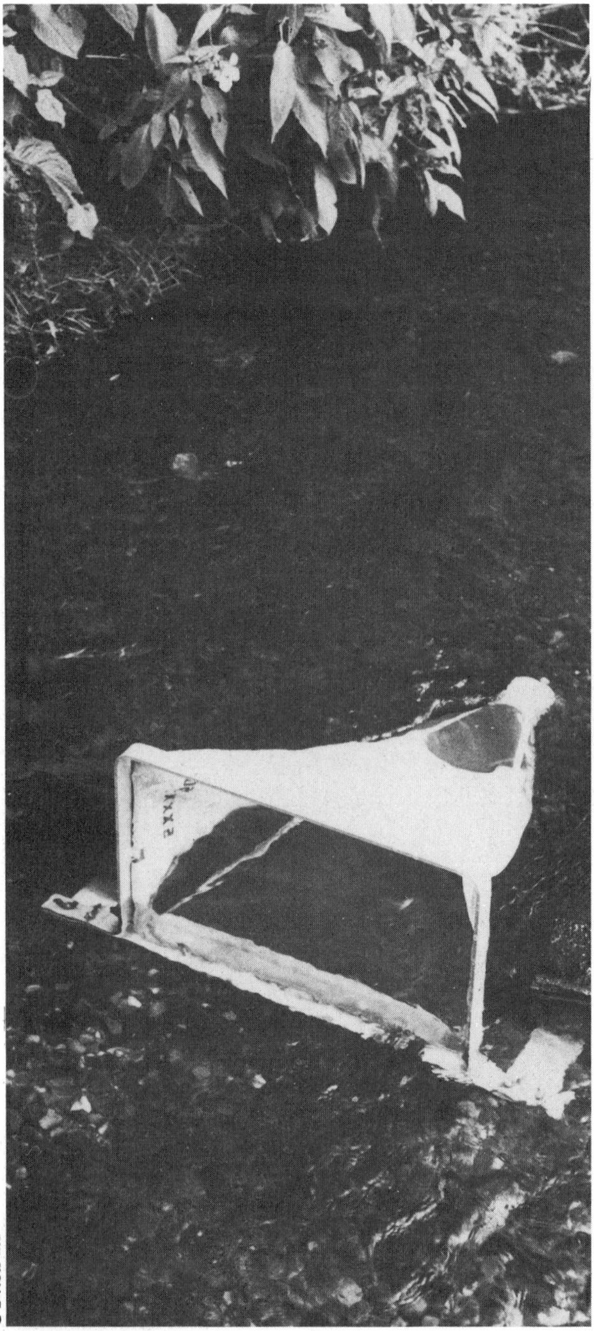

5.9 Current

The speed of flow of water exerts a profound effect upon the distribution of animals and plants. It has been mentioned earlier in the chapter how invertebrates inhabiting fast flowing streams for example have become adapted to living amongst the stones where the current is not so rapid.

Current, apart from the possible dislodgement of animals, can have a number of other indirect effects. It brings food to filter feeders, e.g. the larvae of *Simulium* (Fig 5.16), provides a continual source of well oxygenated water and, as we have seen, can have an eroding effect upon the substratum.

G B Nets Ltd

Fig 5.15 Drift net in use

© Freshwater Biological Association

Fig 5.16 The black fly larva, *Simulium,* filtering its food

Current measurement

Sophisticated current meters have been devised making use of propellers and revolution counters which are highly accurate but also expensive. A number of alternative methods are available for the measuring of current velocity:

Timed float method

1 Select a straight reach of water which is typical of the sample area. Measure the distance *d* with a tape.
2 Obtain some floats whose velocity over the measured distance *d* you can record. Choose those which float mainly below the surface and are therefore less effected by wind: oranges have proved satisfactory and are also conspicuous,.
3 Accurately time the float over the measured distance at least three times to give an average. If the channel is wide it may be useful to measure the velocity at the middle and also towards the banks.
4 Divide the average time by the coefficient 0.85. This ensures a more accurate velocity reading for the stream since the water at the surface flows faster than that beneath (the coefficient can vary from 0.8 for a rough stream bed to 0.9 if it is smooth and subjected to less friction).
5 Calculate the velocity.

$$\text{Velocity (metres per second)} = \frac{\text{distance (metres)}}{\text{time (seconds)}}$$

See Figure 5.17 for a worked example:

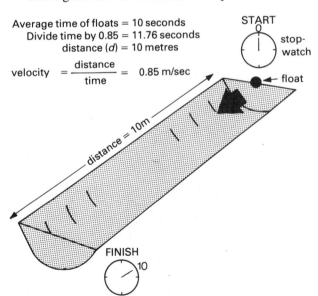

Average time of floats = 10 seconds
Divide time by 0.85 = 11.76 seconds
distance (*d*) = 10 metres

$$\text{velocity} = \frac{\text{distance}}{\text{time}} = 0.85 \text{ m/sec}$$

START
stop-watch
float
distance = 10m
FINISH

Fig 5.17 Measurement of stream velocity (from Lenon and Cleves)

This method only measures the rate of flow at the surface and gives no indication of the velocity at depth.

The Flowvane stream flow meter

This meter is able to record flow velocity down to a depth of 60 cms. It makes use of two operating vanes, the deflection of which is indicated on a dial pointer. The operator stands on the downstream side of the instrument and immerses it vertically with the smaller vane pointing upstream and the larger at approximately right angles to it (Fig 5.18). Water pressure moves the vanes in a clockwise direction and the velocity will be indicated on the dial pointer. A scale on the side of the instrument indicates the depth and the dial reading gives velocity in metres per second (the range is $0.15–2.5 \text{ m s}^{-1}$). The instrument head also contains a compass which can be used to obtain a magnetic bearing on current direction. The Flowvane has the advantage of being simple to operate, portable and not requiring batteries.

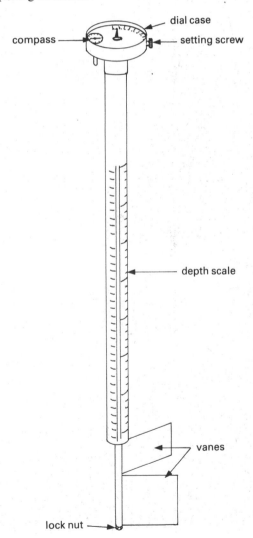

dial case
compass
setting screw
depth scale
vanes
lock nut

Fig 5.18 The Flowvane stream flow meter

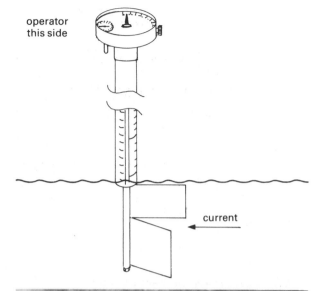

operator
this side

current

The pitot tube

The pitot tube has often been used for measuring current velocity at different depths in streams. It is basically an L-shaped tube with both ends open. It is immersed vertically with the lower opening directly against the current so that water enters and rises up the tube and its height above the water level outside can be recorded. Dowdeswell has designed an improved version making use of two L-tubes, one pointing upstream and the other down. Their other ends are connected to a manometer which displays the difference in pressures between the two tubes. This apparatus is capable of great sensitivity and efficiently demonstrates the reduction of flow velocity with increasing depth of water.

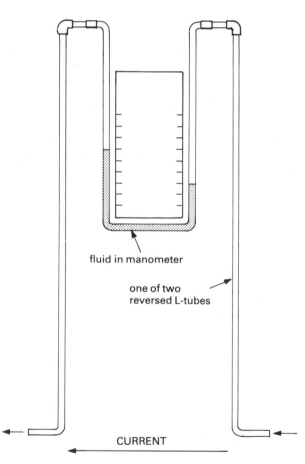

fluid in manometer

one of two
reversed L-tubes

CURRENT

Fig 5.19 Principle of the pitot tube (after Dowdeswell)

D E Rees

Fig 5.18 (cont) The Flowvane in use in the field

Once flow velocity is known it is possible to calculate stream discharge (the volume of water passing a particular point in a given time). To do this the cross-sectional area of the stream needs to be known.

To calculate cross-sectional area

1 Measure the stream width with a tape.
2 Holding the tape taut across the stream, measure water depth at regular intervals across the width, (e.g. every 25 cm in a 2 m width stream).
3 Plot measurements on graph paper to reconstruct the channel cross-section and calculate the area (in square metres). Figure 5.20 shows a worked example.

Stream discharge is calculated by multiplying the stream velocity by the cross-sectional area. An example of a data sheet for use in determining flow velocity and discharge in a stream is shown in Figure 5.21.

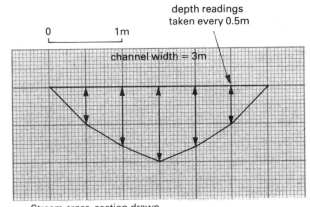

Stream cross-section drawn
from measurements
taken on the stream
Reconstructed cross-section comprises 8
large graph
paper squares
Each large square is equivalent to 0.25 m²

$$\therefore \quad \text{stream cross-sectional area} = 8 \times 0.25$$
$$= 2 \text{ m}^2$$

$$\text{discharge} = \text{stream velocity} \times \text{cross-sectional area}$$
$$= 0.85 \times 2$$
$$= 1.70 \text{ m}^3/\text{sec (cumecs)}$$

Fig 5.20 Measurement of stream cross-sectional area and discharge (from Lenon and Cleves)

Question 4
a Discuss the problems involved in measuring the velocity of the current in a stream.
b Name three invertebrates of different genera which are characteristic of fast flowing water and describe how each is adapted to this environment.
c Name two invertebrates of different genera which are characteristic of still water and describe how each is adapted to this environment.   (JMB 1982)

DISCHARGE DATA SHEET   DATE: ....
NUMBER/NAME OF REACH: ....

1 MEASUREMENT OF VELOCITY
Length of reach studied   .... metres
Time taken for first float   .... seconds
Time taken for second float .... seconds
Time taken for third float   .... seconds
Average time of floats   .... seconds
Divide by 0.85   .... seconds

$$\text{Average velocity} = \frac{\text{distance}}{\text{time}} = \text{.................} \frac{\text{metres}}{\text{seconds}} = \text{.................} \text{ m/sec}$$

3 DISCHARGE
Discharge = velocity × cross-sectional area

$$= \text{.................} \text{ m}^3/\text{sec}$$

2 MEASUREMENT OF CROSS-SECTIONAL AREA
Channel width = ... metres
Channel depth at .... centimetre intervals = 1 ....   6 ....
                                                         2 ....   7 ....
                                                         3 ....   8 ....
                                                         4 ....   9 ....
                                                         5 ....   10 ....

Cross-sectional area = ... m²

Fig 5.21 Field sheet for discharge data

5.10 Water temperature

For reasons outlined earlier temperature variations in water are far less and take place far more slowly than those on land. In general the lowest temperatures occur at the sources of streams and rivers, gradually increasing and also becoming more variable downstream. Not only is there a horizontal range of temperature but also a vertical one. Stratification of temperature with depth readily occurs particularly on sunny days in static bodies of water. Increasing water temperature also effects other variables, e.g. decreasing the oxygen load. A higher temperature will also result in a higher rate of metabolism and rapid growth of many aquatic plants and animals. Water is at its densest at 4°C and becomes lighter as it freezes; thus ice will form at the pond surface but rarely extends very far down. As a result the majority of aquatic animals never experience temperatures below freezing point in contrast to land animals.

Lakes often display seasonal variations in temperature which in turn effect the density of water at different depths. During the winter there may be a uniform temperature throughout the depth of the lake. At the onset of spring the upper layers may become warmed by the sun's rays so that by the summer two distinct layers of water have become established: an upper warmer and therefore less dense layer, the *epilimnion* separated from a colder denser layer, the *hypolimnion*. In between the two is a relatively narrow zone the *thermocline* where the temperature falls rapidly with depth (Fig 5.22). With the onset of autumn the surface water cools and sinks resulting in a breakdown of the thermocline and complete mixing of the epilimnion and hypolimnion again in winter.

Measurement of water temperature down to a depth of about a metre can be made with an electronic temperature probe. Long term records of seasonal temperature changes in a lake could be attempted by safely anchoring maximum and minimum thermometers at different depths. For greater accuracy temperature measurements at deeper levels can be made by the use of reversing thermometers, though these are expensive. When let down to the required depth the thermometer may be inverted so breaking the mercury thread and retaining it in a graduated capillary to be read at the surface.

Question 5

With reference to Figure 5.22 attempt the following:

a By how many °C and over what total depth does the temperature drop through i) the thermocline and ii) the hypolimnion?

b Nutrients tend to accumulate at the bottom of the lake as a result of the decomposition of organic matter.

   i) How does the formation of the thermocline limit the productivity of plants in the epilimnion during the summer?

   ii) How might these nutrients eventually be recycled to surface waters?

c At low latitudes (near the equator) a permanent thermocline exists for most of the year in the sea.

   i) Explain the fact that often there is little seasonal variation in the phytoplankton population.

   ii) How might the arrival of monsoons and heavy rainfall in the tropics bring about a marked increase in the phytoplankton?

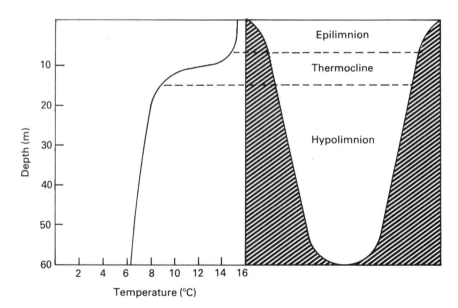

Fig 5.22
Temperatures taken on a July day in Lake Windermere at different depths (from Macan and Worthington, 1951 after Leadly Brown)

5.11 Light

Many factors can effect the penetration of light through water and thus influence the photosynthetic activities of aquatic plants. Turbidity due to the presence of suspended matter, such as silt brought by inflowing streams, will reduce light penetration. Shade from overhanging trees and the presence of the organisms themselves will also reduce the light available for photosynthesis. Submerged plants will need to be adapted to make the most efficient use of the reduced light if it is not to limit their photosynthetic rates.

A rough determination of light penetration may be made by using a *Secchi disc* (Fig 5.23). This consists of a metal disc, about 20 cm in diameter which can be suspended horizontally in the water by means of a graduated line. It is carefully lowered into the water to the depth at which it just disappears from sight and then raised to the depth at which it just reappears. The extinction coefficient can be roughly determined by the formula $K = 1.7/d$ where d is the maximum depth in metres at which the disc is visible. The *euphotic* zone (the layer of water receiving enough light to enable plants to photosynthesise) is estimated to be $2\frac{1}{2}$ × Secchi depth.

Question 5
With reference to Figure 5.24, explain the different levels of Secchi disc transparency recorded in July, September and November by referring to
a phytoplankton growth and
b turbidity of surface waters.

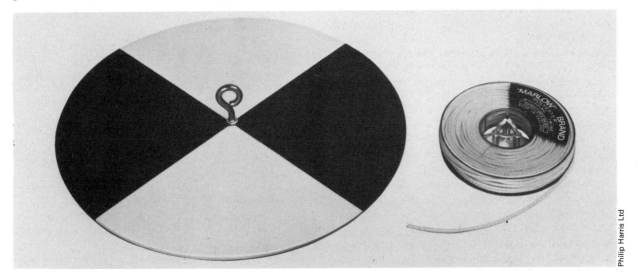

Fig 5.23 The Secchi disc

Fig 5.24 Monthly extinction coefficient values and Secchi disc transparency readings at Duddingston Loch, Midlothian (from Mills, after Mitchell, 1971). Each disk was made at 12 00 hours.

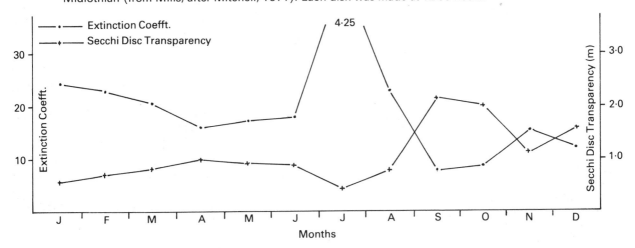

5.12 Dissolved oxygen and biochemical oxygen demand (BOD)

Oxygen is not very soluble in water and that solubility decreases with increasing temperature (Fig 5.25). It becomes dissolved at the surface when air is in contact with water; white water traps air bubbles, frequently achieving saturation levels in excess of 100%. The photosynthetic activity of water plants augments the oxygen supply during daylight hours whilst at night it becomes depleted due to the respiration of plants and animals. Oxygen shortage can occur in water containing a large amount of organic matter. During the process of decomposition micro-organisms make such demands upon the oxygen supply that it may become deficient, adversely affecting other aquatic organisms.

Temperature °C	Dissolved oxygen (mg/l or ppm)
0	14.66
5	12.37
10	10.92
15	9.76
20	8.84
25	8.11

Fig 5.25 Oxygen content of water saturated with air at normal pressure (760 mm Hg)

Chapter 3 describes two methods of estimating dissolved oxygen: the Winkler titration and the electronic oxygen meter. When using the latter manufacturers' instructions warn against possible sources of error:

1 The electrode should not be used directly in fast flowing water, unless it is held at such an angle in the water that prevents the trapping of air bubbles at the membrane.
2 Polargraphic probes are affected by chloride ions so that measurements made in seawater will require correcting (WPA have produced tables showing the corrections required for various chloride concentrations).

As already mentioned the decomposition of organic matter by bacteria can result in deoxygenation since they exert a high oxygen demand on the water. Organic matter is present in a number of effluents including raw sewage, silage and wastes from dairies, paper mills, food processing plants and manure heaps. The polluting effect on such organic matter results from the uptake of oxygen required by the bacteria during decomposition of the material. At its extreme the water may become completely anoxic resulting in death of all forms of animal and plant life and a resultant noxious smell. This sort of pollution is more serious in warmer water since there is less dissolved oxygen present anyway and animals need more oxygen due to an increase in metabolic rate.

We can estimate this type of pollution by measuring the biochemical oxygen demand (BOD). This is the amount of oxygen (in ppm) taken up by a sample of water when incubated for five days at 20°C in the dark. Very clean river samples with a BOD of below 5 ppm may be incubated undiluted, but other samples may have effluents with unusually high oxygen demands exceeding the oxygen available and these must be diluted.

Method

1 Completely fill two 250 cm³ plastic flasks A and B with the water sample (if possible closing them under water to keep them free of bubbles).
2 Record the oxygen concentration for flask A using either the Winkler method or an electronic oxygen probe.
3 Incubate the flask B in the dark for five days at 20°C. Estimate its oxygen concentration.
4 Subtract the reading of flask B from that of flask A to obtain the BOD.

River classification	5-day BOD (ppm)	Guide to biological indicators
Very clean	1	0–3 ppm
Clean	2	trout, grayling
Fairly clean	3	caddis, mayfly present
Doubtful	5	3–6 chub, dace, snails, *Gammarus* present
Bad	10	6–10 coarse fish, *Asellus*

Fig 5.26 BOD classification accepted by the Water Authorities (after Openshaw)

It is worth pointing out that deoxygenation can occur naturally in certain circumstances. Leaf fall in the autumn may add so much organic matter that the water becomes murky and foul smelling. Also excessive algal growth in static bodies of water in summer may result in little oxygen being available for respiration.

Question 6
a What is "biochemical oxygen demand"? Describe how it may be measured and give the units.
b The figures displayed in the following table represent two chemical variables, **A** and **B**, measured above and below a sewage outfall into a river.

Distance from outfall (arbitrary units)			Chemical variable (values shown in arbitrary units)	
			A	B
upstream	↑	2	100	10
		1	100	10
outfall		0	98	80
		1	30	77
downstream	↓	2	27	67
		3	38	50
		4	58	34
		5	72	20
		6	88	17

i)   Plot these figures on a graph, using the upper half of the graph paper.

ii) Suggest the identity of variables **A** and **B** and give your reasons.

iii) Add a line to your graph showing BOD and explain the shape.

iv) On the lower half of the graph paper, draw three lines to represent other variables (one chemical, one physical and one biological). Explain the shape of each curve.

c State two factors which may affect the recovery of a river from organic pollution downstream of a discharge point.   (JMB 1984)

5.13 Dissolved minerals

The ionic composition of water greatly affects the distribution of aquatic animals and plants. Minerals in streams and rivers will be derived from the rock over

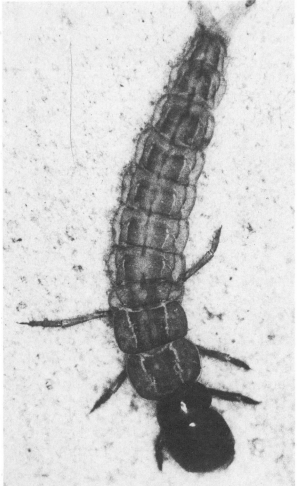

© Freshwater Biological Association

Fig 5.27 Two caseless caddis larvae: left, *Rhyacophila* is tolerant of acid water; right, *Philopotamus* is absent from acid water

which tributaries flow. Hence hard waters flowing over limestone will be rich in calcium and have a high pH. Sutcliffe and Carrick (1973) have shown that streams with little calcium and a low pH tend to have a poor fauna (Fig 5.27). Soft waters like these have drainage areas of acid soil and are characteristic of Northern England and Scotland. No doubt some acidity can be attributed to sulphur compounds derived from industrial smoke brought down as 'acid rain'.

As stated earlier the major constituents of salt water vary very little in relative proportions. Total salinity can vary, however, notably in estuarine conditions when seawater is diluted by river water. Many marine species are intolerant of this dilution and fail to survive in estuaries. These are termed *Stenohaline*. Other marine organisms are hardier and can tolerate the diluting effect. These are able to penetrate up estuaries and are called *Euryhaline* (see Question 7). The industrial pollution of some rivers by large quantities of salt has seen their colonisation by several species of salt marsh plants.

===

Question 7

A study was made of the variation of blood concentration in different salinities of three crustaceans in-

habiting marine and brackish-water (diluted seawater) environments. In each case the osmotic pressure of the blood was determined by measuring its depression of freezing point and plotted against the osmotic pressure of the medium.

a What is meant by the "isosmotic line"?

b i)   What effect does reducing the osmotic pressure of the medium have on the blood of *Maia* (spider crab)?

   ii) Comment on the ability of *Maia* to regulate its blood osmotic pressure.

   iii) What sort of osmotic environment is *Maia* likely to inhabit?

c i)   Compare the ability of *Carcinus* (shore crab) to regulate the osmotic pressure of its blood with that of *Maia*.

   ii) What significance does this have on the occurrence of *Carcinus* in or near estuaries?

d i)   Comment on the tolerance of *Palaeomonetes* (prawn) to the dilution of its external medium.

   ii) What is the likely habitat of *Palaeomonetes*?

e i)   Which of the three species is the "best" osmoregulator?

   ii) Suggest one structural feature of crustaceans which could help them resist dilution of their blood.

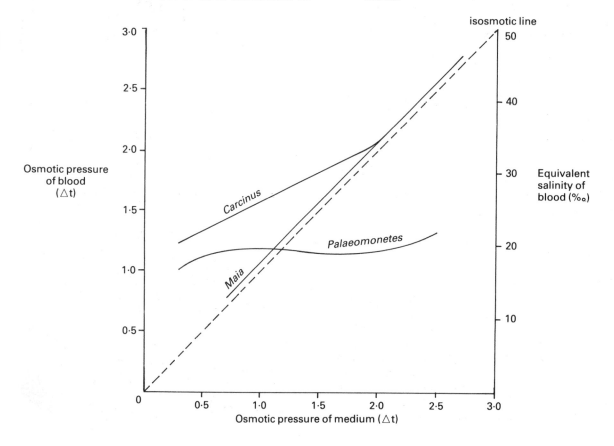

iii) Suggest one physiological method by which some crustaceans are able to resist dilution of their blood.

Conductivity

The conductivity of a water sample refers to its ability to carry an electrical current. Since electricity is carried in solutions by migrating ions, the conductivity of a solution under standard conditions should give an indication of the level of dissolved salts. The conductivity of pure water is zero. The addition of any ions to water will result in an increase in the conductivity of the resulting solution. Since salinity refers to the total weight of salts in a kilogram of water it must follow that conductivity will give a more accurate measure of salinity than would mere chloride estimation. As mentioned, conductivity measurements do not differentiate between dissolved salts so that they can have equal application in estimating the level of carbonates in unpolluted water or the degree of pollution in grossly polluted water.

Conductivity meters for field use are available and are fairly trouble free providing that the probe is well maintained. The unit of conductance is the *siemens* or *ohm*$^{-1}$, being the reciprocal of resistance. Most meters cover the range of conductivities likely to be encountered in field study (for freshwater 10^{-4} to $10^{-2}\Omega^{-1}$ cm^{-1} and for seawater up to $10^{-1}\Omega^{-1}$ cm^{-1}). Conductivity values are strongly affected by temperature changes. Some meters allow for temperature compensation but if not it must be remembered that conductivity measurements taken on different days may not be strictly comparable (conductivity rises by about 2% per °C). In estuarine studies the salinity and hence conductivity will fluctuate with the tidal cycle and with the inflow of freshwater. The degree of dilution may be estimated by referring to a conversion graph like the one in Figure 5.28, constructed by taking conductivity measurements of different dilutions of seawater.

Chloride estimation

The salinity of a sample is a measure of the total weight of salts dissolved in a kilogram of water. For a long time now textbooks have advocated the chemical estimation of dissolved chloride as a measure of salinity and this is probably accurate enough for most purposes. However, the method assumes that the percentage composition of chloride in seawater is constant in relation to all the other dissolved minerals present. Although the ionic composition of seawater does vary

very little this potential source of error needs to be pointed out. It is for this reason that conductivity has largely replaced chloride estimation as a measure of salinity since it relates to the total dissolved salts.

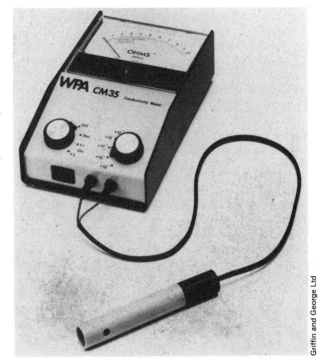

Fig 5.28 WPA Conductivity meter and calibration curve

Griffin and George Ltd

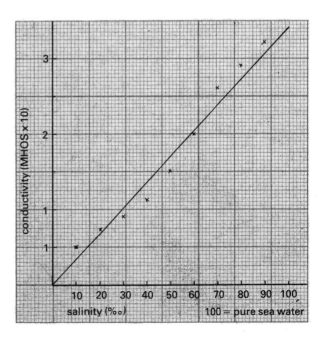

Method for chemical estimation of chloride

1   Dissolve 27.25 g of silver nitrate in distilled water and make up to 1 litre.
2   Place 10 cm³ of the saline water sample into a conical flask.
3   Titrate with the silver nitrate solution from a burette using a few drops of potassium chromate solution as indicator.
4   Swirl the flask as the silver nitrate solution is run in. The end point is reached when the first permanent brick red colour of silver chromate occurs.
5   The volume of silver nitrate (cm³) used in the titration is approximately equal to the salinity in g kg^{-1}.

A more accurate estimation can be made by applying the following formula (Nicol):

$$\text{Salinity (‰)} = 0.03 + 1.805 \times \text{wt of chloride (in g kg}^{-1})$$

Salinity can also be calculated from density measurements made by using an inexpensive hydrometer reading from 1.02 to 1.03 g cm^{-3}. Graphs are available in a number of textbooks (see Bibliography) for the conversion of hydrometer readings to salinity. Alternatively the following formula (Brehaut) can be used:

$$\text{Salinity (‰)} = \frac{\text{Hydrometer reading} - 1}{0.00084 - (0.0000066 \times \text{Temperature})}$$

Worked example for a reading of 1.0268 at 16°C

$$\frac{0.0268}{0.00084 - 0.00011} = \frac{0.0268}{0.00073} = 36.7‰ \text{ salinity}$$

pH and hardness

As mentioned in Chapter 3 pH gives an indication of acidity or alkalinity, being a measure of the number of grammes of hydrogen ions present per litre of solution.

Hardness may be *permanent* due to the presence of chlorides and sulphates of magnesium and calcium, or *temporary* due to the bicarbonates of these cations. The presence of these depends upon the geology of the watershed and calcium and magnesium ions will tend to produce alkaline conditions. Bivalves, gasteropods and organisms such as *Gammarus* and *Asellus* are absent from soft water requiring as they do calcium for the growth of their shells and exoskeletons. Thus the presence of these ions will have an important influence upon the distribution of these organisms.

Method for estimating hardness of water

1   Obtain a 100 cm³ water sample.
2   Carefully add crushed water-hardness tablets (available from **BDH Chemicals Limited**) one by one until there is a change in the colour of the mixture from reddish purple to blue-grey.
3   Record the number of tablets used.
4   Hardness (ppm) = (number of tablets × 20) − 10.

Photosynthesis by plants during daylight hours will reduce the carbon dioxide content of small bodies of water resulting in an increase in pH. Conversely the production of large amounts of carbon dioxide from respiration at night or in areas of bacterial decomposition will result in low pH values. Measurements of pH may be made by using an electronic pH meter (Chapter 3) or universal indicator (Chapter 4).

Question 8

a   Describe briefly a method you could use to determine the snail population of a tarn (small lake).
b   Explain how levels of i) calcium ions and ii) nitrate ions might affect the total biomass of snails in a tarn.
c   The table below shows the species of snail (I to IX) and the concentration of calcium and nitrate ions found in the water of a number of tarns (A to G).

| | SPECIES OF SNAIL, 1 to IX | | | | | | | | | Ca²⁺ ppm | NO₃⁻ ppm | Area of tarn, m² |
TARN	I	II	III	IV	V	VI	VII	VIII	IX			
A		+	+					+	+	20.0	0.40	6 400
B	+	+	+	+				+	+	19.8	0.40	21 000
C								+	+	9.6	0.50	2 800
D				+	+	+		+	+	7.4	0.01	12 800
E								+	+	5.3	0.08	8 300
F				+	+		+	+	+	5.0	0.01	11 600
G									+	5.1	0.01	2 500

+ = presence

i) Discuss briefly whether the table gives direct evidence for the relative abundance of snails in the tarns.
ii) Suggest explanations to account for the variation in the numbers of species found in the seven tarns.
d i) Account for the presence of calcium ions in a lentic freshwater environment.
ii) Explain briefly how the presence of calcium ions may affect the pH of freshwater.   (JMB 1982)

Nitrates and phosphates

Nitrogen and phosphorus, essential for plant growth, are vitally important in aquatic ecosystems. Seasonal variation in the primary productivity of marine and freshwater environments is influenced by the availability of these nutrients (see Question 9).

Nitrogen in natural waters is derived from rainfall, from soil water (originally fixed from the atmosphere by bacteria) and nitrogen fixing blue-green algae. Ammonia is the major breakdown product of plant and animal proteins. Some aerobic soil bacteria are able to convert this to nitrate and this too may be leached out of the soil. Nutrient deficiency can limit the production of aquatic plants. Oligotrophic lakes have low mineral content and are consequently poor in fauna and flora. Enrichment of such a lake with sewage effluent or drainage from nearby arable land results in increasing nutrient levels with a consequent growth of algae (see Question 10). When the algae die they contribute to the dead organic matter in the lake to be broken down by decomposers so creating a high BOD. The process of eutrophication ends with anaerobic bacteria releasing ammonia, methane and hydrogen sulphide, thereby creating a body of water unfit for most forms of aquatic life.

The accurate analysis of water for nitrate and phosphate requires complex spectrophotometric techniques. Practical alternatives include the *Lovibond comparator* which, after the addition of standard reagents, is able to compare the sample water with fixed colour standards. A range of water test kits, still based on this colour matching method, also allow for quick analysis.

Question 9
The graph below shows variations in light intensity, nitrate concentration and numbers of phytoplankton in a fresh water lake over a period of twelve months.
a Comment on the possible relationships between the three curves during the period from the beginning of March to the end of May.
b Suggest a reason for the decrease in the numbers of phytoplankton during May.
c Suggest a reason why the level of phytoplankton remains relatively steady during the period from the beginning of June to the end of August.
d Suggest a reason why there is an increase in the numbers of phytoplankton during September and October.
e In the March following the twelve months for which data is supplied, a farmer used nitrogenous fertilizer on the fields adjacent to the lake. Predict the likely sequence of events in the lake resulting from this action (you may assume the lake receives its water only by drainage from these fields). (London 1983)

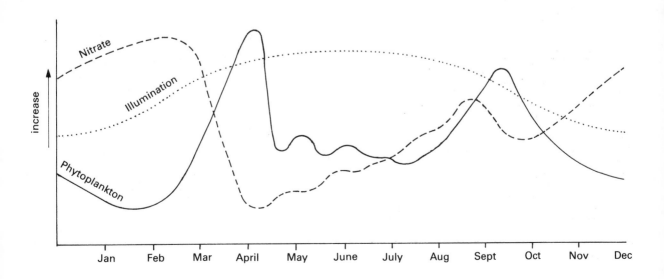

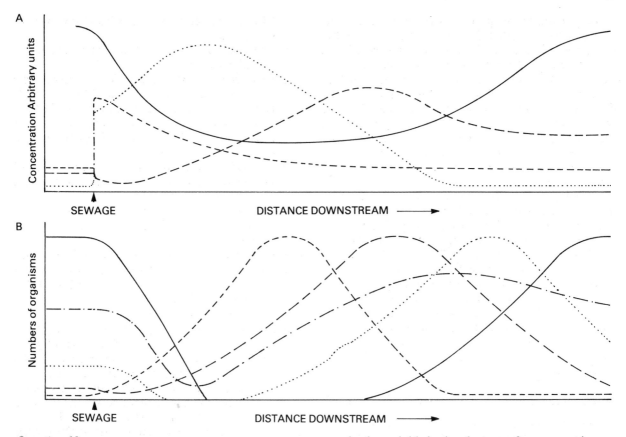

Question 10

The graphs above show the effect on a stream of un-
treated sewage.

a Graph A shows physico-chemical effects (ammonia,
   nitrate, dissolved oxygen, suspended solids). Identify each of the lines 1–4 and give your reasoning.

b Graph B shows changes in flora and fauna (algae,
   Chironomus, clean water invertebrates, *Tubifex,
   Asellus*). Identify each of the lines 5 to 9 and give
   your reasoning.

c Draw a sketch graph to indicate the effect of sewage
   on the number of bacteria in the stream. Explain the
   shape of your curve.   (JMB 1980)

5.14 Water pollution

Pollution has many definitions regarding the degree to
which man releases substances into the environment
which prove harmful to himself and/or other living
organisms. A body of water is polluted if it is turbid,
containing a lot of suspended matter, coloured or has
an objectionable smell and if the pollutant upsets the
delicate ecological balance between the plant and
animal communities. Pollutants of water include
sewage, detergents and toxic chemicals. Some of these

may be degradable in time but are often present in concentrations too high for the ecosystem to cope with.

Water class	Classification criteria
1 Clean water	Waters receiving no significant pol-luting discharges which are known to be well oxygenated with a BOD of less than 3 mg/l.
2 Water of doubtful quality	Waters which may have substantial oxygen reduction at times and a slightly higher BOD than waters of Class 1.
3 Water of poor quality	Waters which may have less than 50 per cent dissolved oxygen and a BOD of up to 12 mg/l. Alternatively they may have been clearly affected by the discharge of suspended solids.
4 Grossly polluted water	Waters with a BOD of 12 mg/l or more under average conditions. Also included are waters incapable of supporting fish and waters which suffer a complete deoxygenation at any time (summer drought excepted).

Fig 5.29 The classification of water quality (after Dale)

uents like
nic matter
pecially of
 In the re-
, sulphur,
ish at the
 pollution
n industry
vater tem-
oducing a
ble in the

suspended
m mines,
iis will re-
photosyn-
rticles can
nimals.
effluent or
he process
containing
gen at the
often have

vater

ole pollut-
expensive
 of many
centration
y projects
oling sites
e reliable,

vith elec-

 a water
iation by
page 41).
mand see

he nature
of the sampling site is to be understood. Use a flow meter or method described on page 85.

4 **Dissolved minerals** A conductivity meter can give an immediate indication of the amount of nutrients present in the water sample. Water test kits are available from biological suppliers for the estimation of calcium, nitrate, ammonium, phosphate and chloride ions. Alternative tests:

a **Calcium** See method for estimating hardness of water (page 94).

b **Nitrate and phosphate** Lovibond comparator or water test kits.

c **Chloride** Obtain a sample for volumetric analysis with silver nitrate (see page 93).

d **Hydrogen sulphide** Place a 50 cm³ water sample into a 100 cm³ conical flask, acidify the sample and place a piece of lead acetate paper in the flask neck. The paper turns black in the presence of hydrogen sulphide. The smell of 'rotten eggs' reinforces a positive result!

e **Ammonia** Detected by placing a small drop of sample water on to tumeric paper. If ammonia is present the paper turns brown.

Heavy metals require complex techniques for identification and estimation beyond the field situation.

5 **pH** Measured with a portable pH meter or universal indicator paper gives an accuracy of within 0.3 pH units. Water above pH 8.0 and below pH 5.0 may well indicate pollution.

6 **Turbidity/suspended solids**

a An optical estimation of turbidity can be gained by using a Secchi disc (page 89) or else by placing a flat bottomed, 70 cm long, clear glass tube on a piece of white paper with a black cross marked on the centre. A well shaken sample is poured into the tube until the cross just fails to be visible and the depth of water measured.

b Filtering a known volume of well shaken water using a Buchner funnel attached to a water jet pump. The piece of filter paper is accurately weighed before and after the filtering process and the total weight of dried solid expressed in mg/dm⁻³.

7 **Bacteriological assessment** Strict hygiene must be practised when investigating water samples for coliform bacteria. Although *Escherichia coli* is a non-pathogen it indicates a type of pollution that could contain pathogens. Coliform abundance can be indicated as follows:

a Add some sample water to tubes containing MacConkey broth (available in tablet form), seal and label. This provides a nutrient medium for coliforms and an acid indicator.

b Place a small inverted Durham tube in each culture (Fig 5.30) and incubate the tubes at 37°C for 48 hours.

c Fermentation of any coliforms present will release gas (collected in the Durham tube) and acid (which turns the indicator from red to yellow).

d Never open the tubes and arrange for the sterile disposal of the broth.

A more detailed treatment of this technique can be found in *The Bacteriological Examination of Water Supplies*, HMSO, London.

8 Detergents A simple comparative test can be carried out by shaking up a half filled, clear water sampling bottle and recording how long it takes the froth to clear (bad water can take several hours to clear).

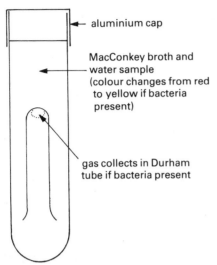

Fig 5.30 Bacteriological assessment of water quality

5.16 Biotic indicators of water pollution

In addition to physical and chemical methods, biological assessment of water quality is possible and observations and counts of the plants and animals associated with different conditions of pollution act as a useful frame of reference.

Most of the information available refers to organic effluents such as domestic sewage. Reference has already been made to the substantial drop in the amount of dissolved oxygen in the water after the discharge point, the high BOD due to microbial activity and the oxidisation of ammonia to nitrate by nitrifying bacteria. Downstream from the sewage outfall the level of dissolved oxygen gradually returns to normal, BOD falls and the decomposers are dispersed in the flow (see Question 10). These chemical changes in the river's composition are accompanied by variations in the composition of the aquatic fauna and flora.

Near the sewage outfall sewage fungus (a filamentous bacteria) flourishes in the anaerobic conditions, also being tolerant to the high concentrations of ammonia. Many algae are intolerant of such conditions and only recover downstream where the minerals produced by the decomposition of the organic matter encourage growth. Variation in the algae community therefore can be used as an index of organic pollution. Macro-invertebrates in the river also show different

tolerances to organic effluents (Fig 5.31) and these have been much used in the past for the indexing of water quality. As is the case with algae the biotic index is based on indicator species which tend to disappear from the river system as the amount of organic pollution increases. In addition the number of different types of animals can be used as a measure of water quality since the species diversity will decrease with increasing pollution. It is upon this principle that the *Trent Biotic Index* works (Fig 5.32).

The Trent Biotic Index, devised by Woodiwiss (1964) and extened (1980), varies from 0 for grossly polluted water to 15 for clean water. A number of sampling stations are marked at various points along a stream or river from the outfall. A standardised sampling procedure is adopted and used at each station, e.g. use a fixed area sampler such as a Surber sampler for estimating actual abundance of the animals or else carry out a 2 minute kick sample to estimate relative abundance (see earlier in Chapter). A species list is then compiled of the invertebrates found and the number of 'groups' present in each sample recorded (see Figure 5.33 for group list). Look through the recorded data and establish which of the key species is present in each sample.

To obtain the Trent Biotic Index, take the highest of the indicator species found, decide if there is more than one species or not and work along the appropriate line. When you come to the column with the correct number of groups, read off the Trent Biotic Index.

e.g. Highest indicator animal = Ephemeroptera
                                  nymph
  Number of indicator species > 1
  Total number of groups $= 12$
  Therefore Trent Biotic Index $= 8$

Fig 5.31 The stonefly nymph larva, *Perla*, inhabits only clean water. Note external gills

		Total number of groups present									
Indicator Species		0–1	2–5	6–10	11–15	16–20	21–25	26–30	31–35	36–40	41–45
		Trent Biotic Index									
Plecoptera nymph present	More than one species	—	7	8	9	10	11	12	13	14	15
	One species only	—	6	7	8	9	10	11	12	13	14
Ephemeroptera nymph present	More than one species*	—	6	7	8	9	10	11	12	13	14
	One species only*	—	5	6	7	8	9	10	11	12	13
Trichoptera larvae present	More than one species†	—	5	6	7	8	9	10	11	12	13
	One species only†	4	4	5	6	7	8	9	10	11	12
Gammarus present	All above species absent	3	4	5	6	7	8	9	10	11	12
Asellus present	All above species absent	2	3	4	5	6	7	8	9	10	11
Tubificid worms and/or red chironomid larvae present	All above species absent	1	2	3	4	5	6	7	8	9	10
All above types absent	Some organisms such as *Eristalis tenax* not requiring dissolved oxygen may be present	0	1	2	—	—	—	—	—	—	—

(Left margin: "Clean" at top, "Heavily Polluted" at bottom)

Baetis rhodani excluded.
†*Baetis rhodani* (Ephem) is counted in this section for the purpose of classification.

Fig 5.32 Trent Biotic Index

Fig 5.33 Groups list

The term "group" here denotes the limit of identification which can be reached without resorting to lengthy techniques.
Thus the groups are as follows:
Each known species of Platyhelminthes (flatworms).
Annelida (worms) excluding genus *Nais*.
Genus *Nais* (worms).
Each known species of Hirudinae (leeches).
Each known species of Mollusca (snails).
Each known species of Crustacea (*Asellus*, shrimps).
Each known species of Plecoptera (stonefly).
Each known genus of Ephemeroptera (mayfly) excluding *Baetis rhodani*.
Baetis rhodani (mayfly).
Each family of Trichoptera (caddis-fly).
Each species of Neuroptera (alder-fly).
Family Chironomidae (midge larvae) except *Chironomus thummi*.
Chironomus thummi (blood worms).
Family Simulidae (black-fly larvae).
Each known species of other fly larvae.
Each known species of Coleoptera (beetles and beetle larvae).
Each known species of Hydracarina (water-mites).

Fig 5.34 Compare the drainage ditch with the fast flowing hill stream

Question 11

The table below shows the numbers of different organisms found at two locations (A and B) on the same river. The two locations were similar except for the presence of organic pollution at one of them.

Organism	Numbers per m² of river bed	
	A	B
Baetis	60	—
Ecdyonurus	19	—
Asellus	15	512
Chironomus	—	229
Gammarus	40	4
Hydropsyche	4	—
Tubifex	—	207
Polycelis	15	—
Limnaea	8	—
Ancylus	6	—
Hydracarina	37	—
Elmis	9	—
Perla	14	—

—= absent

a Explain the following.

i)   biotic index

ii) indicator species

iii) diversity index

Apply each term to the information in the table, making calculations where appropriate. What conclusion can you draw about the nature and extent of the pollution?

b Account for the occurrence of a **named** organism

i)   present only at A,

ii) present only at B,

iii) present at both A and B.   (JMB 1982)

5.17 Project suggestions

1 **Record the variations of temperature in a pond or stream over the period of a year** (see page 88). Record the temperature on the pond bed and also at the surface. Plot the measurements on graph paper. What effects will temperature have upon the vertical movement of the water column over the period studied? How could you take readings to establish the presence of a thermocline in a lake?

2 **Collect water samples from various depths in a pond or lake using the methods outlined earlier in the chapter.** Assess the following:
a dissolved oxygen (using an oxygen meter or Winkler titration).
b pH (using a pH meter) and nitrate.
Is there any evidence for stratification of any of these environmental factors? How could they be linked to the activity of the organisms present in the water?

3 **Using the Secchi disc method, take readings of light penetration and extinction coefficient over the period of a year.** Plot the variations on graph paper (see page 89) and try to establish the reasons for any fluctuations. What are the effects of phytoplankton growth and vertical water movement on the turbidity of the water? What effects might wave action, overhanging trees and inflowing streams have on light penetration in a lake?

4 **Choose a number of sample sites along a river up to its source at a mountain stream.** Record the altitude and measure the rate of flow using one of the methods described earlier in the chapter. Work out the cross sectional area and use this to determine the discharge at each site. Assess the substrate at each site and degree of oxygenation of the waters and discover any adaptations of the representative fauna to deal with the different conditions. A seasonal study could be made of one stream, correlating flow rate and discharge to the amount of precipitation.

5 **From water samples from different locations relate the** a) pH, b) 'hardness' and c) nitrate and phosphate content to the geology of the area. Consider the effects of other sources, e.g. agriculture and industry. Relate your results to the diversity of animals and plants found in the different locations.

6 **Carry out a chemical survey above and below an effluent outfall into a river.** Depending upon the type

of effluent carry out tests to measure some of the following: dissolved oxygen, BOD, pH, nutrients, detergents, hydrogen sulphide, ammonia, turbidity and conductivity.

Analyse the data and attempt to correlate it to the diversity of animals at each of the sites.

7 **Analyse the flow of water from a river into an estuary** (refer to tide tables beforehand and choose a fairly narrow, safe river mouth). Mark out a grid of the river mouth on paper and measure the conductance, with a portable conductivity meter, at points on the grid. From the results draw lines of equal conductance. These should give an indication of the pattern of flow of the fresh water river component into the salt water component.

5.18 Exercises

1 The table below shows information about effluent discharges from industry in the Severn-Trent Water Authority Area in 1974. The eight factories were amongst twelve designated as "the dirty dozen" because their effluents were so far below the quality standard set by the Water Authority.

Factory	Volume of effluent megalitres per day	Consent effluent quality mg l^{-1}	Mean effluent quality mg l^{-1}
A	14	BOD 20	BOD 55
B	3	SS 30	SS 47
C	1	BOD 20 SS 30	BOD 53 BOD 107
D	0.03	SS 30	SS 672
E	3	SS 100	SS 124
F	2	BOD 20 SS 30 TEMP. 25°C	BOD 28 SS 102 TEMP. 28.2°C
G	0.2	SS 50	SS 789
H	0.8	BOD 20 SS 30	BOD 33 SS 34

SS = suspended solids
BOD = Biochemical Oxygen Demand

a i) Suggest what is meant by "constant effluent quality".
   ii) What is meant by "mean effluent quality"? State how, in principle, such figures may be obtained.

iii) Explain how the figures for "suspended solids" are obtained.
b From the table, work out which factory on average is adding most to
i) the BOD of the river into which it is discharging, and
ii) the suspended solids.
c i) Explain how the discharge of hot water (e.g. factory F) may affect the organisms present in the river.
   ii) Explain briefly what other information you would require in order to assess the effects of a proposed rate of effluent discharge into an unpolluted river. (JMB 1981)

2a What do you understand by the following terms used in relation to the assessment of river pollution?
i) Biochemical Oxygen Demand (BOD)
ii) Biotic Index
iii) Diversity Index
Upon what general principles is each based?
b A sketch map of the upper reaches of a River X and its tributary Y is shown below.

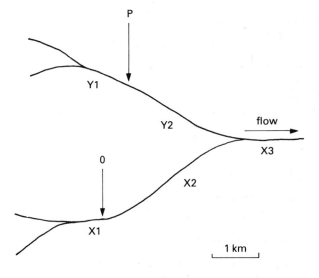

Above the confluence, the two streams are of equal flow.

River X receives an organic effluent (O) from a food processing factory whilst its tributary (Y) receives drainage from lead mining activities at P. The benthic invertebrate communities were examined at X1, X2 and X3 on the main river and at Y1 and Y2 on the tributary. In addition, measurements were made of Dissolved Oxygen and Biochemical Oxygen Demand at each site. The results of these studies are given in the following tables.

Organisms	Number of each organism per 0.1 m² of river bed at each site (— = absent)				
	X1	X2	X3	Y1	Y2
Agapetus fuscipes	27	—	—	32	—
Amphinemura sp.	4	—	—	7	—
Ancylus fluviatilis	9	—	—	12	—
Asellus aquaticus	—	514	17	—	—
Baetis rhodani	68	—	3	53	3
Chironomus spp.	—	218	15	—	—
Ecdyonurus venosus	17	—	—	22	1
Elmis sp.	15	—	—	23	1
Erpobdella octoculata	—	19	3	—	—
Dendrocoelum lacteum	—	5	—	—	—
Gammarus pulex	55	2	1	71	—
Glossiphonia sp.	—	—	1	3	—
Helobdella stagnalis	—	12	1	—	—
Heptagenia sulphurea	14	—	—	8	—
Hydracarina	43	—	—	41	7
Hydropsyche sp.	2	—	—	3	—
Isoperla grammatica	8	—	—	9	—
Leuctra inermis	—	—	—	27	38
Limnodrilus sp.	—	71	3	—	—
Lymnaea pereger	—	—	2	—	—
Nemoura cinerea	11	—	—	14	27
Pedicia sp.	2	—	—	—	—
Piscicola sp.	—	—	—	1	—
Plectrocnemia sp.	3	—	—	5	—
Polycelis felina	17	—	—	23	—
Rhyacophila dorsalis	7	—	—	9	—
Tubifex sp.	—	218	14	—	—

	Dissolved Oxygen and Biochemical Oxygen Demand at each site (mg l⁻¹ oxygen)				
	X1	X2	X3	Y1	Y2
Dissolved Oxygen	11.8	4.3	8.7	12.1	12.4
Biochemical Oxygen Demand	1.2	5.6	4.9	1.0	1.0

i) Comment on, and offer explanations of, the changes in benthic community structure caused by the two discharges. (It is not necessary to refer individually to each of the animals listed.)

ii) How useful would each of the pollution indexes – BOD, Biotic Index and Diversity Index – be in assessing the pollution effects of the two discharges? (JMB 1978)

Part B

Processing the information

So far we have been concerned with methods of collecting data either in the field or laboratory. Most of the techniques used will have been quantitative and many could have taken the investigator a great deal of time. However, data collection can be relatively easy compared to data interpretation. Before interpretation can be attempted the raw data will need processing. Decisions will have to be made about which material needs processing and in what form.

The method of data processing will depend upon the objectives of the project or exercise in question. Tables, graphs and statistical calculations can all summarise data far more effectively than a written account but care must be taken to choose the appropriate method.

In this section two main methods of processing ecological information are looked at: graphical presentation and statistical analysis. The limitations and merits of each of the techniques are discussed to help in choosing between them.

I used to work on charts but I decided it was prostituting my art.

6 Graphical presentation

Once the collection of data has been completed it is often worth summarising it and putting it into a more manageable form by means of an illustration. Graphs make it easier for us to understand the relationships between large numbers of figures since they provide an immediate visual impression. Some of the main methods of graphical presentation are outlined in this chapter. It is important that the choice of any one method can be justified before you start. A simple design will make it far easier for others to interpret your data than a complex one. Other important considerations when using graphical methods are accuracy, neatness and an anticipation of what the final display will look like on the paper (the choice of scale is important here).

6.1 Line graphs

These represent a quick and simple means of showing the relationship between two variables, e.g. time and temperature. Interpretation of a line graph is relatively easy since any trends are quickly identifiable. However, even though they are much used, some important rules govern their use:

1 One of the two variables (the independent variable) causes the other (the dependant variable) to change rather than vice versa. Thus when plotting soil depth against angle of slope, the depth of soil is designated the dependent variable since its changes in response to the independent variable, slope angle. When plotting a line graph it is conventional to plot the dependent variable on the vertical or y axis and the independent variable on the horizontal or x axis. However, this may be disregarded and often is in the case of height or depth which may be plotted on the y axis if it aids interpretation (Fig 6.1). Time, however, is conventionally plotted on the x axis.

2 A graph must be given a title which should be self-explanatory and the axes should be clearly labelled.

3 It is usually best to join successive points with a straight line.

4 The scales used must be carefully chosen since they will very much determine the visual impression conveyed by the graph. Figure 6.2 shows the same data plotted on two graphs with axes of different scales. Note the difference in the final appearances of the two graphs.

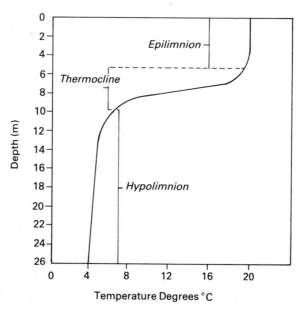

Fig 6.1 Graph to show the changes of temperature with depth during summer in a temperature lake (from Welch 1952)

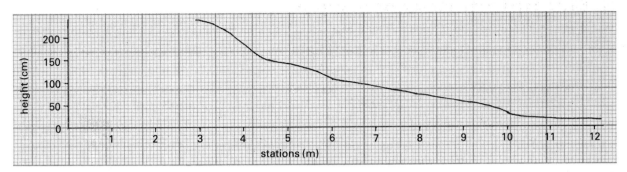

6.2 Bar charts

These are often used for presenting discontinuous data for the purpose of comparison. Discontinuous data may be grouped into one category or another as opposed to continuous data which has no such distinct boundaries, e.g. weight, height, time. The data are represented by drawing bars proportional in height to the value which they represent (Fig 6.3). This form of presentation is particularly appropriate for comparing group data such as the density of successive samples of a population.

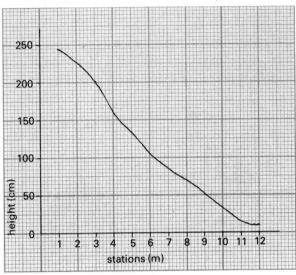

Fig 6.2 Line graphs charting part of a transect profile on a moorland slope

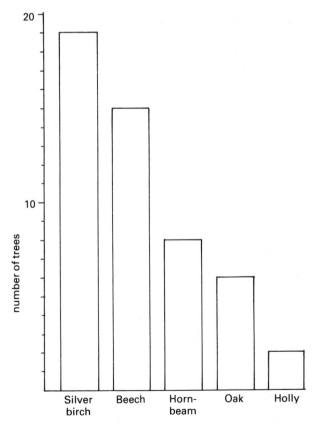

Fig 6.3 Bar chart to show abundance of trees in a small woodland site

6.3 Histograms

The histogram is similar to a bar chart but in this case it is continuous data that is being recorded. Unlike bar charts the proportion of the data is depicted not only by the height of the column but also by its area. If more than one set of data is to be displayed on the same axes it is often convenient to superimpose the graphs one on another. Where there is a clear pattern the largest division of the column should be at the bottom and the smallest at the top. When two sets of data are to be compared, this may be facilitated by drawing two adjacent histograms. Here again it is important to anticipate the final appearance of the histogram when choosing the scales.

6.4 Kites

Kite diagrams are much used when displaying transect data. The information on the frequency histograms illustrated in Figure 2.16 could just as easily have been represented as kites. Many people prefer them for their economy of space and they have been particularly popular in connection with population studies on sea shores. In practice the transect line is laid out and estimations of plant or animal abundance made in the usual way, e.g. percentage cover of plant species. The data is then plotted as symmetrical line graphs either side of a base line to give the kite diagram (Fig 6.5).

Crothers has warned of the inaccuracies of plotting kites based upon abundance scale data since lines

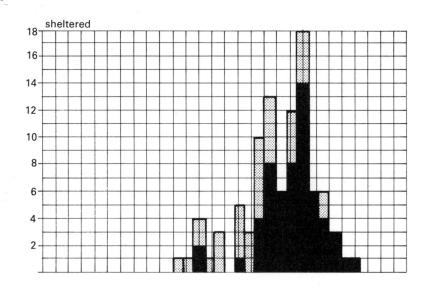

Percentage frequency of different shell heights

Percentage frequency of different shell heights

Distribution of thick-lipped shells is shown by black shading

Fig 6.4 Percentage frequency histograms for different heights of dog-whelk shells (*Nucella lapillus*) on sheltered and exposed shores (from Brown, Evans and Jenkins 1984)

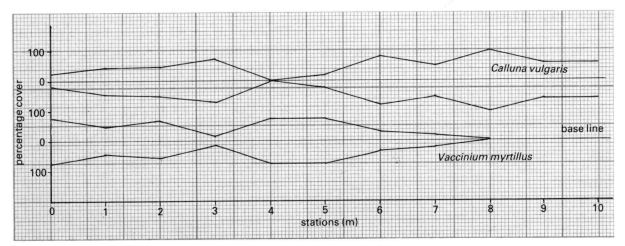

Fig 6.5 Kite diagrams for two species of moorland plants along parts of a transect

drawn between abundance grades have little meaning. For a detailed review of the methods of graphical presentation the reader is advised to refer to this account (see Bibliography).

6.5 Circular graphs

These are useful when the variable to be displayed is continuous over time, e.g. temperature and light. On normal graphs, e.g. charting the monthly rainfall figures, there is a false break: it starts at one end on January 1st and ends at the other on December 31st. Circular graphs eliminate such breaks (Fig 6.6).

On these graphs the two axes are represented by the circumference and radius of the circle. In our example the values for temperature radiate outwards whilst time is represented on the circumference so that each month will be 30° of the circumference ($360 \times \frac{1}{12}$). With circular graphs the rise and fall apparent on a normal graph is replaced by a line moving away from or nearer to the centre of the circle. Detailed appreciation of this comes with practice.

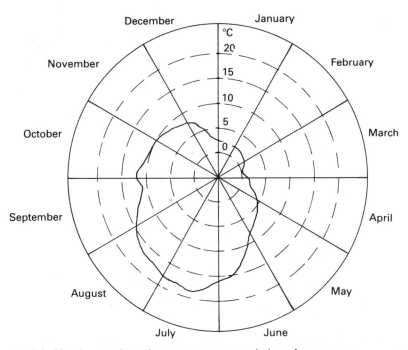

Fig 6.6 Circular graph to show temperature variations for one year

6.6 Logarithmic graphs

These are of two types, those where both axes are logarithmic ('log-log graphs', Fig 6.7) and those where only the vertical axis is logarithmic ('semi-log graphs', Fig 6.8). In a semi-log graph the horizontal axis is normal but on the vertical axis the numbers are not evenly spaced. Larger quantities are successively more contracted so that the interval from 1 to 10 is the same as from 10 to 100 and from 100 to 1000. In each suc-

cessive cycle the values are 10 times greater than the cycle below. Logarithmic graphs are particularly useful in two respects:

1 They allow the plotting of a very great range of data on one piece of graph paper. It would be impossible to plot such values as 1, 12, 72 and 110 000 on normal graph paper but possible on logarithmic paper.

2 Equal rates of change are depicted by lines of equal slope.

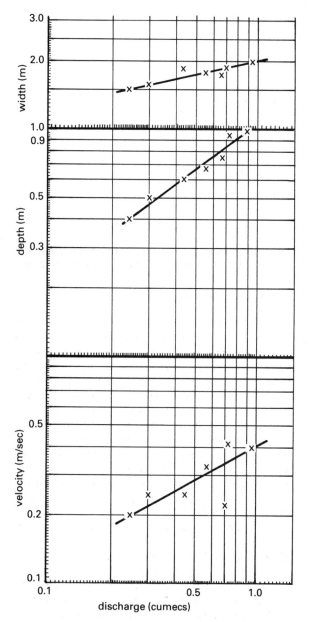

Fig 6.7 Width, depth, velocity and discharge readings taken along Ashes Brook, Church Stretton, Shropshire (from Lenon and Cleves)

Hypothetical biomass estimates (g/0.5 m²) for two shrubs X and Y

	1981	1982	1983
X	10	20	40
Y	50	100	200

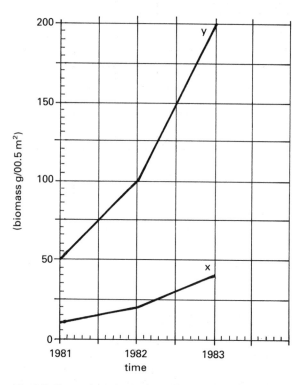

Fig 6.8 Data plotted on two different types of graph: (a) a simple line graph

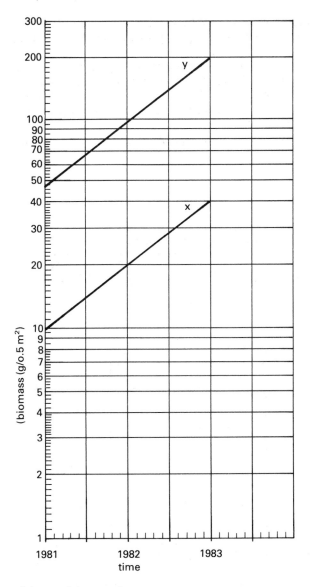

(b) a semi-log graph

6.7 Scatter graphs

Sometimes it is preferable to plot points as dots without linking them up with a line. This may be the case when investigating the relationship between two variables and one has data from many locations. In Figure 6.9 the dependent variable is the number of nymphs and the independent variable, current flow. The pattern of scatter of the points demonstrates any relationship between the two variables. In Figure 6.9 the dots show a tendency to form a band, sloping at an angle to the horizontal, highlighting a positive correlation between the two variables (as one goes up, the

other goes up). In our example there appears to be two separate groupings which could correspond to two separate species. Lines of 'best-fit' may be drawn to highlight the general trend of the dots.

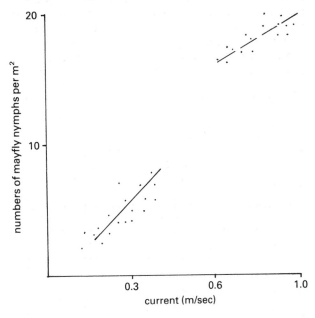

Fig 6.9 Scatter graph to show relationship between numbers of mayfly nymphs and current velocity

6.8 Pie graphs

These differ from other graphs since they do not employ x and y axes. They are used to display proportional data, the whole quantity being divided into its component parts, e.g. the component parts of a soil can be usefully portrayed with a pie graph (Fig 4.3). A circle is drawn which represents the whole quantity and it is then divided into segments each of which is proportional to the size of the components. The method for dividing the circle is as follows:

1 Draw the circle, proportional in area to the total quantity you wish to represent.
2 Compile a table of the component values which will form the segments of the circle. Convert these to percentages of the whole.
3 Calculate the angle which will correspond to this percentage of 360°.
4 Draw a vertical line from the centre of the circle to the top of its circumference.
5 Draw in the segments, measuring the angles calculated in 3. Start from the vertical line and work in a clockwise direction. Draw the segments in order of size starting with the largest.
6 Different segments may have different shading with an appropriate key or else they may be labelled.

Species	Numbers trapped	%	% of 360°
Field vole (*Microtus agrestis*)	188	47.2	169.9
Common shrew (*Sorex araneus*)	103	25.8	92.9
Woodmouse (*Apodemus sylvaticus*)	83	20.8	74.9
Bank vole (*Clethrionomys glareolus*)	11	2.9	10.4
Others	13	3.3	11.9
TOTAL	398	100	360

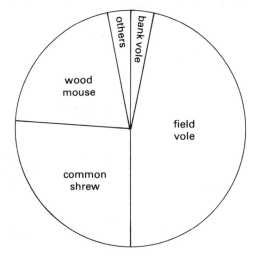

Pie graphs are particularly useful if superimposed upon a map enabling proportional data to be displayed for a number of locations simultaneously (Fig 6.11).

Fig 6.10 Pie graph showing species composition of a small mammal population

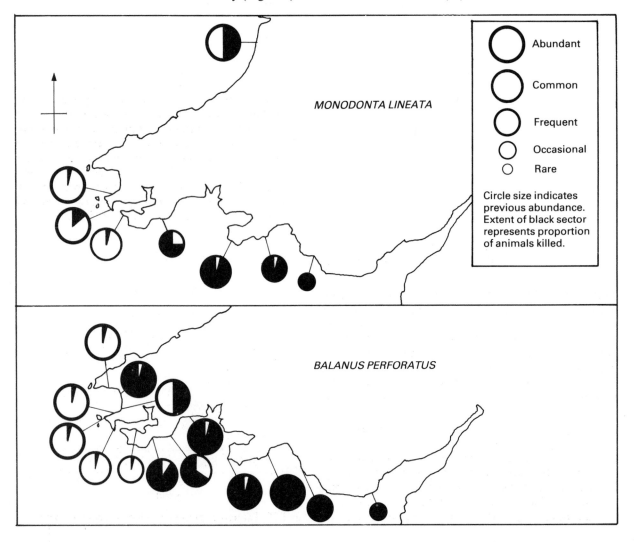

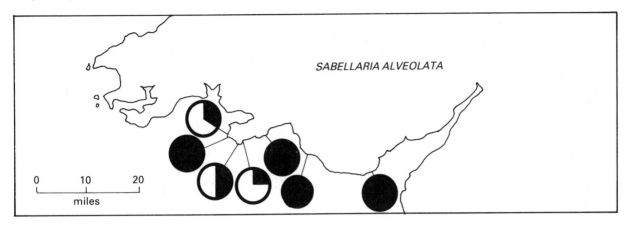

Fig 6.11 Mortalities of *Monodonta lineata, Balanus perforatus* and *Sabellaria alveolata* in South Wales (from Crisp 1964)

6.9 Triangular graphs

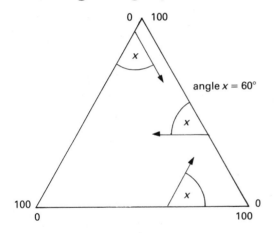

Fig 6.12 Diagram of a triangular graph showing the way in which the values are carried across the graph

These are graphs with three axes instead of two, which make up an equilateral triangle (Fig 6.12). They can be used for plotting any data which can be easily divided into three proportions. They are most valuable when data from several sources are plotted on one graph, the position of the points in relation to one another giving a quick impression of the dominance of any one component over the others. Points to remember about triangular graphs are:

1 Each axis is divided into 100 units representing percentages.
2 From each axis lines are drawn at an angle of 60° so carrying the values across the graph (Fig 6.12).
3 The data must be divisible into three components each of which is represented by a percentage, all three adding up to 100%. A useful example may be drawn from the constituent particles of a soil sample:

Particle	%
Silt	5
Clay	33
Sand	62
	100

These values have been plotted on Figure 6.13. The dotted lines indicate the way the values are carried across the graph to meet at one point. The position of this point indicates the relative dominance of sand in this particular soil sample. Samples taken from other locations could be analysed for these component particles and assigned a position on the graph, e.g. X shows the position of a hypothetical sample when all three components represent a third of the total.

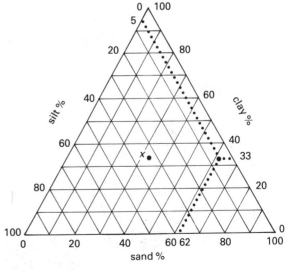

Fig 6.13 Triangular graph showing soil composition

6.10 Pyramids

These are often used to give a proportional representation of the organisms present at successive trophic levels. Quantitative measurements of the producers, primary, secondary and tertiary consumers are represented on graph paper by areas proportional to the data collected. The data consists of numbers, biomass or energy of the organisms sampled in a defined area (see Exercise 2, Chapter 1). In our example all the living material within a 0.5 m² quadrat has been harvested and the individuals sorted into producers, primary and secondary consumers. The organisms in each group were weighed (these weighings include water content and exoskeletons but in many cases dry weight measurements will be possible and more representative). The weights were then expressed on graph paper in g m^{-2} with the secondary consumers displayed on top of the primary consumers, which are in turn placed on top of the producers.

In Figure 6.14 the biomass pyramid in (a) is from a rocky shore community dominated by the fucoid alga, *Ascophyllum nodosum* (standing crop expressed in g/m²) and in (b), from a densely covered mussel bed.

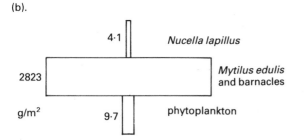

(a).

3·1 | carnivores

8·3 | herbivores and scavengers

4727 | *Ascophyllum nodosum*

g/m²

(b).

4·1 | *Nucella lapillus*

2823 | *Mytilus edulis* and barnacles

g/m²   9·7 | phytoplankton

Fig 6.14 Biomass pyramids

Biomass pyramids enable meaningful comparisons of different ecosystems to be made. In practice, however, such quantitative biomass estimates are often different from the theoretical models. The possible explanations for such anomalies provide in themselves an excellent source of discussion.

6.11 Proportional symbols

These are symbols drawn on a map or along a transect line proportional in size to the variable being represented. Dansereau symbols have been used to produce a diagrammatic profile of the vegetation occurring along a line transect. Data is collected for each of the main vegetation layers: tree, shrub, herb, ground layers and also epiphytes (plants such as mosses and lichens found upon the stems and branches of other plants). For each layer record the distance along the transect and with the exception of the ground vegetation record the maximum height. The clinometer method described in Chapter 3 will be useful here. For trees and shrubs also measure the radius of the canopy. Results may then be plotted as either true scale graphical representations or as a symbol diagram using the Dansereau vegetation classification system (Fig 6.15). These profiles are useful in studies where the structure of the vegetation is the main consideration as opposed to the species composition, e.g. when comparing the structure of different areas of woodland to determine the degree of regeneration of saplings.

6.12 Exercises

1 Duckweed grows on or near the surface of ponds. Its growth can be measured by counting the number of fronds. Two species of duckweed, *Lemna trisulca* and *Lemna minor* were grown separately and together, in identical beakers in the laboratory. The results are shown in the table below.

	Total Number of Fronds			
	Species grown separately		Species grown together	
Days	*L. trisulca*	*L. minor*	*L. trisulca*	*L. minor*
0	30	30	30	30
16	63	78	48	105
36	126	142	84	234
46	177	225	84	324
54	165	276	48	360
60	129	219	45	354

a Draw graphs to compare the rates of growth of the two species when grown separately and when grown together.

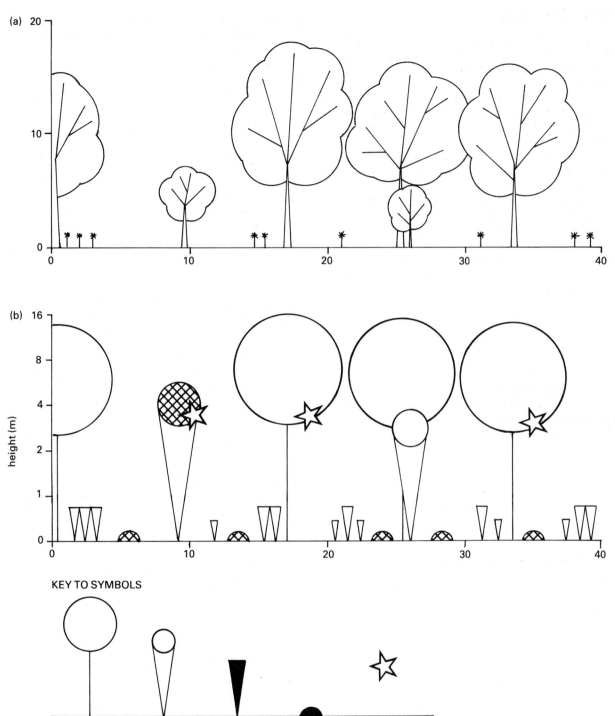

Fig 6.15 Vegetation profiles along a transect line (after Hall)
(a) True scale graphical section
(b) Symbolic section based on Dansereau system (NB Logarithmic height scale)

b i) What do the graphs suggest about the growth of the two species when grown separately?
  ii) Offer an explanation for this difference.
c Offer an explanation for the interaction of the two species when grown together.
d Account for the changes in growth rate between 46 and 60 days for *Lemna trisulca* grown separately.
(WJEC 1985)

2a Draw a triangular graph and label the 3 axes % sand, % clay, and % silt respectively. Plot the composition of each of the following soil types on the graph:

Soil type	% Sand	% Clay	% Silt
A	35	30	35
B	40	40	20
C	75	10	15
D	10	75	15
E	10	30	60
F	60	15	25

b By reference to Figure 4.11 classify each soil type.
c Use an alternative method to proportionately display the above data.

3 The table below shows the concentration of mineral ions in a nutrient solution in which barley plants were grown at the start and at the end of an experiment:

a Represent this data in a suitable graphical form to highlight any changes in nutrient ions during the course of the experiment.
b Comment upon the displayed data.

4 Fruits of the foxglove (*Digitalis purpurea*) were collected from a mixed hedgerow and their lengths measured in millimetres and recorded as follows:

14	18	13	16	15	16	13	17
19	14	18	14	16	15	16	19
14	15	11	19	12	19	15	19
16	19	14	21	19	18	15	16
18	17	15	13	19	20	18	20
15	15	14	12	16	15	15	20
19	17	16	15	13	19	18	15

a Assemble the data to show the frequency of each length.
b Use a suitable graphical form to display the data giving reasons for your choice.
c Discuss the illustrated results. What environmental factors could have brought about the range of fruit lengths?

	Nutrient ions						
	K^+	Ca^{2+}	Mg^{2+}	NO^{3-}	$H^2PO_4^{-}$	SO_4^{2-}	HCO_3^{-}
Initial concentration (mol dm^{-3})	3.0	5.0	2.0	7.0	1.0	2.0	3.0
Final conc. (mol dm^{-3})	0.2	5.8	2.2	1.8	1.5	2.6	0.2

7 Statistical analysis

Tabulation and graphical presentation are useful methods of highlighting the comparisons of data. Statistical methods involving the mathematical processing of data give far greater precision and allow us to discover things that might otherwise go unnoticed.

This being the case, it is as equally important to recognise the fact that statistics are merely an *aid* to analysis. Sometimes statistical calculations are made in fieldwork projects without adequate justification. Before making use of a statistical method you should ask yourself two questions:

1 **Why am I using the technique?** It is important to recognise what it is that you hope to prove and how the statistical method can help you do it.

2 **Is this particular technique appropriate to the data that I have collected?** Each technique requires that the data be arranged in a particular form. If it is not, the data can not be used. Above all if your data is no good in the first place then the manipulation of a complex statistical technique will not help it.

In this section each technique is described step by step and worked examples are given corresponding to these steps.

7.1 Summarising the data

When faced with a large amount of data such as the numbers of an individual species in a series of sampling units you may well wish to summarise it and in doing so, organise it into a more manageable form. This can be done relatively easily by any of three commonly used methods:

1 The mean
The mean is often known as the average and is found by adding up all the values you are dealing with and dividing the total by the number of values. The mean is shown by the symbol $\bar{x}$.

The mean is the most commonly used data summary as it can be used for further statistical analysis. However, it can be distorted if you have just one extreme value.

EXAMPLE
Data: 3, 4, 4, 4, 6, 6, 9

Working: $\dfrac{3+4+4+4+6+6+9}{7} = \dfrac{36}{7} = 5.1$

$$\bar{x} = 5.1$$

2 The mode
The mode is the most frequently occuring event. In a series of numbers the mode is the most frequently occuring number. In a series of classes the mode is the most common class.

The mode is not affected by extreme values but cannot be used for further mathematical processing.

EXAMPLE
Data: 3, 4, 4, 4, 6, 6, 9
Mode: Most frequently occurring number = 4

Data:	*Class (no. of springtails per sampling unit)*	*Frequency*
	0–19	0
	20–39	5
	40–59	9
	60–79	13
	80–99	7
	100–119	2
	120–139	1

Mode: most frequently occurring class = 60–79

3 The median
The median is the central value in a series of ranked values. If the series has an even number of values then

the median is the mid-point between the two centrally placed values.

The median is unaffected by extreme values but cannot be used for further mathematical processing.

EXAMPLES
Data: 3, 4, 4, 4, 6, 6, 9
Median: Central value = 4
Data: 3, 3, 4, 6, 8, 9
Median: = mid-point between the two central values = 5

7.2 Spread around the median and mean

The mean, mode and median all provide us with a summary value for a set of data. However, on their own they can be misleading since they give us little idea of the spread of data around the summary value.

EXAMPLE
Monthly rainfall totals were determined for a particular area as part of a fieldwork project:

Months	Rainfall (mm)
March	60
April	35
May	5
June	0
July	0

The mean of these (20 mm) does not provide an accurate representation of what actually happened, since there was a great deal of deviation about the mean. The median (5 mm) is also misleading and the deviation even greater.

We are able to measure deviation by a number of statistical methods:

Spread around the median: the inter-quartile range

The measure of the spread of values around the median is known as the *inter-quartile* range. The greater the spread the higher the inter-quartile range.

Method
Stage 1 Place the variables in rank order with the smallest first and the largest last.
Stage 2 Find the 'upper quartile'. To do this you take the 25% highest values and find the mid-point between the lowest of these and the next lowest value.
Stage 3 Find the 'lower quartile'. In this case by taking the 25% lowest values and finding the mid-point between the highest of these and the next highest value.
Stage 4 Find the difference between the upper and lower quartile. This is the 'inter-quartile'

range, a crude index of the spread of values around the median. The higher the inter-quartile range, the greater the spread.

EXAMPLE
Monthly average temperatures (°C) for a study area:

January	3	July	19
February	5	August	16
March	9	September	13
April	9	October	11
May	15	November	7
June	15	December	3

Ranked: 3 3 5 | 7 9 9 | 11 13 15 | 15 16 19

lower quartile   median   upper quartile
6   10   15

Inter-quartile range = (15 − 6) = 9

Spread about the mean; the standard deviation σ

The standard deviation enables us to measure the spread of our data around its mean. This is important since the greater the range or spread of the data, the less useful is the mean as a summary of it.

Method
Stage 1 Tabulate the values (x) and their squares (x^2). Add these values $(\Sigma x$ and $\Sigma x^2)$.
Stage 2 Find the mean of all the values of x $(\bar{x})$ and square it $(\bar{x}^2)$
Stage 3 Calculate the formula:

$$\sigma = \sqrt{\left(\frac{\Sigma x^2}{n} - \bar{x}^2\right)}$$

where σ = standard deviation
$\sqrt{}$ = square root of
Σ = the sum of
n = the number of values
$\bar{x}$ = the mean of the values

The higher the standard deviation, the greater the spread of data around the mean. The standard deviation is the best measure of this spread because it takes into account *all* the values under consideration.

EXAMPLE
Shell height of dog-whelks on a sheltered rocky shore:

Size classes (mm)	x	x^2
26	5	25
27	3	9
28	10	100
29	13	169
30	11	121
31	12	144
32	17	289
33	6	36
34	6	36
35	3	9
36	2	4
	$\Sigma x = 88$	$\Sigma x^2 = 942$

mean $\bar{x} = \dfrac{88}{11} = 8$ and $\bar{x}^2 = 64$

$n = 11$

$$\sigma = \sqrt{\left(\frac{\Sigma x^2}{n} - \bar{x}^2\right)}$$

$$= \sqrt{\frac{942}{11} - 64}$$

$$= 4.7$$

This figure 4.7 is the standard deviation of the data from the mean. Thus the true mean lies within the range 8 ± 4.7.

Spread about the mean

1 Coefficient of variation (V)

The coefficient of variation is the standard deviation expressed as a percentage of the mean. A high coefficient indicates a greater spread of data.

To calculate the coefficient of variation:

$$V = \frac{\sigma}{\bar{x}} \times 100$$

Where
V = coefficient of variation
σ = standard deviation
$\bar{x}$ = the mean of the values

Since they are expressed as percentages, coefficients of variation from different sets of data are more easily comparable.

EXAMPLE

Shell height of dog-whelk (from previous example)
$\bar{x} = 8$
$\sigma = 4.7$
$V = \dfrac{\sigma}{\bar{x}} \times 100$
$= \dfrac{4.7}{8} \times 100$
$= 59\%$

2 Standard error of the mean

We are able to estimate the range of deviation from the mean by calculating the standard error (SE). This will give us some indication of how various samples from different populations vary in their means.

$$SE = \frac{\sigma}{\sqrt{n}}$$

σ = standard deviation
n = number of values

From previous data:

$$SE = \frac{4.7}{\sqrt{11}} = \pm 1.4$$

For a 95% range of confidence the mean

$$\simeq \bar{x} \pm 2 \times SE = 8 \pm 2.8$$

In other words in 95% of all similar samples the mean will lie between 5.2 and 10.8. (This method is only valid for samples larger than about 30.)

If in a similar exercise on a different population of dog-whelks, the data produced a quite different range of the mean (Fig 7.1), then it may well be that the difference is due to some genetic factor (dog-whelks have no planktonic larval stage and thus, each group of individuals on the shore usually interbreed within the limits of that small population. (Crothers referred to these groups as *gamodemes*). Alternatively a different range of the mean in a population could be the result of environmental (*phenotypic*) influences, e.g. degree of wave exposure.

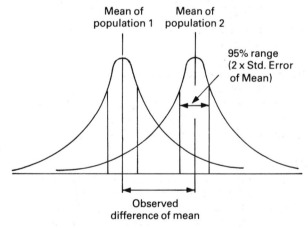

Fig 7.1 Diagram of two frequency distributions showing significant difference between the means (from Bennett and Humphries)

Standard error of the difference

The difference between the means of two populations where the standard deviations are known can be investigated by determining the standard error of the difference, given by

$$SE \text{ of difference} = \sqrt{\frac{\sigma_1^2}{n_1} + \frac{\sigma_2^2}{n_2}}$$

where σ_1 and σ_2 are the standard deviations of the samples and n_1 and n_1 are the number in each sample. From previous data:

$$SE \text{ of difference} = \sqrt{\frac{4.7^2}{11} + \frac{5.2^2}{30}} = 1.7$$

(where 5.2 is the standard deviation and 30 the size of the sample of a second population of dog-whelks with mean shell height of 11.7 collected from a nearby shore).

Therefore a 95% confidence interval for the difference between the two population means is $(11.7 - 8) \pm 2 \times 1.7 = 3.7 \pm 3.4$.

7.3 Probability and the normal curve

If we plot the frequency distribution of some continuously variable data, e.g. shell height, with data groupings on one axis and frequency on the other, we would very likely end up with a regular bell-shaped curve. This is known as the *normal distribution curve* and the frequency distribution is symmetrical about the mean. Other components of the shape of a normal distribution curve do not matter; all the curves in Figure 7.2 are normal curves.

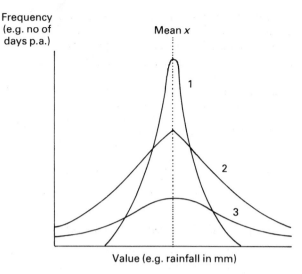

Fig 7.2 Normal distribution curves

Certain probability statements can be made about data which, when plotted, forms a normal distribution curve. These statements all make use of the standard deviation of the data which is a measure of the dispersion of values about the mean. If a set of data has a near normal distribution, then just over 68% of the values will fall within one standard deviation of the mean (plus and minus), just over 95% of the values will fall within two standard deviations of the mean and 99.5% will fall within three standard deviations of the mean (see Figure 7.3).

In probability terms these statements can be expressed as follows:

There is a 0.68 or 68% probability that a value will be within one standard deviation of the mean (or a 0.32 or 32% probability that it will be more than one standard deviation from the mean).

There is a 0.95 or 95% probability that a value will be within two standard deviations of the mean (or a 0.05 or 5% probability that it will be more than two standard deviations from the mean).

There is a 0.995 or 99.5% probability that a value will be within three standard deviations of the mean (or a 0.005 or 0.5% probability that it will be more than three standard deviations from the mean).

Fig 7.3 A normal distribution curve showing the proportion of values (in percentages) which fall within a given distance (measured in standard deviations) from the mean ($\bar{x}$) from (Lenon and Cleves)

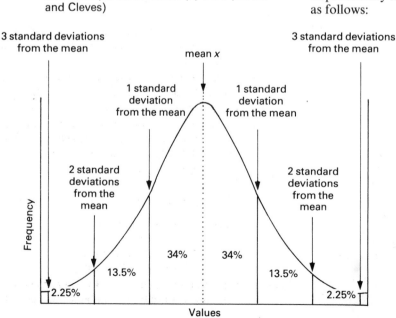

Thus if we know the mean and standard deviation of a set of data, and if its distribution is normal, we can make some useful probability statements.

EXAMPLE

If the mean plant height for a certain species is 50 cms and the standard deviation is 15 cm. We can say:

There is a 32% probability that other plants of the same species will be less than 35 cm or more than 65 cm high.

There is a 5% probability that other plants will be less than 20 cm or more than 80 cm high.

There is a 0.5% probability that other plants will be less than 5 cm or more than 95 cm high.

7.4 Tests of significance

Many projects involve the collecting of two or more sets of data from different locations with a view to their subsequent comparison. Examples may include:

1 The current flow of a stream at different points.
2 The biomass of a plant species in conditions of light and shade.
3 The numbers of woodlice in damp and dry conditions.
4 The lichen cover on a north facing and south facing wall.

Significant tests are used to find out whether the differences between two or more sets of sample data are truly significant or if these differences are purely due to chance. For example, samples of earthworms in soils on chalk and limestone gave the following results.

Rock	Nos of earthworms
Chalk	22
Limestone	17

Would it be true to say that the *actual* (rather than the sampled) number of earthworms on chalk is higher than that on limestone? Or could the difference between the figures be due to chance? Tests of significance tell us the probability that differences between sample data are due to chance. If as a result of the tests we determine that the occurrence was due to chance then we conclude one of two things:

Either 1   That the relationship is not significant and there is little point in looking for explanations of it.

or 2   That our sample is too small and that if we were to take a larger sample then the result of the significance test changes, i.e. the relationship becomes more certain.

The results of the test alone do not tell us which of these two conclusions applies to our data. Biological considerations need to be examined to decide this question.

The chi-squared (χ^2) test

In order to use this our data must have the following characteristics:

1 It must be frequency data counted in each of several categories.
2 The total number of observations should be more than 20.
3 The expected frequency in any one category (see *Stage 3* below) should be no less than 5.
4 The observations should not be such that one influences another.

χ^2 for two variables

Method

Stage 1   State the null hypothesis, i.e. that any difference between the sample data sets was purely due to chance.

Stage 2   Tabulate the data as shown in the example. The data to be tested for significance is termed 'observed frequency'.

Stage 3   Calculate the 'expected frequency', that is the values that would be *expected* to have occurred if the null hypothesis was correct.

Stage 4   Calculate the formula:

$$\chi^2 = \Sigma \frac{(O - E)^2}{E}$$

where χ^2 = chi-squared figure
Σ = sum of
O = observed frequency
E = expected frequency

Stage 5   Calculate the 'degrees of freedom' which is one less than the total number of categories:

Our statistics use 27% more distortion than anyone else's..

$$df = n - 1$$

Where df = degrees of freedom

n = no. of test categories

Stage 6   Using the calculated value of chi-squared and the degrees of freedom use the graph on page 147 to read off the probability that the data frequencies you are testing could have occurred by chance.

EXAMPLE

The numbers of the smooth periwinkles (*Littorina obtusata*) found amongst the fronds of four species of seaweed were as follows:

Seaweed	No. of smooth periwinkles
Spiral wrack	5
Bladder wrack	16
Egg wrack	23
Serrated wrack	56

Are these results a true reflection of the distribution of the smooth periwinkle on seaweed fronds or are they simply the result of chance?

Stage 1   The null hypothesis is that the distribution was purely chance.

Stage 2   Tabulation (see *Stage 4*).

Stage 3   If the species of seaweed had no effect upon the density of smooth periwinkles then an equal number of animals would be expected to be found upon the fronds of each species of seaweed, i.e. 100 individuals divided by the number of seaweed species (4). Therefore you would expect 25 periwinkles on each seaweed species, $E = 25$.

Stage 4

Seaweed species	Observed frequency (O)	Expected frequency (E)	$\dfrac{(O-E)^2}{E}$
Spiral wrack	5	25	$(5-25)^2 \div 25 = 16.0$
Bladder wrack	16	25	$(16-25)^2 \div 25 = 3.2$
Egg Wrack	23	25	$(23-25)^2 \div 25 = 0.2$
Serrated wrack	56	25	$(56-25)^2 \div 25 = 38.4$
			$\Sigma\ 57.8$

$$\chi^2 = \Sigma \frac{(O-E)^2}{E} = 57.8$$

Stage 5 $df = n - 1 = 3$

Stage 6   From the graph on page xx read off the degrees of freedom (3) on the horizontal axis against the χ^2 value (57.8) on the vertical axis. The resulting point lies above the line marked 0.1 chance in 100. Therefore the probability that the data could be due to pure chance is less than 1 in 1000. Thus the evidence is strongly against the null hypothesis and it must be discarded.

χ^2 for more than two variables

In the previous example only two variables were used (seaweed species and numbers of periwinkle). In this example we use three (temperature groupings and readings taken at the soil surface and at a depth of 30 cm).

Method

Stage 1   State the null hypothesis.

Stage 2   Tabulate the data as shown in the example.

Stage 3   Calculate the expected frequency (E), by multiplying the sum of the column (Σr) by the sum of column (Σk) in which the observed frequency lies and dividing by N, the sum of all observed frequencies.

Stage 4   Calculate the formula:

$$\chi^2 = r\Sigma k\Sigma \left(\frac{(O-E)^2}{E} \right)$$

Where $r\Sigma k\Sigma$ = the sum of the fraction for all values of r and k

O = observed frequency

E = expected frequency

Stage 5   Calculate the degrees of freedom (df). This is the number of rows less one, times the number of columns less one:

$$df = (r-1)(k-1)$$

Stage 6   Turn to page 147 and, using the calculated value of χ^2 and the degrees of freedom, read off the probability that the data frequencies you are testing could have occurred by chance.

EXAMPLE

Soil temperatures were taken at the soil surface and at a depth of 30 cm below short grass over a period of thirty days. The results were grouped into 1°C intervals and tabulated as follows:

Temperature °C	At soil surface	At 30 cm depth
10.0–10.9	2	8
11.0–11.9	3	7
12.0–12.9	4	7
13.0–13.9	7	6
14.0–14.9	14	2

Stage 1   The null hypothesis states that any differences between the two sets of temperatures are due to chance.

Stage 2 Tabulation of data:

Row number (r)	Column number (k)	At soil surface O k_1	At soil surface E	At 30 cm depth O k_2	At 30 cm depth E	Σr
r_1	10.0–10.9	2	5	8	5	10
r_2	11.0–11.9	3	5	7	5	10
r_3	12.0–12.9	4	5.5	7	5.5	11
r_4	13.0–13.9	7	6.5	6	6.5	13
r_5	14.0–14.9	14	8	2	8	16

$$\Sigma k_1 = 30 \qquad \Sigma k_2 = 30 \qquad N = 60$$

Stage 3 For example, the observed frequency for the value k_1, r_1 is 2. The expected frequency is the sum of its row (10) multiplied by the sum of its column (30), divided by the sum of all the observed frequencies (60).

$$E = \frac{30 \times 10}{60}$$
$$= \frac{300}{60}$$
$$= 5$$

Stage 4 $\chi^2 = r\Sigma k\Sigma \left(\frac{(O-E)^2}{E} \right)$

$$= \frac{(2-5)^2}{5} + \frac{(8-5)^2}{5} + \frac{(3-5)^2}{5} +$$
$$\frac{(7-5)^2}{5} + \frac{(4-5.5)^2}{5.5} + \frac{(7-5.5)^2}{5.5} +$$
$$\frac{(7-6.5)^2}{6.5} + \frac{(6-6.5)^2}{6.5} + \frac{(14-8)^2}{8} +$$
$$\frac{(2-8)^2}{8}$$
$$= 13.1$$

Stage 5 $df = (r-1)(k-1)$
$$= (5-1)(2-1)$$
$$= 4$$

Stage 6 Read off the graph on page 147 the degrees of freedom (4) on the horizontal axis against the χ^2 value (14.32) on the vertical axis. The resulting point is below the line marked 1 chance in 100. This means that the probability that the apparent difference between the two sets of temperature readings was unlikely to be due to chance and the null hypothesis is rejected.

The *t*-test

The calculations of standard deviation and standard error assume that the data was drawn from distributions that are approximately normal. These calculations also require that the samples used be large. With a small sample the distribution will tend to deviate more from the mean than a large sample. A measure of deviation can be gained from the *t*-test. The *t*-test is concerned with the difference between a *sample mean* and a *population mean*. An investigator may wish to know if the mean score of his sample is different from that of the population as a whole. It is a useful statistic to use when comparing the population of a particular plant or animal in two different locations. The *t*-test is a parametric test, i.e. the data has to conform to certain conditions and in this case it must be normally distributed. The calculations involved in the *t*-test are somewhat laborious unless carried out with a pocket calculator.

Method

Stage 1 State the null hypothesis which you wish to disprove.

Stage 2 Tabulate the data as shown in the example so that the calculations for each population can be compared at each stage.

Stage 3 Calculate the mean $\bar{x}_1$ or $\bar{x}_2$ for each population along with the deviation from the mean $(x-\bar{x}_1)$ or $(x-\bar{x}_2)$ and square it. Sum the squares of deviation.

Stage 4 Calculate the variance, standard deviation and standard error of mean for each population. From the latter, work out the standard error of difference.

Stage 5 Calculate
$$t = \frac{\text{Differences between means of population 1 and 2}}{\text{Standard error of difference}}$$
$$= \frac{\bar{x}_1 - \bar{x}_2}{SE\,\bar{x}_1 - x_2}$$

Stage 6 Calculate the degrees of freedom for t
$$df = (n_1 - 1) + (n_2 - 1)$$
where n = number of observations

Stage 7 Look up the critical values in the *t*-tables (page 149) and using degrees of freedom and your calculated value of t, find out the corresponding probability. For instance in our example below with 18 degrees of freedom, our calculated value of $t = 2.78$ exceeds 2.55 and is near to 2.88 (see *t*-tables). Since our calculated value of t exceeds 2.55 the probability is 0.02, (i.e. 1 in 50). Thus the null hypothesis is rejected and the difference in the two sample means is significant.

EXAMPLE

Ten samples of earthworms were taken from the underneath of a compost heap (population 1) and from an area of uncultivated soil adjacent to the heap (population 2). The null hypothesis states that any difference in the number of earthworms in each population was due to chance.

POPULATION 1			POPULATION 2		
Observation (x)	Deviation of observation from mean $(x-\bar{x}_1)$	Square of deviation $(x-\bar{x}_1)^2$	Observation (x)	Deviation of observation from mean $(x-\bar{x}_2)$	Square of deviation $(x-\bar{x}_2)^2$
3	−4.2	17.64	4	−0.2	0.04
8	0.8	0.64	6	1.8	3.24
11	3.8	14.44	2	−2.2	4.84
5	−2.2	4.84	5	0.8	0.64
13	5.8	33.64	4	−0.2	0.04
4	−3.2	10.24	5	0.8	0.64
9	1.8	3.24	3	−1.2	1.44
7	−0.2	0.04	6	1.8	3.24
7	−0.2	0.04	4	−0.2	0.04
5	−2.2	4.84	3	−1.2	1.44
Sum of observations $\Sigma x_1 = 72$		Sum of squares of deviation $\Sigma(x-\bar{x}_1)^2 = 89.6$	Sum of observations $\Sigma x_2 = 42$		Sum of squares of deviation $\Sigma(x - \bar{x}_2)^2 = 15.6$
No. of observations $n_1 = 10$	Sum of squares $(SS_1)= \Sigma(x-\bar{x}_1)^2$ $= 89.6$ Variance $(V_1)=\dfrac{SS}{n_1-1}=\dfrac{89.6}{10-1}=9.96$		No. of observations $n_2 = 10$	Sum of squares (SS_2) $= \Sigma(x-\bar{x}_2)^2 = 15.6$ Variance $(V_2)=\dfrac{SS}{n_2-1}=\dfrac{15.6}{10-1}=1.73$	
Mean of population 1 $(\bar{x}_1)=\dfrac{\Sigma x_1}{n_1}=7.2$	Standard Deviation $(SD_1)=\sqrt{V_1}$ $=3.16$		Mean of population 2 $(\bar{x}_2)=\dfrac{\Sigma x_2}{n_2}=4.2$	Standard Deviation $(SD_2)=\sqrt{V_2}$ $=1.32$	

Standard error of mean of population 1

$$(SE\,\bar{x}_1)=\sqrt{\frac{V_1}{n_1}}=0.998$$

Standard error of mean of population 2

$$(SE\,\bar{x}_2)=\sqrt{\frac{V_2}{n_2}}=0.416$$

Standard error of difference between means of populations 1 and 2 $(SE\,\bar{x}_1-\bar{x}_2)=\sqrt{(SE\bar{x}_1)^2+(SE\bar{x}_2)^2}=1.08$

$$t=\frac{\text{Difference between means of populations 1 and 2}}{\text{Standard error of difference}}=\frac{\bar{x}_1-\bar{x}_2}{SE\,\bar{x}_1-\bar{x}_2}=2.78$$

Degrees of freedom for $t=(n_1-1)+(n_2-1)=18$

Probability $= 0.02$

Mann-Whitney *U*-test

This test can be used as an alternative to the parametric *t*-test. It too can be used to compare small sample sizes and being a non-parametric test the data does not have to conform to certain conditions, i.e. does not have to come from a normal distribution. It can be used to test whether two independent groups have been taken from the same population. Whereas the *t*-test can tell us whether the *means* of the two tests differ significantly, the Mann-Whitney *U*-test tells us whether the *medians* differ significantly.

EXAMPLE

Comparing the numbers of *Gammarus* sp. collected by kick sampling at two different sites.

Stage 1 Arrange the counts in each sample in order from the lowest to the highest for each sites.

Site 1 8,10,11,16,19,27,34,34,39,40
Site 2 0,1,4,5,7,7,10,12,12,14

Stage 2 Combine the counts from the two sites and substitute a rank for each count (equal numbers are given average rank values).

Counts in
ascending
order: 0 1 4 5 7 7 8 10 10 11 12 12 14 16 19 27 34 34 39 40
Rank
value: 1 2 3 4 5 6 7   8   9 10 11 12 13 14 15 16 17 18 19 20
        5½   8½   11½   17½

Stage 3 Total the ranks for each site.

Site 1		Site 2	
8	7	0	1
10	8½	1	2
11	10	4	3
16	14	5	4
19	15	7	5½
27	16	7	5½
34	17½	10	8½
34	17½	12	11½
39	19	12	11½
40	20	14	13

$$R_1 = 144.5 \qquad R_2 = 65.5$$

R_1 = sum of ranks for site 1
R_2 = sum of ranks for site 2
n_1 = number of counts for site 1
n_2 = number of counts for site 2

Stage 4 Calculate the values of U_1 and U_2

$$U_1 = n_1 \times n_2 + \frac{n_2(n_2+1)}{2} - R_2$$

$$= 10 \times 10 + \frac{10(10+1)}{2} - 65.5$$

$$U_1 = 89.5$$

$$U_2 = n_1 \times n_2 + \frac{n_1(n_1+1)}{2} - R_1$$

$$= 10 \times 10 + \frac{10(10+1)}{2} - 144.5$$

$$U_2 = 10.5$$

Stage 5 Refer the smallest for these two calculated values, U_1 or U_2 to the appropriate value in the tabulated U-statistic (page 148).
In our example U_2 has the smallest value (10.5). The tabulated value for n_1 and $n_2 = 10$ is 23, there being a 95% chance that the difference between the results is due to something other than chance. Since U_2 is smaller than the tabulated value, the difference between the samples of *Gammarus* at the two sites is significant at the 5% level.

7.5 Correlation

Two things can be said to *correlate* when they vary in

relation to each other, e.g. oxygen consumption in fish increases with a rise in temperature. A *positive* correlation exists if the increase in one value is accompanied by an increase in the other variable. If, however, as one goes up the other goes down a *negative* correlation is said to exist. Some things correlate quite well, e.g. the decrease in light intensity with depth of water. Other things do not correlate very well, e.g. pH and current speed (Fig 7.4).

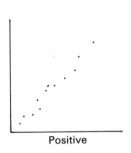

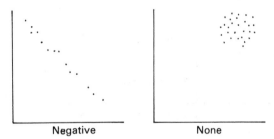

Fig 7.4 Types of correlation

Any existing correlations can be seen if the two variables are plotted as a scatter graph. Sometimes it is difficult to decide merely by looking at the pattern of the points whether or not a straight line can be drawn between them. Greater precision is required here, so a numerical index can be used to express the level of correlation. This index is termed the **correlation coefficient** and it has a number of uses:

1 It has greater precision than a graph. Two graphs showing correlations may appear similar but the correlation coefficients for the sets of data may be different.
2 It enables us to compare several pairs of data more easily. Drawing and comparing twenty graphs would be far more tedious than comparing twenty numbers expressing the same relationship.
3 It is possible to test the correlation to see if it is significant or due to chance.

Care should be exercised when interpreting any apparent correlations. Proving that two variables correlate statistically does not mean to say that one must be affecting the other, e.g. the numbers of two different species may correlate very well but this may be due to them both being influenced by the same environmental variable, e.g. soil pH. Therefore all project work involving correlations must seek to discover the processes behind the correlations.

Spearman's rank correlation coefficient (r_s)

This method enables us to calculate one number that summarises the strength and direction of any correlation between two variables.

Method

Stage 1 Tabulate the data as shown in the example. Rank the two sets of data separately giving the highest value the rank of 1 and so on.

Stage 2 Work out the difference between the ranks of each of the paired variables (d). Square these differences (d^2) and sum them (Σd^2).

Stage 3 Calculate the coefficient (r_s) from the following formula:

$$r = 1 - \frac{1 - 6\Sigma d^2}{n^3 - n}$$

Where d = the difference in rank of the values of each matched pair
n = the number of pairs
Σ = the sum of

The result can be interpreted from the following scale.

$$+1.0 \longrightarrow 0 \longrightarrow -1.0$$

| Perfect positive correlation | No correlation | Perfect negative correlation |

How do we decide whether the correlation we have calculated is significant or has occurred by chance?

Stage 4 Decide on the rejection level (α). This reflects how certain you wish to be that the calculated correlation could not have occurred by chance. So if you wish to be 95% certain the rejection level is calculated as follows:

$$\alpha = \frac{100 - 95}{100}$$
$$= 0.05$$

Stage 5 Calculate the formula for t:

$$t = r_s \sqrt{\frac{n-2}{1-r_s^2}}$$

where r_s = Spearman's rank correlation coefficient
n = number of pairs

Stage 6 Calculate the degrees of freedom (df):
$$df = n - 2$$
where n = the number of pairs.

Stage 7 Look up the critical values in the t-tables (page 149) using the degrees of freedom (df, *Stage 6*) and rejection level (α, *Stage 4*). If the critical value is less than your t-value (*Stage 5*) then the correlation is significant at the level chosen (95%). If the critical value is more than your t-value then you cannot be certain that the correlation could not be due to chance. This may mean one of two things:

a The relationship is not a good one and probably not worth pursuing.

b The size of your sample is too small. If you increase the sample size perhaps a significant correlation may occur.

EXAMPLE

Data: Using a standardised sampling technique the numbers of mayfly larvae were estimated at a number of sites with different current speeds.

Current speed (cm/s)	Numbers of mayfly larvae
20	6
60	16
90	44
10	9
40	19
80	37
95	51
30	13
65	29
75	38

Stages 1–2

1	2	3	4	5	6
Current Speed	Rank	Mayfly Nos.	Rank	Difference between ranks (d)	d^2
10	10	9	9	1	1
20	9	6	10	1	1
30	8	13	8	0	0
40	7	19	6	1	1
60	6	16	7	1	1
65	5	29	5	0	0
75	4	38	3	1	1
80	3	37	4	1	1
90	2	44	2	0	0
95	1	51	1	0	0
					$\Sigma d^2 = 6$

Stage 3

$$r_s = 1 - \frac{6\Sigma d^2}{n^3 - n}$$

$$= 1 - \frac{6 \times 6}{10^3 - 10}$$

$$= +0.96 \text{ (a strong positive correlation)}$$

Stage 4 Rejection level (α) = 95%

$$= 0.05$$

Stage 5 $t = r_s \sqrt{\left(\frac{n-2}{1-r_s^2}\right)}$

$$= 0.96 \sqrt{\left(\frac{10-2}{1-0.96^2}\right)}$$

$$= 9.70$$

Stage 6 $df = (n-2)$

$$= (10-2)$$

$$= 8$$

Stage 7 $df = 8$

Rejection level = 0.05
Therefore critical value of $t = 2.31$
The critical is less than our t-value (9.70)
Therefore we can conclude that there is a significant correlation between current speed and number of mayfly nymphs.

7.6 Species diversity index

A measure of species diversity is useful when investigating the interaction of physical and biotic factors in an ecosystem. Diversity of species is usually proportional to the stability of the ecosystem in question. Most stable communities have a large number of different species with relatively similar numbers of organisms in each. In comparison an ecosystem under stress, e.g. due to pollution, has few species which become abundant and low diversity.

Methods to measure diversity are based upon the relationship between the total number of individuals present and the number of individuals per species.

Two methods are commonly used.

1 **The Simpson index** is more often used for gauging plant diversity. A sample area is taken and all plants within it counted and identified (they need not be accurately named so long as they differ in appearance sufficiently enough to be recognised as a separate species).

   Calculate the diversity with the following formula:

$$D = \frac{N(N-1)}{\Sigma n(n-1)}$$

   where D = diversity index
   N = total number of plants
   n = number of individuals per species
   Σ = sum of

EXAMPLE

Species	A	B	C	D	E	F	G	H	I	J
Number	7	98	14	57	12	73	24	4	9	16

$$D = \frac{314(314-1)}{7(7-1) + 98(98-1) + 14(14-1) \text{ etc}} \qquad \text{Total } 314$$

$$= \frac{98282}{19186} = 5.1$$

2 **An alternative method** is to select 200 organisms from the community and as you catch each organism score whether it is different in appearance from the previous one. To obtain the index of diversity, divide the number of differences by the number of organisms.

EXAMPLE

Record of each species A, B, C etc, and 'differences':

A B C C D D E D C C A B E C C C C D C C C
 + + +   +   + + +   + + + +   + +

$$= \frac{13}{20}$$

$$= 0.65$$

7.7 Calculators and computers

The rapid increase in data processing technology has meant that scientific calculators and desk-top computers are now readily available in most schools. Both have been used successfully in the statistical processing of ecological data, dispensing with the need for lengthy calculations.

Calculators

Pocket calculators are simple to use and enable an on the spot analysis of the collected data to be made in the field. A large volume of data can be processed with a considerable saving in time. The basic mathematical abilities enable a calculator to, e.g. find the mean of a set of data, but in addition some calculators now have a statistical function. Once the data is entered the appropriate key can be pressed to obtain *standard deviation*, the *sum of the data* and the *sum of each value squared*. This would be particularly useful for instance in carrying out a rank-size correlation test. Some more sophisticated calculators are capable of manipulating paired data and giving the correlation coefficient to find out how closely the two data match.

Computers

Computers can be valuable aids to the processing of

ecological data. They can save much time and allow the manipulation of data in ways that otherwise would be so time consuming as to be prohibitive. Programmes are now available which process data collected by students in the field. Diagrams and graphs can be displayed on the monitor screen or printed out. There may be facilities for data storage, so that results collected at different sites or at different times of the year may be compared. Science Education Software have produced a package of five programmes dealing with plant ecology for the BBC Model B microcomputer on 40 or 80 track disc. One programme determines the optimum size and number of quadrats required for vegetation sampling and generates random coordinates for their location. Another coordinates quadrat records of cover values, relief, soil and other site characteristics. Species density mapping and vegetation profile surveying are also covered, together with species distribution (shown by kites) along a transect line compared with environmental factors, e.g. soil pH and slope angle.

Other computer programmes are available for use as simulation exercises of field conditions. They can be useful in supplementing the actual field exercises and can be used to practice recording and presentation of data and as a source of discussion. Programmes include species distribution mapping for shores of different wave exposure and the effects of desiccation and changes in salinity. Simulation exercises also exist for studying population dynamics: these include predator-prey and parasite-host interactions, the interactions of abiotic and biotic factors in determining population size and the effects of both inter-and intra-specific competition.

7.8 Exercises

1   The following data shows the percentage cover values for the cross-leaved heath (*Erica tetralix*) in two moorland sites, the second of which occupied a much damper position. The data were recorded using randomly placed frame quadrats.

Site 1	Site 2
15	35
25	5
0	60
5	75
15	35
30	50
25	20
35	45
10	15
10	70

Calculate the mean, mode, median, inter-quartile range and standard deviation of the two sets of data.

2   The following data shows the length of corolla tube for 100 flowers taken from different plants of the same species.

Corolla tube length (mm)	Frequency
37	1
38	4
39	8
40	15
41	23
42	22
43	14
44	9
45	3
46	1

Calculate the mean, standard deviation and standard error of these data.

3   The length of frond and number of pairs of air bladders were recorded for specimens of the brown seaweed, *Fucus vesiculosus* on a particular beach:

Frond length (cm)	No. of pairs of bladders
38	6
20	4
15	2
36	8
30	6
22	5
17	3

Use the chi-squared test to determine whether these data sets are a true reflection or simply the result of chance. Also calculate Spearman's rank correlation coefficient for these data and check its significance.

4   An investigation was carried out in which the populations of earthworms in two large plots were compared. Plot 1 had been regularly manured and cultivated, whereas plot 2 had been lying fallow for two years. Eight quadrats were thrown at random in each plot. The areas within each quadrat were soaked with dilute potassium permanganate solution. After about 30 minutes the earthworms which had risen to the surface were counted. The results are shown below:

Plot 1 (manured)		Plot 2 (untreated)	
Sample	Worms per m²	Sample	Worms per m²
1	5	1	4
2	9	2	3
3	11	3	6
4	9	4	7
5	10	5	5
6	7	6	3
7	5	7	3
8	8	8	5

a State a null hypothesis that could be tested using these data.

b Carry out a *t*-test to enable you to comment on the significance of the difference between the means of the two data sets. (WJEC 1985)

5 Data were obtained for the total numbers of invertebrates caught in pitfall traps at two different sites. 10 pitfalls were used in short grass and 10 inch long grass. The data obtained were as follows:

Trap No.	1	2	3	4	5	6	7	8	9	10
Site 1 (Short grass)	47	15	26	16	112	43	71	85	28	52
Site 2 (Long grass)	11	13	15	17	42	18	23	31	19	37

Use the Mann-Whitney *U*-test to determine whether there is a significant difference between the numbers of invertebrates collected at the two sites, or if it was merely due to chance.

6 The rate of water loss by the woodlouse, *Philoscia muscorum*, was studied by placing a number of individuals in conditions of differing temperature. By weighing each individual before and after the period of exposure, the rate of evaporation (mg/cm² per hour) was recorded. The results were as follows:

External temperature (°C)	Rate of evaporation (mg/cm²/hr)
10	3
20	4.5
30	5.8
40	8.2
50	14.5
60	20.0

Calculate Spearman's rank correlation coefficient for these data and check its significance.

I read your last survey and just loved it – especially the happy ending..

8 Project suggestions

This chapter gives outlines of a number of projects which have been attempted in a range of habitats. Many of these investigations are well known and long established; others are of more recent origin. It is hoped that they can give the student some insight into the types of investigations which can yield interesting results. They are not intended to be prescriptive but rather to act as a guide and inspiration so that the student can formulate his own hypotheses, test them out practically and analyse and interpret his findings. It may well be that techniques described in one particular habitat can be applied with equal success to others accessible to the investigator. The use of complex techniques and expensive pieces of equipment has been avoided and the duration of the investigations varies from short self-contained exercises to ones which are long term and more open ended.

8.1 Woodland

Woodlands cover only 9% of Britain today but are importat reservoirs of our indigenous plant and animal species. They are amongst the most complex of ecosystems and are unique in that their main primary producers, the trees, are so large and aged. These provide shading, the degree and duration of which varies with species of tree and time of year. In addition to affecting light, trees also make for a more humid atmosphere with less extreme fluctuations of temperature than in open habitats. Semi-natural woods composed of such tree species as oak, beech and ash contain the greatest diversity of plants and animals and are vital in terms of conservation.

1 Investigating the structure of a woodland community

Describe the location, topography, soil and drainage characteristics of the woodland in question (Fig 8.1). Draw a profile diagram (Fig 8.2) to illustrate the vertical structure of the various strata. Lay out a 50 m tape and note the positions of all trees, shrubs and herbs. Use a clinometer (Chapter 3) to measure the heights so that a scaled profile can be drawn. Dansereau symbols may be usefully employed in the data presentation (see Chapter 6).

2 Investigating the change of species composition in a woodland community as the habitat changes

The area should be chosen to show a transition, e.g. along a slope from a dry to a frequently waterlogged

Fig 8.1 Mixed deciduous woodland – note tree, shrub, and herb layer

area or from grassland into woodland. Use the belt transect method described in Chapter 2 to estimate percentage cover of each species in a 0.25 m² quadrat at 1 metre intervals. Record which layer (tree, shrub, herb or moss) each species belongs to, also the extent of leaf expansion and whether they are flowering. Are leaf expansion and flowering related to the layer which the species occupy? (see data sheet, Fig 8.4. Do the details of cover recorded reveal any zonation?

Changes in height of the ground should also be recorded at metre intervals (Chapter 3) so that a profile can be drawn. Soil pits may be dug at intervals along the transect to give information of amount of litter, depth of humus, pH and texture of the soil. Depth of the water table, soil and air temperatures and humidity (whirling hygrometer) may also be relevant measurements to record.

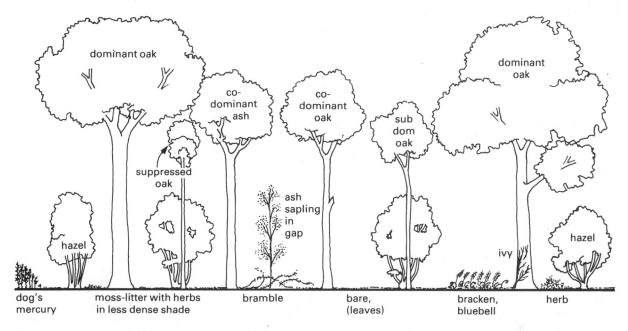

dog's
mercury

moss-litter with herbs
in less dense shade

bramble

bare,
(leaves)

bracken,
bluebell

herb

Fig 8.2 Profile diagram for an oak wood showing strata – ground flora not to scale (from Cousens)

3 The distribution of invertebrates in relation to the plant cover

Is it possible to relate the distribution of animals to the vegetation and physical variables recorded along a transect as in 2? Select a number of types of ground cover represented in the transect and for each, sample the field layer (using a sweep net), the litter (by hand sorting and also by pitfall trapping) and the soil (take core samples for later extracting by Tullgren funnel). Sort and identify the catches. Is the distribution of animals closely tied to the species composition of the plant cover, to the structure of the plant cover or is it quite independent of it?

4 An investigation of woodland microhabitats

Correlations exist between the amount of light penetrating through the canopy (Fig 8.4) to the woodland floor and the growth of plants in the field and ground layers. A study can be made of the many microhabitats created in a deciduous woodland habitat. Pitfall trap and mark-recapture techniques can give information about the diurnal activity of many of the cryptozoic animal populations. Light intensity and humidity measurements may well be of related interest (Chapter 3).

5 Influence of shading on *Mercurialis perennis* (dog's mercury)

Examine the extent to which growth and distribution of *M. perennis* is associated with shading (Fig 8.5).

Fig 8.3 Light penetration through the tree canopy in a mixed deciduous woodland

				LAYER	LEAF EXPANSION	FLOWERS
DISTANCE ALONG TRANSECT (m)						
DEPTH OF WATER TABLE (cm)						
VEGETATION (cover %)						
Symphytum officinale (Comfrey)						
Carex acutiformis (Lesser Pond Sedge)						
Salix fragilis (Crack Willow)						
Rumex sanguineus (Red-veined Dock)						
Angelica sylvestris (Wild Angelica)						
Filipendula ulmaria (Meadow-sweet)						
Iris paeudacorus (Yellow Flag)						
Alnus glutinosa (Alder)						
Urtica dioica (Stinging Nettle)						
Mercurialis perennis (Dog's Mercury)						
Dryopteris filix-mas (Male Fern)						
Sambucus nigra (Elder)						
Crataegus monogyna (Hawthorn)						
Quercus robur (Common Oak)						
Rubus fruticosus agg. (Blackberry)						
Glechoma hederacea (Ground Ivy)						
Prunus domestica ssp. *insititia* (Bullace)						
Chamaenerion angustifolium (Fireweed)						
Grasses						
Mosses (on the ground)						

Fig 8.4 Data sheet for project 2

Select a number of places in a wood where *M. perennis* grows well and also where it is rare. At each site measure the light intensity (Chapter 2) and lay down a 0.25^2 quadrat and determine the number of *M. perennis* shoots within it, their average height and the sex of the plants. Plot graphs of light intensity against number of shoots per m² and also against shoot height. Do the sexes have a differing light requirement?

6 The effect of coppicing on the field layer of a woodland

Investigate the distribution of differing species of plants found in the field layer in a well grown coppice and in a coppice a few years old (Fig 8.6). By means of random quadrat analysis (frame or point) estimate the

Fig 8.5 *Mercurialis perennis* (dog's mercury), mainly female plants but one male on extreme right

J H Oldham

percentage cover of such species as foxglove (*Digitalis purpurea*), rosebay (*Chamaenerion angustifolium*) or wood anemone (*Anemone nemorosa*) in the two habitats. As a long term study set up permanent quadrats on a recently coppiced area. Initially look for the presence of plants requiring good light and as shade increases investigate the effects of low light intensity upon their rate of flowering.

Fig 8.6 17-year old coppiced sweet chestnut *Castanea sativa*, Great Martin's Wood

7 Population dynamics of the holly leaf miner *(Phytomyza ilicus)*

The size of the leaf miner populations are assessed by counting the proportions of infested to total holly leaves produced in any one year. Since food supply does not appear to limit the size of the population, mortality factors should be examined. The fate of leaf miner larvae can be classified into four groups: larvae, diseased, predated, parasitised and successful. The effect of each factor is considered in relation to the number of larvae available. Discover whether the number of larvae killed by parasites, for example, correlates strongly with the number of larvae available in that year.

8 Competition between two elm bark beetles *Scolytus scolytus* and *S. multistriatus*

These two beetles feed upon the sapwood of elm trees transmitting the fungus which causes Dutch Elm Disease which often kills infected trees within a few years. Remove a number of squares of bark (20 × 20

cm) from the trunks of a dead elm and do the same for the side branches. Examine the galleries tunnelled by the adults and their larvae, either on the bark or on the exposed trunk. For each insect species record the number and length of mother galleries and larval galleries present on both the trunk and side branches. Make distribution histograms of tunnel length for each species and assess the effect of size upon the spatial distribution of each species. If elms are unavailable a similar study could be carried out on ash, spruce and pine bark beetles.

9 The distribution of gall spangles on oak leaves

Many plants produce galls in response to the laying of eggs by insects in their tissues. Oak leaves produce gall spangles in late summer in reaction to the activity of the gall wasp, *Neuroteus*. An investigation of the distribution of different species of gall can be carried out by first collecting a large quantity (> 500) of oak leaves. Subdivide each leaf into 10 bands and count the number of each gall species in each band. The distribution of gall-bearing leaves at various heights above ground could also be investigated. Identification of these and other galls can be carried out using the key in Darlington (see Bibliography).

8.2 Grassland

Grassland constitutes one of the commonest and most accessible of our habitats. Playing fields, meadows, gardens and roadside verges all represent potential areas for study for the student. Grassland has special significance for the production of human food and much agricultural research has been devoted to the effects of weeds, herbicides, pests and pesticides. Downs are areas of grassland associated with chalk and limestone; they have alkaline soils which result in a great diversity of plant species. This diversity is also a result of grazing pressures by sheep or rabbits, there being less competition for light in short vegetation.

1 The effects of grazing pressure on a grassland sward

The effects of non-selective grazing can be studied by setting up permanent grassland plots and subjecting them to different mowing regimes. Figure 8.7 shows the arrangement of plots set up for the Nettlecombe Grassland Experiment (see Crothers and Lucas). Within fenced off grassland, 16 plots (3 m × 3 m) were set up and separated by 2 m wide paths. Four of each of the following treatments were applied:

A = Mown fortnightly during growing season.
B = Mown annually in June.
C = Cleared to bare soil and unmown.
D = Left unmown.

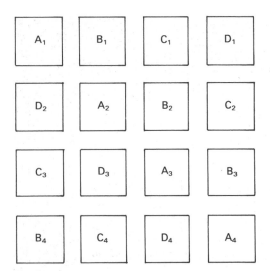

Fig 8.7 Arrangement of plots for the Nettlecombe Grassland Experiment (after Crothers and Lucas)

Fig 8.8 Trampled and untrampled areas of grassland

Weekly sampling of each plot with a point quadrat (Chapter 2) gives estimates of percentage cover and enables the changes in species composition to be studied over a prolonged period. Height of the vegetation and biomass could also be compared.

2 The effect of trampling upon grassland species

Select an area where trampled and untrampled vegetation occur close together, e.g. a path around arable land or by the side of the school field (Fig 8.8) and carry out a line transect of suitable length along a well trampled path. Then move the tape to an adjacent untrampled area and repeat the exercise. At 10 cm intervals along the tape record the species present, their height, growth form (rosette or matt) and if possible devise a method of determining the amount of soil compaction. Use suitable symbols to plot a profile of the vegetation at each site and suggest reasons for any differences that you find.

3 Comparing the biomass of two grassland sites

Choose two contrasting localities, e.g. at the top and bottom of a slope or south facing and shaded. Place a $0.25 \, m^2$ quadrat down at each site in turn and crop all the vegetation which it delineates. Place the cuttings into polythene bags and back in the laboratory dry the plant material to constant weight at 105°C in an oven. The biomass of vegetation at two sites may thus be determined at intervals and their seasonal growth compared.

4 Comparing the invertebrates inhabiting long and short grass

A defined area $(10 \times 10 \, m)$ is marked out with string and pegs on each site in turn and the animals sampled. The sampling may be made semi-quantitative by sweeping the area with a sweep net for a certain period of time. The animals caught can be periodically put in a collecting bottle after being removed from the sweep net with a pooter. After sorting and identification down to the order, the results may be conveniently expressed by bar charts or pie graphs. The exercise could be extended to compare the animals collected by sweeping with those collected by searching frame quadrats placed randomly in the sampling area. The discussion could evaluate the effectiveness of the two collecting techniques.

5 Animal analysis of two different locations

Pitfall traps and water traps (Chapter 2) are cheap and easy to set up. A number of traps can be placed in each of two contrasting locations and the catch after a fixed period of time examined and identified. As can be seen in Chapter 2, various permutations are possible: comparing the effectiveness of baited and unbaited pitfalls or of differently coloured water traps. A 24 hour periodicity study might also be attempted to investigate the patterns of animal activity. In all these exercises the relative effectiveness of the traps should be discussed.

6 Estimating the size of froghopper (*Philaenus spumarius*) populations

Froghoppers are abundant in grassland between June and September. They are particularly suitable for mark-recapture methods since they are not very active

Fig 8.9 The froghopper, *Philaenus spumarius*

flyers. A large number of froghoppers need to be collected by sweep netting a known area of grassland. The captured individuals can be marked on the forewings or protonotum with waterproof felt tip pen and released back into the population (if too active to mark, the insects can be anaesthetised with a small amount of ethyl acetate on cotton wool). A suitable period of time must elapse for the marked individuals to redistribute themselves in the population before a second sample is taken. For details of mark, release, recapture techniques and the formulae for estimating population size see Chapter 2.

7 The colonisation of cow pats

A two month survey of the fauna associated with cow dung can be carried out on pasture land. The dung pats should be marked on deposition to identify their ages and then a sequential record kept of the colonisers. Many flies lay their eggs in the dung in the first hour and these are closely followed by numerous beetles. At the end of two months the pats contain a network of fungal hyphae and a luxurient growth of grasses penetrates through them. Cow pats provide a convenient ecological unit for the study of succession and interspecific competition.

An excellent introduction may be found in Peter Skidmore's *Insects of the Cowdung Community*, an AIDGAP publication from the Field Studies Council.

8 Studying the activity of small mammal populations in grassland

Depending upon the available numbers, set up a grid of Longworth traps in an area of long grass. Leave the traps with the pre-bait catch set for two days to enable the animals to become used to them. Set the traps and examine them at least twice daily at say 9 am and 9 pm. Mark, release, recapture techniques can be used to gain an estimate of population size (see Chapter 2).

Fig 8.10 The heather, *Calluna vulgaris*

Other possible exercises could compare the populations trapped in contrasting grassland localities or examine the seasonal variations in population size.

8.3 Moorland and heathland

Moorlands occur on acid soils in upland areas. They are most often found in the north and west of Britain in regions of heavy rainfall. In contrast, lowland heaths are located on light sandy soils in areas of lower rainfall. Both habitats are subjected to extremes of temperature and wind and it is these two factors that are largely responsible for the resultant flora. Few plant species are able to tolerate the harsh conditions, so that the habitat tends to be dominated by two or three particular plant species such as the heather, *Calluna vulgaris*, the bell heather, *Erica cinerea*, (dominant in drier areas) or the cross-leaved heath, *Erica tetralix* (dominant in wetter areas). Moors and heaths are consequently 'species-poor' in comparison to many other habitats, a feature which can be advantageous to the student in that it restricts the time needed for identification. Added to this both habitats are robust to sampling, (e.g. for biomass estimates) and on areas of steeply sloping ground the temporal succession of the flora, from heath ⟶ wet heath ⟶ bog, may be studied.

1 A study of the regeneration of heather moorland after burning

Choose about six sites which have been subjected to burning as a form of management at different times (date of burning might be obtained from landowners or local fire brigade). Analyse the vegetation at each site by the frame quadrat method to obtain values of percentage cover for each species. The quadrats may either be randomly placed or used at 0.25 m intervals along a line transect of the site. The resultant data gives an indication of secondary succession on upland following fire. The significance of any observed differences between sites could be analysed statistically using the Mann-Whitney U-test. Burning too frequently often gives rise to extensive nutrient-poor grassland.

2 A study of the productivity of the heather, *Calluna vulgaris*

Biomass or standing crop (g m^{-2}) is determined for *Calluna* sites of different ages (Fig 8.10). A non-destructive estimate of standing crop can be gained by measuring the overall shoot length. If the end of the shoot bearing green side shoots is also measured then an indication of the grazing potential of the plant is gained. The percentage of the plant bearing green side shoots could be plotted against age to reveal the long term changes in grazing potential.

3 Plant–soil interrelationships along a moorland valley

Choose a small moorland valley, preferably with a boggy valley floor. Lay a transect down the valley side and estimate the plant cover at suitable intervals by means of a point quadrat. Measure also such soil variables as moisture and humus contents, acidity and infiltration rates. Take core samples back to the laboratory to investigate soil structure. Is there any relationship between the plants present and the transition from dry to wet conditions down the valley?

4 A comparison of the microclimate within heather stands of different age

At different phases in its development the community dominant, *Calluna vulgaris*, influences the microclimate to varying degrees, e.g. at the building phase (7–13 years) the closed, dense canopy will greatly affect such conditions as light, temperature etc, beneath it. Measurement of microclimates were mentioned in

Chapter 3 and a comparative study could be made of illumination, temperature, humidity and air movement. This information could be linked to the distribution of ground layer plants (mosses and lichens) and invertebrate communities (by use of pitfalls).

5 Association analysis between two plant species

A statistical test (χ^2 test) can be applied to sample data to determine whether two plants are growing together or not. Use 50 random quadrat samples of the site to record the following information.

Quadrat	*Calluna* with *Agrostis*	*Calluna* only	*Agrostis* only	Neither *Calluna* nor *Agrostis*
1.				
2.				
.				
.				
.				
50.				
TOTAL	A	B	C	D

Record frequency by ticking appropriate column.

If the plants are associated then A + D will be greater than B + C. If not associated A + D will be less than B + C. Use the χ^2 test to compare the observed result with the expected result in each case. If the two species are associated, investigate the possible environmental causes (Fig 8.11).

Fig 8.11 4-year old moorland site following burning: mainly fine-leaved grasses and bell heather. Are the two associated?

6 The influence of microtopography on the distributions of two species of *Erica*

This investigation looks into the effect of soil moisture upon the distribution of the bell heather (*Erica cinerea*), and the cross-leaved heath (*Erica tetralix*). Choose a number of sample sites in well drained positions and a number in poorly drained positions. At each site determine the percentage cover of each species using a number of randomly placed point quadrats. Draw scatter graphs and carry out correlation determinations between the plant cover and soil moisture.

7 The trophic structure of a heathland or moorland community

Choose a site where one plant is dominant, e.g. *Molinia* grassland, heather moorland or cotton sedge bog. Mark off the area to be sampled and systematically sweep net the vegetation for invertebrates. Collect soil samples and examine the roots of dominant plants for further animals. Examine mouthparts and study feeding behaviour to determine whether animals are herbivores, carnivores or scavengers. Draw a food web of the community showing the roles of the producers, consumers and decomposers.

8 The effect of altitude on certain plant species

Choose a common plant species, e.g. the moor rush, *Juncus squarrosus*, and examine several individuals at stations of varying altitude. Record such features as density (per m²), height, length of flower stalk and numbers of fruits per stalk. Plot these characteristics against altitude to produce scatter graphs and carry out correlation determinations. Other correlations may be examined between the frequency of a species and environmental factors, e.g. bracken and soil depth or wind exposure, milkwort and soil moisture or heath bedstraw and pH.

9 Xeromorphic adaptations of heathland and moorland plants

In contrast to sand dunes, the xeromorphic adaptations in many moorland or heathland species are a result of restricted water uptake by roots from the cold windswept soils. Compare the species present in moorland and wet heath: do species from wet areas show less development of water conserving mechanisms? Take specimens back to the laboratory and prepare sections of leaves for microscopic examination. Look for the presence of such features as reduced leaf surface area (*Calluna, Erica*), leaves modified to form spines (gorse *Ulex* sp.), thick waxy cuticle (*Erica*) or sunken stomata (*Nardus, Descampsia*).

10 An investigation into grazing pressure on moorland sites

Examine two moorland sites, one which has been subjected to grazing, the other which has not. Use a standardised sampling procedure such as a number of randomly placed frame quadrats over the sample area. How do the two sites compare with regard to a) the diversity of plant species and b) the cover of each species? Evaluate the use of grazing as a form of management in upland areas.

8.4 Freshwater

Freshwater habitats can be divided into two main groups:
1   Standing water – ponds and lakes.
2   Running water – streams and rivers.
In still water many environmental factors show stratification, (i.e., vary with depth). Temperature, light, oxygen and pH all tend to decrease with depth in direct contrast to carbon dioxide, nutrients and organic matter which increase with depth. Not surprisingly, in running water the dominant factor is the rate of current flow. Where water movement increases most animal populations are found attached to or sheltering under stones on the bottom. All these environmental factors influence the species composition of different communities and have resulted in adaptations in those species. Most people have access to freshwater habitats.

1 Trophic structure of a river community

The exercise can be made quantitative by taking randomly placed kick samples from the habitat. Animals can be identified down to the family and classified as carnivores, herbivores or detritivores on the basis of their feeding behaviour and mouth parts. The total number of animals at each trophic level can then be worked out. Results can be expressed as pyramids of numbers or (if samples are collected together and weighed) as pyramids of biomass. Draw up a food web for the system and discuss the limitations of the techniques you have used with reference to standing crop, productivity, energy content and flow in ecosystems.

2 Ecosystem structure in eutrophic and oligotrophic lakes

Devise quantitative sampling techniques (refer to Chapter 5) for estimating the benthic, pelagic and neustic invertebrates in both eutrophic and oligotrophic lakes. How could you best express the data graphically? What relevant chemical tests would you carry out on the water samples collected from each type of lake? Explain how the diversity index for each lake is related to associated environmental factors.

J H Oldham

Fig 8.12 Upper reaches of an upland stream. Note flats and riffles

3 Comparing the fauna of fast and slow sections of a stream

Benthic invertebrates are collected from fast water (*riffles*) and slow water (*flats*) (Fig 8.12) by the kick sampling or stone washing technique (see Chapter 5). Hand sort in trays and identify and count individuals on site. Adaptations of the two different groups can be considered, e.g. streamlining and hooks in mayflies and stoneflies, hydroplane and cushion pad effect in the mayfly *Ecdyonurus* (the current is deflected up over the head thereby forcing the animal against stream bed). Correlate numbers of individuals with adaptations and test the latter in experimental streams.

4 Periodicity study involving the collection of invertebrate drift

Set up a drift net (Chapter 5) and remove samples at hourly intervals over a 24 hour period, (preferably working as a team!). Are there any diurnal fluctuations in the numbers of each species caught? Are species day active or night active? Results could be related to current flow, light, temperature and stream discharge. Devise methods of testing whether activity is triggered by external factors, e.g. light, or internal factors, e.g. hormones.

5 Mapping the vegetation of a canal

Lay a length of line, marked at metre individuals, at right angles across the canal. Place a second line parallel and one metre apart from the first, making sure that the graduations are in line. Record the distribution and abundance of the different plant species within the belt transect and construct a transverse profile. A series of parallel transects can be set up repeating the procedure and the data mapped to show the main zones of vegetation. Seasonal changes in the vegetation could be studied by repeating the exercise at suitable intervals.

6 Hydrosere zonation into a pond or lake

Mark out a belt transect 5 m wide with parallel lines, commencing a convenient distance away from the water's edge. Map on graph paper the areas occupied by the main species. Examine soil profiles along the transect noting the depth of each horizon, the pH and the depth of water table. Is there any evidence of succession from water to land (hydrosere)? What gradients in environmental conditions could have brought about any observed plant succession?

7 Diurnal fluctuations in zooplankton density

Devise a method for quantitatively sampling zooplankton at various depths in a pond or lake. Estimate the numbers of individuals in each sample in a counting chamber as described in Chapter 2. Take a series of samples at different depths at convenient intervals over a 24 hour period. Are there any diurnal variations in the vertical distribution of the zooplankton over 24 hours? What environmental factors might affect such variations and how might they be measured?

8 Microhabitats and niches in a pond

Identify a number of microhabitats in part of a pond, e.g. surface film, under stones, on submerged plants or in mud. Using suitable sampling techniques (Chapter 5) investigate the abundance and distribution of the animals in each microhabitat. What are the roles of the animals in each microhabitat and what adaptations do they possess to enable them to be successful?

9 The distribution and behaviour of the freshwater shrimp, *Gammarus pulex*

Devise a sampling strategy (kick sampling or stone washing?) to obtain semi-quantitative estimates of the distribution of *Gammarus* in a section of a stream (Fig 8.13). How does increase in current flow effect the distribution of *Gammarus*? Is there any evidence of crevice-seeking to avoid current? How could you test out your findings in the laboratory? Investigate the swimming activity of *Gammarus* when placed over white and black backgrounds; assess the speed and direction of movement. Relate any observed differences to the natural environmental conditions.

Fig 8.13 The freshwater shrimp *Gammarus pulex*, male carrying female

10 Biotic indicators of organic pollution

Sample the aquatic invertebrates above and at several stations below an organic effluent outfall. Identify and count the biotic indicator species with reference to Chapter 5 and assess the water quality using the Trent

Fig 8.14 Little flow in this drainage ditch: evidence of water pollution

Biotic Index. Is species diversity a reliable pointer to the degree of pollution? Discuss the adaptations of the pollution tolerant animals.

8.5 Seashore

Any work on the seashore is dominated by the diurnal movement of the tides which subject the shore populations to alternating periods of exposure to the air and submersion by the sea. This harsh environment contains a great abundance and diversity of living organisms (representatives of virtually all the invertebrate phyla can be found here). Fluctuations in temperature and salinity along with the effects of desiccation and wave action have provided just some of the selective pressures influencing the evolution of these organisms. Because of its remoteness the seashore environment is probably far less familiar to many biologists than freshwater or terrestrial habitats. If the problem of access can be overcome then the adaptations and inter relationships of intertidal organisms provide great potential for study.

1 The effect of wave action on *Fucus vesiculosus*

Two or three shores are chosen with different degrees of exposure to wave action. The *F. vesiculosus* zone in the midshore is located and the following measurements noted after examining each of about 30 plants.

a Frond length (from holdfast to apex).

b Number of bladders on frond (in this species bladder formation occurs each April).

From these figures the mean number of bladders per unit length of frond can be calculated for each shore. Other features which alter with exposure include the amount of branching, thickness of stipe and holdfast diameter. These could also be measured and an indication of the degree of exposure for the shore in question could be gained by using the exposure scale on page 45.

2 Zonation patterns on a rocky shore

This involves the use of an interrupted belt transect (see Chapter 2) to record the abundance and distribution of plant and animal species. Consult tide tables to obtain a prediction of the time of low tide and level of low tide above chart datum for the area to be studied. Construct a profile of this shore slope by using one of the surveying techniques outlined in Chapter 3. Try to reach the bottom of the shore, (i.e. last station) at exactly the predicted time of low tide. Work back up the shore laying down a 0.25 m² quadrat at each station at metre intervals and recording the abundance of plants as percentage cover and of animals by using abundance scales (page 15). Back in the laboratory the data can be plotted as described on page 18 on a large sheet of graph paper. A similar exercise conducted on an exposed shore illustrates how basic zonation patterns are modified by wave action.

3 Factors affecting the desiccation of seaweeds

The loss of water from pieces of thallus in air can be used as an index of the amount of evaporation. Several pieces of thallus of identical size are cut from the ends of healthy fronds of each of the common brown seaweeds. The cut ends only are smeared with vaseline and excess water removed. Each piece is weighed separately and exposed to air on a petri dish. Re-weigh at regular intervals, estimate the percentage loss in fresh weight and plot this against time (Fig 8.15). Does the rank order of water retention reflect the zonation of these species?

How might cell wall thickness and increased lipid content reduce water loss in some of these algae?

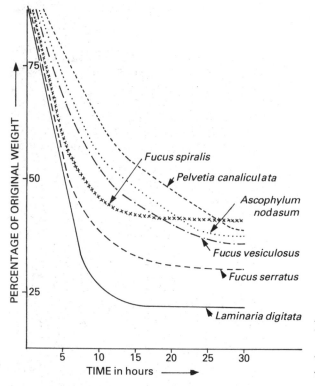

Fig 8.15 Percentage loss in weight due to evaporation of six species of brown seaweeds

4 Shell shape in the dog-whelk, *Nucella lapillus*

A large number of dog-whelks (100) are examined from each of an exposed and a sheltered shore. Measurements of shell height and aperture are taken in

the field using a vernier caliper and the animals carefully replaced. The ratios of shell height/aperture are calculated and plotted as histograms. Individuals from wave-exposed shores tend to have a larger foot for attachment in conditions of increased wave action (Fig 8.16). Measurements of shell thickness and rows of teeth on the shell aperture have been found to correlate with the degree of exposure (Fig 8.17). Individuals from exposed shores tend to have more tooth rows and thicker shells, the reasons for these observations may well prompt interesting discussion. See Crothers J H (1985), 'Dog-whelks: An introduction to the biology of *Nucella lapillus* (L)', *Field Studies* Vol 6, 291–360).

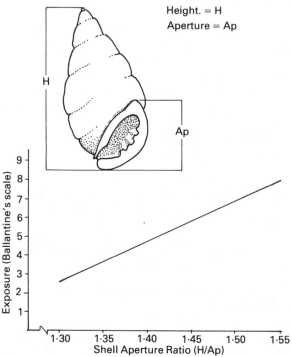

Fig 8.16 The dog-whelk (*Nucella lapillus*) predating on barnacles. Note the number of empty barnacle cases

Fig 8.17 Positive correlation between shell aperture ratio and degree of exposure

Animal	Total water loss % wt	Average water loss % day − 1	Mortality %	Shore position
Nerite periwinkle (*Littorina neritoides*)	26	3.71	0	Splash zone
Rough periwinkle (*L. rudis*)	39.7	5.6	8–17	Upper and midshore
Edible periwinkle (*L. littorea*)	37.5	5.35	70	Midshore
Flat periwinkle (*L. obtusata*)	56.5	8.35	80	Mid and lower shore

Fig 8.18 Effects of dessication on *Littorina* sp after 7 days at 18°C (after Lewis)

5 Water loss in air and tolerance of desiccation in periwinkles, *Littorina* sp.

Periwinkles within the genus *Littorina* show differing ability to resist desiccation which can be correlated with position on the shore. A number of individuals of each of the species *L. neritoides*, *L. rudis*, *L. littorea* and *L. obtusata* were collected and left for a few hours in oxygenated seawater to become fully hydrated. Excess water was then removed from each batch with absorbent paper and the mean fresh weight for each species recorded. The periwinkles were then left exposed to still air and re-weighed daily (Fig 8.18). In addition to their position on the shore, results could take into account behavioural aspects, such as the aggregation of some species in rock crevices or amongst heaps of seaweeds.

6 Integrated activity in the lugworm, *Arenicola marina*

Arenicola displays two types of activity cycle. The first concerns feeding and involves the oesophagus, proboscis and first three body segments. The second involving the other segments of the body wall is concerned with irrigation of the burrow and defaecation.

Introduce the worm into a U-tube tail first and fill the tube with seawater. After a settling down period record the following observations.:

a Number of proboscis extrusions per minute over a ten minute period. Express your results in the form of a histogram.

b Record over a period of 1 hour:
   i) frequency and direction of peristaltic waves of contraction passing along the body and
   ii) the worm's position in the tube.

The effect upon rate of proboscis extrusion of injecting 0.01% adrenaline into the body cavity surrounding the oesophagus could also be studied (Fig 8.19)

7 Holdfasts of *Laminaria* sp, a study of microhabitats

Spaces between the rhizoids of Laminarian holdfasts provide shelter for a whole variety of small invertebrates including sea squirts, barnacles, hydroids, polychaete worms, bryozoans, and small mussels (Fig 8.20). A number of holdfasts from a variety of shores are collected together with attached substrate and each individual placed in a labelled plastic bag. In the laboratory the holdfasts are broken up in dishes of seawater and the animals identified and listed. Since many of these animals are small a binocular microscope is useful for identification purposes. It may be possible to classify the animals as herbivores, carnivores or detritivores and finally draw up a food web for the system.

Fig 8.19 Sampling sand-dwelling animals such as the polychaete *Arenicola* involves digging and sieving out the substrate

Fig 8.20 A Laminarian holdfast

8 Salinity tolerance in the shore crab, *Carcinus maenus*

Collect ten similar sized specimens of the shore crab. In this way each crab should have about the same surface area of tissue in contact with the external medium. Make a range of dilutions of seawater from full strength to 0.1 full strength and place 200 cm³ of each into a labelled beaker. Use a hypodermic syringe to gently remove stored water from the gill chamber of each crab (see Jenkins). Different amounts of water in the gill chambers of each crab will give erratic initial weights. Weigh each labelled crab and record the weight. Immerse each crab in a different dilution of seawater for one hour after aerating the water. Remove the water from the gill chamber as before and re-weigh. Calculate the percentage change in weight of each individual.

9 Factors affecting the activity of barnacles, *Semibalanus balanoides*

Barnacles may be conveniently collected on stones or mussels and placed in fresh seawater. A study may be made of the effects of different conditions upon the sweep rate of their feeding appendages (*cirri*). These conditions could include different dilutions of seawater, different oxygen concentrations and a range of temperatures. Between each treatment, time must be allowed for the barnacles to recover and produce a constant sweep rate. Discussion could relate cirrus sweep rate to gas exchange and feeding. Do all the barnacles under observation feed at the same time? Do more feed at the time corresponding to high tide?

10 A study of intertidal rock pools

Some species escape desiccation and are able to extend further up the shore by living in rock pools. However, these pools provide fluctuating conditions and few animals are able to tolerate continuous submersion in them. Upper pools experience wide fluctuations in seawater, in temperature, salinity, pH and concentrations of dissolved gases over a 24 hour period.

Three pools are chosen, one from each of the upper, mid and lower shore. A surface plan of the pool is then drawn to show the shape and measurements made of the length, width and depth at a number of points to enable a scale drawing to be made later. In addition a record is made of the direction of north and also that of the sea. The positions of any shadowing rocks and the positions of animals and plants within the pool are included upon the diagram.

The following parameters may be usefully measured, preferably over a 24 hour period (see Chapter 3).

Temperature with a field thermometer or electronic thermometer.

b Salinity or conductivity either by taking samples for later chloride estimation with silver nitrate or by using a conductivity meter.

c pH with an electronic meter.

d Oxygen by means of an oxygen meter or by 'fixing' a sample of water for titration by the Winkler method back in the laboratory. (Carbon dioxide is generally thought to have a greater influence upon the pool inhabitants than oxygen but its estimation is complex (see Daniel and Boyden).

A scale drawing of each pool is made on graph paper (Fig 8.22) and discussion attempted of the distribution of species within each pool and the diurnal variation in environmental factors. (See Daniel M J and Boyden C R (1975), 'Diurnal variations in physico-chemical conditions within intertidal rock pools', *Field Studies* Vol 4, 161–176).

Fig 8.21 Measuring the dimensions of a midshore rock pool at Cable Bay, Anglesey

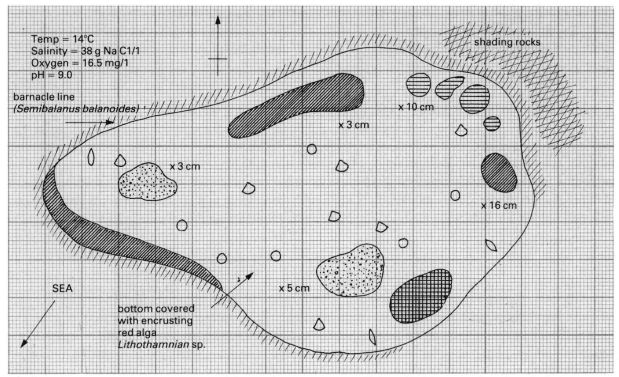

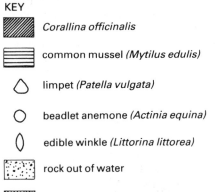

KEY

▨ *Corallina officinalis*

☰ common mussel *(Mytilus edulis)*

△ limpet *(Patella vulgata)*

○ beadlet anemone *(Actinia equina)*

◊ edible winkle *(Littorina littorea)*

▦ rock out of water

▦ *Enteromorpha compressa*

Fig 8.22 Scaled drawing of rock pool from the midshore

8.6 Sand dune and salt-marsh

Both these habitats are influenced by the sea and show a transition to increasingly more stable conditions on the landward side. They are excellent habitats for providing a spatial demonstration of the temporal phenomenon of succession. They are also fragile sites and easily susceptible to trampling damage.

Sand dunes

The formation of sand dunes results from the movement of sand particles by the wind. A few pioneer plants, such as the sea rocket *(Cakile maritima)* and

couch grass, *(Agropyron junceiforme)*, provide a wind check which accelerates the build up of blown sand. Gradually such hardy grasses as marram become established binding the sand together with their fibrous rhizomes and forming the so called yellow dunes which may reach heights of up to 50 feet. Behind these the more stabilised substrate encourages a greater diversity of new plants producing the grey dune stage. The slack vegetation in the sheltered hollows between these dunes gives rise to a variety of angiosperms which flourish in damp conditions and the increased organic content of the 'soil'. Thus, by walking inland over the dunes from the driftline, we are able to observe the different stages in dune development.

Sand dunes harbour a rich variety of plants and animals and are deserving of conservation. In many areas they form the first line of defence from the sea. Damage to plant cover by human trampling and rabbit grazing and burrowing can lead to exposure of the sand and consequently dune erosion. The fragile nature of the dunes should be recognised since too much recreational use could bring about their destruction.

1 A study of dune succession

Lay a transect line down from the strand line to the grey (fixed) dunes. At convenient intervals sample the vegetation by means of a point quadrat to obtain estimates of percentage cover. Identify the pioneer species. How are these plants adapted for rapid growth and how do they aid the stabilisation of young dunes?

Bob Gibbons

Fig. 8.23 Yellow dunes colonised mainly by marram

Robin Fletcher/Natural Image

Identify any stages in succession along with the transect and assess any transition into a climax vegetation. Present the results as kite diagrams or bar chart equivalents.

2   Comparison of dune and slack vegetation

Take random quadrat samples within these two zones estimating the percentage cover of the plant species found. Results could again be related to topography, water table level, substrate stability, soil moisture, humus contents and humidity. This project could be carried out for most of the year and may be backed up by a study of the anatomy of the plants back in the laboratory. Many sand dune species are xeromorphic showing structural adaptations to reduce water loss, many of which can be revealed by taking sections.

3   The effect of dune development on soil composition

Along a transect line running from fore dunes to secondary dunes take soil samples from root level at suitable intervals. In the laboratory estimate the water content, humus content, pH and salt content (dissolve 10 g samples in distilled water and filter off the sand, then titrate against silver nitrate). Examine any changes in the soil composition with age of dune and suggest how these changes may affect plant growth.

4   Investigation into the diet of rabbits

Collect faecal pellets of rabbits from embryo dunes, mature dunes, and dune slacks. Analyse back in the laboratory by carefully dissecting each pellet and washing the contents out in a sieve. Attempts could be made to discern any grazing preferences by using trays of grasses raised from seed, to add some experimental work to the exercise.

5   Seed germination and seedling survival

Long term projects (at least a year) could be set up to study the optimal conditions for seed germination and seedling survival of sand dune plants. Experiments could be set up investigating the success of different species under varying soil moisture, drainage and substrate stability. Plants raised from seed could also be transplanted into different microhabitats. Attempts could be made to relate the success of various sand dune species to reproductive capacity (by estimating the number of seeds per plant) or to times of flowering, fruiting and germination.

Salt-marshes

Salt-marshes are fertile habitats and energy flow rates within the ecosystem are often more rapid than in the surrounding area since the tidal action provides a rapid circulation of nutrients and aids the removal of waste material. They develop most commonly in estuaries where clay and silt, brought down by rivers, settles and is exposed to the air at low tide. Pioneer species colonise the lower levels of the marsh, their fibrous roots stabilising the mud (Fig 8.24). These plants are halophytes and are able to tolerate excessive salinity by means of mechanisms which are still poorly understood. At the top of the marsh, agriculture often reclaims the land so that the natural transition into climax vegetation rarely occurs.

Salt-marshes are extremely delicate sites and far more susceptible to damage by trampling than sand dunes. Great care needs to be exercised not to cause any damage when investigating the soft muddy areas being colonised. Salt-marshes and mud flats have importance conservationally as they provide feeding and roosting in the winter months for numerous migrant waders and wildfowl.

Fig 8.24 Lower salt-marsh view

1   A study in plant performance in the cord grass, *Spartina townsendii*

Set up three permanent quadrats located at the top, middle and bottom of the marsh. The performance of *Spartina* in these quadrats could be studied over a period of time by measuring density, height of shoot and density of flowering shoots. Individual plants could be tagged using plastic coated wire and subsamples taken at random within the permanent quadrat to enable subsequent statistical analysis.

Fig 8.25   The cord grass, *Spartina townsendii*

2   The effects of density upon plant growth in the glasswort, *Salicornia europaea*

Another of the pioneer colonisers of a salt-marsh is *Salicornia*. The performance of this annual could be compared with that of the perennial grass, *Spartina*, using the procedures outlined in the previous exercise. A useful exercise involves studying the influence of density upon plant growth in *Salicornia*. This involves quadrat sampling areas when the plant is at obviously

different density and relating the mean height of individuals to that density. Taken over a period of time, the amount of self-thinning occurring during the growing season could be established.

3   A study in the succession of salt-marsh plants

Decide upon the approximate length of your transect, from creek to upper marsh, and divide it into about 20 sampling stations. Measure the vertical rise or fall between each of these points using a technique outlined in Chapter 3, so that you can construct a transect profile (this needs to be done accurately since the total height difference along the complete transect may not exceed 30 cms). At each sampling station use a frame quadrat or else a point quadrat to estimate abundance (as percentage cover). Present the results as kite diagrams or bar chart equivalents.

4   Changes in soil composition along a salt-marsh

Run a transect line along the marsh from the creek to

Fig 8.26
Common sea lavender (*Limonium vulgare*) amongst *Triglochin maritima* on upper saltmarsh

the upper marsh. At suitable points along this line record soil temperature and take a soil sample. Back in the laboratory estimate the organic content, pH and salinity (with silver nitrate titration) of the different samples. Salinity may be measured in the field by means of a hydrometer if a hole is dug in the soil and intertidal water allowed to drain into it. Suggest how any observed changes in soil composition may affect plant distribution along the marsh.

5   Salinity tolerance in estuarine invertebrates

Estuarine animals have to be more plastic in their physiology to withstand immersion in waters of fluctuating salinity. Suitable organisms for this sort of exercise would be the shore crab *Carcinus maenas*, the ragworm *Nereis diversicolor* or the bivalve *Scrobicularia plana*. A series of dilutions of sea water are made from full strength (35‰) to fresh water (0‰). Animals of similar size are then weighed (firstly evacuating water from the gill chamber in the case of *Carcinus* or the mantle cavity for *Scrobicularia*). Immerse each animal in a beaker of known salinity for one hour and re-weigh (firstly removing excess water as before). Evaluate the ability of the species investigated to osmoregulate in conditions of changing salinity. Compare its performance with a closely related species which is truly marine.

8.7 Urban environments

Since 80% of the population of Britain lives in urban areas it is not perhaps surprising that there has been an upsurge of interest in urban ecology over the past decade. Traditional fieldwork has focussed upon natural ecosystems despite the fact that urban habitats have many merits. Accessibility means that long term projects can be attempted with a consequent saving of time and money. In addition urban environments often contain a multitude of microhabitats and are also subjected to many environmental pressures, e.g. pollution.

1   The study of a hedgerow

Sample along a belt transect across a hedgerow with an approximate north and south aspect. At equal distances along the transect use a frame quadrat of suitable size or a point quadrat to estimate the percentage cover of the different species. Draw a profile on graph paper and plot frequency histograms for each species. Suggest the reasons for any observed differences in the vegetation on each side of the hedge. Is there any evidence of succession along the transect?

Work out the index of species diversity for each side of the hedge.

2   Investigating feeding relationships in a compost heap

Determine the relative abundance of the different animal species living in the compost heap. Collect the animals by hand sorting and by Tullgren funnel extraction. Determine their feeding relationships either by direct observation of feeding behaviour and structure of mouth parts or from reference books. Attempt to build up a food web based upon the detritus. What are the conditions of humidity, pH and temperature like inside the heap? Compare the abundance of soil animals underneath the heap with samples taken from the surrounding soil. Attempt to relate these differences to conditions in the two soils.

3   Determination of the plant succession on waste tips

Choose a suitable industrial pit heap which is likely to show the pattern of succession. Lay down the transect line commencing at the youngest part of the tip. At metre intervals estimate the percentage cover either by using a 0.25 m² frame quadrat or a point quadrat (sampling can be carried out at 3 or 5 m intervals if the length of the transect is extensive). Use one of the surveying techniques described in Chapter 3 to record changes in height along the transect. Draw a profile to scale and plot frequency histograms for each of the

species as demonstrated in Chapter 2. Identify the pioneer species and set up experiments to investigate their ability to colonise this environment. Examine the pattern of succession illustrated by the histograms and examine the changes in *edaphic* (soil) conditions along the transect.

4   Plant growth experiments on wasteland soil plots

Experimental plots of a convenient size can be set up for long term study on suitable nutrient-poor wasteland tips (permission to use the waste tip must be obtained especially since many tips contain hazardous chemicals). Once the plots are marked out and dug over, various treatments may be applied, e.g.

A Plot – No nutrients
B Plot – Nitrogen fertiliser
C Plot – Phosphate fertiliser
D Plot – Nitrogen and phosphate fertilisers

Grass seed, e.g. *Festuca rubra*, is then sown on each plot and the height of the vegetation recorded weekly. Metal tolerant grass species could be tested. Biomass determinations could also be made along with such records as pH estimation and lime requirement.

5   Atmospheric pollution and lichen growth

Lichens are sensitive to sulphur dioxide in solution which they absorb across the entire body surface. Since sulphur dioxide is a common pollutant in urban areas, its effect upon the growth and distribution of lichens can be studied by selecting sampling stations at regular intervals from the town centre to the surrounding countryside. At each station the same sort of substrate should be selected, e.g. the bark of one particular species of tree (Fig 8.27) and the diversity and levels of lichen growth in a defined area assessed. The line transect method may reveal a gradient of atmospheric pollution in an urban area.

6   The colonisation of gravestones by lichens

At an old cemetery select a number of gravestones which give a large age span. Use a 10 cm quadrat drawn on acetate paper and divided into 100 squares to estimate the percentage cover of each lichen species (Fig 8.29). Record also the following information from each gravestone: the age from the inscription, aspect, and if possible pH. Attempt to explain any differences in the rate of growth of the various species.

7   A comparison of the distribution of plants on two aspects of a wall

This is best attempted in summer and preferably on a wall with a north and south facing aspect. Identify the species of mosses, liverworts and lichens present. Investigate the spatial distribution of these species by quadrat analysis from the base to the top of the wall. Analyse samples of accumulated soil at different heights in the wall for organic content, pH, lime and water content. Record the surface temperature of each side of the wall at hourly intervals and take readings of humidity for each side by means of an evaporimeter (Chapter 3). A similar exercise could be carried out to compare the distribution and levels of growth of mosses and lichens on north and south facing roofs.

8 Investigation into the distribution and abundance of weeds in a playing field

Using point quadrat or frame quadrat techniques for estimating percentage cover, investigate the pattern of weed distribution in different sites on a playing field. What factors influence the distribution of some of the weeds? Evaluate the effects of mowing and trampling. What proportion of the weeds have a rosette habit? What is the ratio of root size to shoot size in typical specimens?

J Rowan

Fig 8.27 Luxuriant lichen growth on oak bark in pollution free atmosphere

Fig 8.28 Rosebay willowherb, *Chamaenerion angustifolium*, a common coloniser of sunny open ground

J H Oldham

Fig. 8.29 Lichen growth on a gravestone

Bob Gibbons

Appendix 1

Random sampling numbers

```
20 17   42 28   23 17   59 66   38 61   02 10   86 10   51 55   92 52
74 49   04 49   03 04   10 33   53 70   11 54   48 63   94 60   94 49
94 70   49 31   38 67   23 42   29 65   40 88   78 71   37 18   48 64
22 15   78 15   69 84   32 52   32 54   15 12   54 02   01 37   38 37
93 29   12 18   27 30   30 55   91 87   50 57   58 51   49 36   12 53

45 04   77 97   36 14   99 45   52 95   69 85   03 83   51 87   85 56
44 91   99 49   89 39   94 60   48 49   06 77   64 72   59 26   08 51
16 23   91 02   19 96   47 59   89 65   27 84   30 92   63 37   26 24
04 50   65 04   65 65   82 42   70 51   55 04   61 47   88 83   99 34
32 70   17 72   03 61   66 26   24 71   22 77   88 33   17 78   08 92

03 64   59 07   42 95   81 39   06 41   20 81   92 34   51 90   39 08
62 49   00 90   67 86   83 48   31 83   19 07   67 68   49 03   27 47
61 00   95 86   98 36   14 03   48 88   51 07   33 40   06 86   33 76
89 03   90 49   28 74   21 04   09 96   60 45   22 03   52 80   01 79
01 72   33 85   52 40   60 07   06 71   89 27   14 29   55 24   85 79

27 56   49 79   34 34   32 22   60 53   91 17   33 26   44 70   93 14
49 05   74 48   10 55   35 25   24 28   20 22   35 66   66 34   26 35
49 74   37 25   97 26   33 94   42 23   01 28   59 58   92 69   03 66
20 26   22 43   88 08   19 85   08 12   47 65   65 63   56 07   97 85
48 87   77 96   43 39   76 93   08 79   22 18   54 55   93 75   97 26

08 72   87 46   75 73   00 11   27 07   05 20   30 85   22 21   04 67
95 97   98 62   17 27   31 42   64 71   46 22   32 75   19 32   20 99
37 99   57 31   70 40   46 55   46 12   24 32   36 74   69 20   72 10
05 79   58 37   85 33   75 18   88 71   23 44   54 28   00 48   96 23
55 85   63 42   00 79   91 22   29 01   41 39   51 50   36 65   26 11

67 28   96 25   68 36   24 72   03 85   49 24   05 69   64 86   08 19
85 86   94 78   32 59   51 82   86 43   73 84   45 60   89 57   06 87
40 10   60 09   05 88   78 44   63 13   58 25   37 11   18 47   75 62
94 55   89 48   90 80   77 80   26 89   87 44   23 74   66 20   20 19
11 63   77 77   23 20   33 62   62 19   29 03   94 15   56 37   14 09

64 00   26 04   54 55   38 57   94 62   68 40   26 04   24 25   03 61
50 94   13 23   78 41   60 58   10 60   88 46   30 21   45 98   70 96
66 98   37 96   44 13   45 05   34 59   75 85   48 97   27 19   17 85
66 91   42 83   60 77   90 91   60 90   79 62   57 66   72 28   08 70
33 58   12 18   02 07   19 40   21 29   39 45   90 42   58 84   85 43

52 49   70 16   72 40   73 05   50 90   02 04   98 24   05 30   27 25
74 98   93 99   78 30   79 47   96 62   45 58   40 37   89 76   84 41
50 26   54 30   01 88   69 57   54 45   69 88   23 21   05 69   93 44
49 46   61 89   33 79   96 84   28 34   19 35   28 73   39 59   56 34
19 64   13 44   78 39   73 88   62 03   36 00   25 96   86 76   67 90

64 17   47 67   87 59   81 40   72 61   14 00   28 28   55 86   23 38
18 43   97 37   68 97   56 56   57 95   01 88   11 89   48 07   42 07
65 58   60 87   51 09   96 61   15 53   66 81   66 88   44 75   37 01
79 90   31 00   91 14   85 65   31 75   43 15   45 93   64 78   34 53
07 23   00 15   59 05   16 09   94 42   20 40   63 76   65 67   34 11

90 98   14 24   01 51   95 46   30 32   33 19   00 14   19 28   40 51
53 82   62 02   21 82   34 13   41 03   12 85   65 30   00 97   56 30
98 17   26 15   04 50   76 25   20 33   54 84   39 31   23 33   59 64
08 91   12 44   82 40   30 62   45 50   64 54   65 17   89 25   59 44
37 21   46 77   84 87   67 39   85 54   97 37   33 41   11 74   90 50
```

After Lindley and Miller (1953).

146

Appendix 2

Critical values of chi-squared

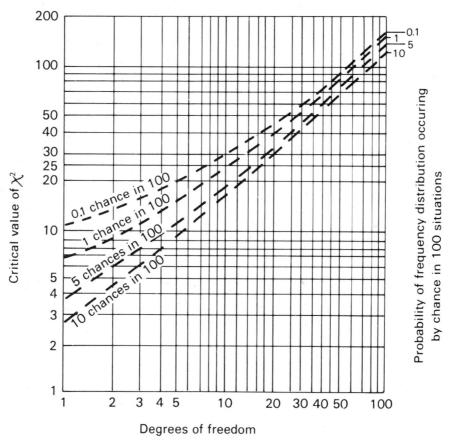

Source: based on McCullagh, P., *Data Use and Interpretation*

Appendix 3

VALUES OF THE *U*-STATISTIC AT THE 5% LEVEL OF SIGNIFICANCE.

n_1 and n_2 are the number of counts in each sample. Remember that small values of U cause rejection of H_0 at the 5% level.

n_1 \ n_2	2	3	4	5	6	7	8	9	10	11	12	13	14	15	16	17	18	19	20
2							0	0	0	0	1	1	1	1	1	2	2	2	2
3				0	1	1	2	2	3	3	4	4	5	5	6	6	7	7	8
4			0	1	2	3	4	4	5	6	7	8	9	10	11	11	12	13	13
5		0	1	2	3	5	6	7	8	9	11	12	13	14	15	17	18	19	20
6		1	2	3	5	6	8	10	11	13	14	16	17	19	21	22	24	25	27
7		1	3	5	6	8	10	12	14	16	18	20	22	24	26	28	30	32	34
8	0	2	4	6	8	10	13	15	17	19	22	24	26	29	31	34	36	38	41
9	0	2	4	7	10	12	15	17	20	23	26	28	31	34	37	39	42	45	48
10	0	3	5	8	11	14	17	20	23	26	29	33	36	39	42	45	48	52	55
11	0	3	6	9	13	16	19	23	26	30	33	37	40	44	47	51	55	58	62
12	1	4	7	11	14	18	22	26	29	33	37	41	45	49	53	57	61	65	69
13	1	4	8	12	16	20	24	28	33	37	41	45	50	54	59	63	67	72	76
14	1	5	9	13	17	22	26	31	36	40	45	50	55	59	64	67	74	78	83
15	1	5	10	14	19	24	29	34	39	44	49	54	59	64	70	75	80	85	90
16	1	6	11	15	21	26	31	37	42	47	53	59	64	70	75	81	86	92	98
17	2	6	11	17	22	28	34	39	45	51	57	63	67	75	81	87	93	99	105
18	2	7	12	18	24	30	36	42	48	55	61	67	74	80	86	93	99	106	112
19	2	7	13	19	25	32	38	45	52	58	65	72	78	85	92	99	106	113	119
20	2	9	13	20	27	34	41	48	55	62	69	76	83	90	98	105	112	119	127

(Source: Elliott J M (1977), see Bibliography)

Appendix 4

Student's *t*-tables

Degrees of Freedom	Rejection level probabilities				
	$p=0.1$	$p=0.05$	$p=0.02$	$p=0.01$	$p=0.001$
1	6.31	12.71	31.82	63.66	636.62
2	2.92	4.30	6.97	9.93	31.60
3	2.35	3.18	4.54	5.84	12.94
4	2.13	2.78	3.75	4.60	8.61
5	2.02	2.57	3.37	4.03	6.86
6	1.94	2.45	3.14	3.71	5.96
7	1.90	2.37	3.00	3.50	5.41
8	1.86	2.31	2.90	3.36	5.04
9	1.83	2.26	2.82	3.25	4.78
10	1.81	2.23	2.76	3.17	4.59
11	1.80	2.20	2.72	3.11	4.44
12	1.78	2.18	2.68	3.06	4.32
13	1.77	2.16	2.65	3.01	4.22
14	1.76	2.15	2.62	2.98	4.14
15	1.75	2.13	2.60	2.95	4.07
16	1.75	2.12	2.58	2.92	4.02
17	1.74	2.11	2.57	2.90	3.97
18	1.73	2.10	2.55	2.88	3.92
19	1.73	2.09	2.54	2.86	3.88
20	1.73	2.09	2.53	2.85	3.85
21	1.72	2.08	2.52	2.83	3.82
22	1.72	2.07	2.51	2.82	3.79
23	1.71	2.07	2.50	2.81	3.77
24	1.71	2.06	2.49	2.80	3.75
25	1.71	2.06	2.49	2.79	3.73
26	1.71	2.06	2.48	2.78	3.71
27	1.70	2.05	2.47	2.77	3.69
28	1.70	2.05	2.47	2.76	3.67
29	1.70	2.05	2.46	2.76	3.66
30	1.70	2.04	2.46	2.75	3.65
40	1.68	2.02	2.42	2.70	3.55
60	1.67	2.00	2.39	2.66	3.46

Addresses

ASSOCIATION FOR SCIENCE EDUCATION College Lane, Hatfield, Herts, AL10 9AA (publishes *School Science Review*)

ADVISORY CENTRE FOR EDUCATION 32 Trumpington St., Cambridge (lichen identification chart)

BRITISH ECOLOGICAL SOCIETY Harvest House, 62 London Road, Reading RB1 5AS

BRITISH MOUNTAINEERING COUNCIL Crawford House, Precinct Centre, Booth St., East Manchester M13 9RZ (*Safety on Mountains*)

FIELD STUDIES COUNCIL Preston Montford, Montford Bridge, Shrewsbury SY4 1HW (information on courses)

FIELD STUDIES Nettlecombe Court, Williton, Taunton, Somerset TA4 4HT (journal of the Field Studies Council)

FRESHWATER BIOLOGICAL ASSOCIATION Windermere Laboratory, The Ferry House, Far Sawrey, Ambleside, Cumbria LA22 OLP

INSTITUTE OF BIOLOGY 20 Queensberry Place, London SW7 2DZ (publishes *Biologist* and *Journal of Biological Education*)

LINNEAN SOCIETY OF LONDON Burlington House, Piccadilly, London W1V OLQ

MAMMAL SOCIETY Harvest House, 62 London Road, Reading

MARINE BIOLOGICAL ASSOCIATION The Laboratory, Citadel Hill, Plymouth, Devon PL1 2PB

NATURAL ENVIRONMENT RESEARCH COUNCIL Polaris House, North Star Avenue, Swindon SN2 1ET (*Safety in the Field*)

ROYAL ENTOMOLOGICAL SOCIETY 41 Queen's Gate, London SW7 5HU

SCIENCE EDUCATIONAL SOFTWARE Marian Mawr Industrial Estate, Dolgellau, Gwynedd (computer programs)

SOIL ASSOCIATION Walnut Tree Manor, Haughley, Stowmarket, Suffolk IP14 3RS

B D H CHEMICALS LTD Broome Road, Poole, Dorset BH12 4NN (soil testing kits)

S M DAVIES 45 Quest Hill Road, Malvern, Worcs WR14 1RL (pond nets)

EDUCATIONAL ELECTRONICS LTD, 28 Lake St., Leighton Buzzard, Beds LU7 8RX (environmental sensors)

EDUCATIONAL FIELD EQUIPMENT 1 Puddle, Lanlivery, Bodmin, Cornwall PL30 5BY

G B NETS Gill Baldwin, 50 Henshaw Road, Small Heath, Birmingham B10 0TB

GRIFFIN AND GEORGE LTD Ealing Road, Alperton, Wembley, Middx HA0 1HJ

PHILIP HARRIS LTD Lynn Lane, Shenstone, Staffs WS14 OEE

W P A LTD The Old Station, Linton, Cambridge CB1 6NW (meters)

Bibliography

A General ecology

Bennett D P AND Humphries D A (2nd Edition 1983)
Introduction to Field Biology, Edward Arnold.
Chalmers N and Parker P (1986) *The OU Project Guide, Fieldwork
and Statistics for Ecological Projects*, Field Studies Council.
Cloudsley-Thompson J L (1974) *Microecology*, Edward Arnold.
Dowdeswell W H (1984) *Ecology: Principles and Practice*,
Heinemann.
Elton C S (1966) *The Pattern of Animal Communities*, Methuen.
Kershaw K A (1984) *Quantitative and Dynamic Ecology* (3rd
Edition), Edward Arnold.
King T J (1980) *Ecology*, Nelson.
Krebs C J (1978) *Ecology, the experimental analysis of distribution
and abundance*, Harper & Row.
Lewis T and Taylor L R (1967) *Introduction to experimental
ecology*, Academic Press.
Odum E P (1975) *Ecology*, Holt, Reinhart & Winston.
Sands M K (1978) *Problems in Ecology*, Bell & Hyman.
Southwood T R E (1966) *Ecological Methods*, Methuen.

B Techniques

1 Sampling and monitoring
Archer M (1971) 'The use of pitfall, water and cover traps as an
introduction to animal ecology' *School Science Review*, **53**, No.
183, 307–315.
Atkinson C (1983) 'Integrated light measurement in the field'
Journal of Biological Education, **17**, 285.
Baker J and Sinker C *'Harris Point Frame' Equipment Notes*,
Philip Harris Ltd.
Begon M (1979) *Investigating Animal Abundance*, Edward Arnold.
Bishop O N (1975) 'A photometer for biological investigations'
School Science Review, **57**, No. 199, 241–53.
Blower J G, Cook L M and Bishop J A (1981) *Estimating the Size
of Animal Populations*, George Allen and Unwin.
Crellin J R (1978) 'Environmental measurement in schools:
electronics in field studies' *Journal of Biological Education*, **12**,
190–8.
Crellin J R and Tranter J (1978) 'Monitoring the environment: the
use of electronic meters and chemical or bacteriological tests'
Journal of Biological Education, **12**, 291–304.
Freeland P W (1975) 'Some applications of colorimeters and light
meters in biology teaching' *School Science Review*, **57**, No. 198,
22–37.
Grieg-Smith F (2nd Edition 1964) *Quantitative Plant Ecology*,
Butterworth.

Gurnell J and Flowerdew J R (1982) *Live Trapping Small
Mammals – a practical guide*, the Mammal Society.
Nichols D (1983) *Safety in Biological Fieldwork – guidance notes
for codes of practice* (2nd Edition), Institute of Biology, London.
Nuttall I E I (1964) *Environmental Multiprobe*, Waldren Precision
Apparatus.
Richardson J (1981) 'Oxygen meters: some pratical considerations'
Journal of Biological Education, **15**, 107–16.
Unwin D M (1978) 'Simple techniques for microclimate
measurement' *Journal of Biological Education*, **12**, 179–189.
Wrigglesworth (1981) *The Griffin Environmental Multimeter*,
Griffin and George Ltd.
Wood-Robinson C (1981) 'Surveying Rocky Shores' *Journal of
Biological Education*, **15**, 100–1.

2 Soil analysis
Archer M E (1967) 'Collecting, extracting and counting soil
animals' *School Science Review*, **48**, No. 166, 871–875.
Courtney F M and Trudgill S T (1984) *The Soil – an introduction
to soil study*, Edward Arnold.
Jackson R M and Raw F (1966) *Life in the soil*, Edward Arnold.
Leadley Brown A (1978) *Ecology of Soil Organisms*, Heinemann.
Mc. E. Kevan D K (1962) *Soil Animals*, H F & G Witherby.
Townsend W N (1973) *An Introduction to the Scientific Study of
Soil*, Edward Arnold.
Tribe H T (1967) 'Pratical studies on biological decomposition in
soil: a simple technique for observation of soil organisms
colonising buried celluloid film' *School Science Review*, **49**, No.
167, 95–112.
Wallwork J A (1970) *Ecology of Soil Animals*, Mcgraw-Hill.

3 Water analysis
Dale C R (1980) 'The biotic indexing of water quality and its
application to fieldwork in schools and colleges' *Journal of
Biological Education*, **14**, 205–212.
Gill B F (1977) 'A plastic syringe method for measuring dissolved
oxygen in the field or laboratory' *School Science Review*, **58**,
No. 204, 458–60.
Hambler D J and Dixon J M (1982) 'Limnological projects'
Journal of Biological Education, **16**, 116–122.
Hynes H B N (1960) *The Biology of Polluted Waters*, Liverpool
University Press.
Humphreys J J (1981) 'Estuarine ecology as project work' *Journal
of Biological Education*, **15**, 225–233.
Lapworth C H (1981) 'Measuring salinity by conductivity'
Journal of Biological Education, **15**, 186–7.
Lind O T (1974) *Handbook of common methods in limnology*,
Mosby, Saint Louis.

Mackereth F J H, Heron J and Talling J F (1978) 'Water Analysis: some revised methods for limnologists' *Freshwater Biological Association Scientific Publication*, No. 36.

Maitland P S (1978) *The Biology of Fresh Waters*, Blackie.

McKenny A M A *The Griffin Pollution Test Kit Handbook*.

Price J H, Irvine D E G and Farnham W F (1980) *The Shore Environment: Methods* Vol 1; *Ecosystems* Vol 2, Academic Press.

Openshaw P H (1983) 'River pollution Part I' *School Science Review*, **65**, No. 231, 243–254.

Openshaw P H (1984) 'River pollution Part II, Biological methods for assessing water quality' *School Science Review*, **65**, No. 232, 460–474.

Sutcliffe D W (1983) 'Acid precipitation and its effects on aquatic systems in the English Lake District (Cumbria) *Freshwater Biological Association* Scientific Publication, No. 51, 30–62.

Williams N V and Dussart G B J (1976) 'A field course survey of three English river systems' *Journal of Biological Education*, **10**, 4–14.

Woodiwiss F S (1964) 'The biological system of river classification used by the Trent River Board' *Chemistry and Industry*, **11**, 443–7.

4 Statistics and graphical presentation

Bailey N T J (1959) *Statistical Methods in Biology*, English Universities Press.

Bishop O N (3rd Edition 1981) *Statistics for Biology*, Longman.

Campbell R C (2nd Edition 1974) *Statistical Methods in Biology*, Cambridge.

Crothers J H (1981) 'On the graphical presentation of quantitative data' *Field Studies*, **5**, 487–511.

Elliott J M (1977) 'Some methods for the statistical analysis of samples of benthic invertebrates' *Freshwater Biological Association Scientific Publication*, No. 25.

Lenon B J and Cleves P G (1983) *Techniques and Fieldwork in Geography*, Bell & Hyman.

Parker R E (2nd Edition 1980) *Introductory Statistics for Biology*, Studies in Biology, No. 43, Edward Arnold.

C Communities

1 Woodland

Aston T J (1978) 'Energy flow in a woodland ecosystem' *Journal of Biological Education*, **12**, 163–178.

Couzens J (1974) *An Introduction to Woodland Ecology*, Oliver and Boyd.

Darlington A (1972) *The World of a Tree*, Faber.

Packham J R and Harding D J L (1982) *Ecology of Woodland Processes*, Edward Arnold.

Prince C T (1970) *Investigations in Woodland Ecology*, Heinemann.

Wells P (1982) 'An ecological energetics field course for sixth forms' *Journal of Biological Education*, **16**, (4), 265–74.

2 Grassland

Ashby M (1961) *Intrdoduction to Plant Ecology*, Macmillan.

Brodie J (1985) Grassland Studies, George Allen & Unwin.

Crothers J H and Lucas A M (1982) 'Putting the biology students out to grass: the Nettlecombe experiment after thirteen years' *Journal of Biological Education*, **16**, 108–14.

Kershaw K A (1974) *Quantitative Plant Ecology*, Edward Arnold.

Moore I (1966) *Grass and Grasslands*, Collins.

Spedding C R W (1971) *Grassland Ecology*, Oxford University Press.

3 Moorland and heathland

Darlington A (1978) *Mountains and Moorlands*, Hodder and Stoughton.

Gimingham C H *Ecology of Heathlands*, Chapman and Hall.

Miles P M and Miles H B (1967) *Chalkland and Moorland Ecology*, Hulton.

Pearsall W H (1950) *Mountains and Moorlands*, New naturalist, Collins.

4 Freshwater

Arnold F and Macan T T (1970) Studies on the fauna of a Shropshire hill stream', *Field Studies*, **3**, 159–184.

Clegg J (4th Edition 1974) *Freshwater Life*, Warne.

Hynes H B N (1971) *The Ecology of Running Waters*, University of Liverpool Press.

Leadley Brown A (1971) *Ecology of Fresh Water*, Heinemann.

Macan T T (1963) *Freshwater Ecology*, Longman.

Macan T T and Worthington E D (1951) *Life in Lakes and Rivers*, New Naturalist, Collins.

Mills D N (1972) *An Introduction to Freshwater Ecology*, Oliver and Boyd.

Townsend C R (1980) *The Ecology of Streams and Rivers*, Studies in Biology, No. 122, Edward Arnold.

5 Sea-shore

Ballantine W J (1962) 'A biologically defined exposure scale for the comparative description of rocky shores' *Field Studies*, Vol 1, No. 3.

Barrett J H (1974) *Life on the Sea Shore*, Collins.

Brafield A E (1978) *Life Sandy Shores*, Studies in Biology, No. 89, Edward Arnold.

Brehaut R N (1982) *Ecology of Rock Shores*, Studies in Biology, No. 139, Edward Arnold.

Eltringham S K (1971) *Life in Mud and Sand*, English University Press.

Jenkins M (1983) *Seashore Studies*, George Allen & Unwin.

Lewis J (1964) *The Ecology of Rocky Shores*, Hodder and Stoughton Educational.

Moyse J and Nelson-Smith A (1973) 'Zonation of animals and plants on rocky shores around Dale', *Field Studies*, Vol 1, No. 5

Newell R C (1978) *Biology of Intertidal Animals*, Marine Ecological Surveys Ltd.

Yonge C M (1949) *The Sea Shore*, New Naturalist, Collins.

6 Sand dune, salt-marsh and estuary

Barnes R S K (1974) *Estuarine biology*, Studies in Biology, No. 49, Edward Arnold.

Dalby D H (1970) 'The salt-marhses of Milford Haven, Pembrokeshire', *Field Studies*, **3**, 297–330.

Evans S M and Hardy J M (1970) *Seashore and Sand Dunes*, Heinemann.

Green J (1968) *The Biology of Estuarine Animals*, Sidgwick & Jackson.

Hepburn I (1952) *Flowers of the Coast*, New Naturalist, Collins

Jenkins M (1986) *Salt-marsh and Estuarine Studies*, George Allen & Unwin.

Ranwell D (1974) *Salt-marsh and Sand Dunes*, Chapman & Hall.

7 Urban ecology

Collins M (1984) *Urban Ecology: A Teacher's Resource Book*, Collins.

Chinery M (1977) *The Natural History of Towns and Gardens*, Collins.

Darlington A (1969) *Ecology of Refuse Tips*, Heinemann.

Darlington A (1981) *Ecology of Walls*, Heinemann.

Gemmell R P (1977) *Colonisation of Industrial Wasteland*, Edward Arnold.

Hawksworth D L and Rose F (1976) *Lichens as Pollution Monitors*, Edward Arnold.

Mabey R (1974) *The Pollution Handbook*, The ACE/Sunday Times Clean Air and Water Surveys, Penguin.

Smith D P (1984) *Urban Ecology*, George Allen & Unwin.

D Keys for identification

1 Flowering plants

Clapham A R, Tutin T G and Warburg E F (1981) *Excursion Flora of the British Isles*, (3rd Edition), Cambridge University Press.

Fitter R, Fitter A and Blamey M (1974) *The Wild Flowers of Britain and Northern Europe*, Collins.

Haslam S, Sinker C A and Wolseley P (1974; 1982) 'British Water Plants' *Field Studies*, **4**, 243–351.

Hayward J (1986) *A New Key to Wild Flowers*, Cambridge University Press.

Hubbard C E (1984) *Grasses* (3rd Edition), Penguin Books.

Keble Martin W (1982) *The New Concise British Flora*, Ebury Press and Michael Joseph.

Mitchell A (1978) *A Field Guide to the Trees of Britain and Northern Europe*, Collins.

Pankhurst R J and Allinson J E (1985) 'British grasses: a punched card key to grasses in the vegetative state' *Occasional Publications of the Field Studies Council*, No. 10.

Phillips R (1977) *Wild Flowers in Britain*, Pan Books.

Phillips R (1980) *Trees in Britain, Europe and North America*, Pan Books.

Phillips R (1980) *Grasses, Ferns, Moses and Lichens of Great Britain and Ireland*, Pan Books.

Rose F (1981) *The Wild Flower Key*, Warne.

Schauer T (1982) *A Field Guide to the Wild Flowers of Britain and Europe*, Collins.

2 Non-flowering plant

Dickinson C I (1963) *British Seaweeds*, Eyre & Spottiswoode.

Ferry B W and Sheard J W (1969) 'Zonation of supra-littoral lichens on rocky shores around the Dale peninsular (with a key for identification)' *Field Studies*, **3** (1), 41–67.

Hiscock S (1979) 'A Field Key to the British Brown Seaweeds (Phaeophyta)' *Field Studies*, **5**, 1–44.

Hiscock S (1986) 'A Field key to the British Red Seaweeds' *Occasional Publications of the Field Studies Council*.

Jahns H M (1983) *Collins Guide to Ferns, Mosses and Lichens*, Collins.

Lange M and Hora F B (1963) *Collins Guide to Mushrooms and Toadstools*, Collins.

Page C N (1982) *The Ferns of Britain and Ireland*, Cambridge University Press.

Phillips R (1980) *Grasses, Ferns and Mosses and Lichens of Great Britain and Ireland*, Pan Books.

Phillips R (1981) *Mushrooms and other Fungi of Great Britain and Europe*, Pan Books.

Sykes J B (1981) 'An illustrated guide to the Diatoms of British Coastal Plankton' *Field Studies*, **5**, 425–468.

Watson E V (1981) *British Mosses and Liverworts* (3rd Edition), Cambridge University Press.

3 Marine invertebrates

Barret J H and Yonge C M (1958) *Collins Pocket Guide to the Seashore*, Collins.

Beedham G E(1972) *Identification of the British Mollusca*, Hulton.

Campbell A C and Nicholls J (1986) *The Hamlyn Guide to the Seashore and Shallow Seas of Britain and Europe*, Hamlyn.

Crothers J and Crothers M (1983) 'A key to the crabs and crab-like animals of British inshore waters' *Field Studies*, **5**, 753–806.

Eales N B (1967) *The Littoral Fauna of the British Isles*, Cambridge Univeristy Press.

Gibson R (1981) *British Nemerteans* Synopsis of the British Fauna (New Series) No 24, published for the Linnean Society of London and the Estuarine and Brackish Water Sciences Association by Cambridge University Press.

Graham A (1971) *British Prosobranchs* Synopses of the British fauna (New Series), No 2, published for the Linnean Society of London by Academic Press.

Ingle R W (1983) *Shallow-water Crabs* Synopses of the British fauna (New Series), No 25, published for the Linnean Society of London and the Estuarine and Brackish Water Sciences Association by Cambridge University Press.

Manuel R L (1981) *British Anthozoa* Synopses of the British fauna (New Series), No 18, published for the Linnean Society of London and the Estuarine and Brackish Water Sciences Association by Cambridge University Press.

Naylor R (1972) *British Marine Isopods* Synopses of the British fauna (New Series), No 10, published for the Linnean Society of London by Academic Press.

Nelson-Smith A and Gee J U (1966) 'Serpulid tubeworms around Dale' *Field Studies*, **2** (3), 331–7.

Newell G E and Newell R C (1973) *Marine Plankton*, Hutchinson.

Rainbow P S (1984) 'An introduction to the biology of British Littoral Barnacles' *Field Studies*, **6**, 1–51.

Smaldon G (1979) *British Coastal Shrimps and Prawns* Synopses of the British Fauna (New Series), No 15, published for the Linnean Society of London and the Estuarine and Brackish Water Sciences Associated by Cambridge University Press.

Tebble N (1966) *British Bivalve Seashells*, British Museum (Natural History).

Thompson T E and Brown G H (1976) *British Opisthobranch Molluscs* Synopses of the British fauna (New Series), No 9, published for the Linnean Society of London by Academic Press.

4 Freshwater invertebrates

Ball I R and Reynoldson T B (1981) *British Planarians* Synopses of the British Fauna (New Series), No. 19, published for the Linnean Society of London and the Estuarine and Brackish Water Sciences Association by Cambridge University Press.

Croft P S (1986) 'A key to the major groups of freshwater invertebrates' *Field Studies*, **6**.

Ellis A E (1978) *British Freshwater Bivalve Mollusca* Synopses of the British Fauna, No 11, published for the Linnean Society of London by Academic Press.

Hammond C O (1985) *The Dragonflies of Great Britain and Ireland*, Harley Books.

Hicken N E (1967) *Caddis Larvae*, Hutchinson.

Macan T T (1959) *A Guide to Freshwater Invertebrate Animals*, Longman.

Mellanby H (1983) *Animal Life in Fresh Water*, (3rd Edition) Methuen.

Quigley M (1977) *Invertebrates of Streams and Rivers, A Key to Identification*, Edward Arnold.

Redfern M (1975) 'Revised field key to the invertebrate fauna of stony hill streams' *Field Studies*, **4**.

Freshwater Biological Association Scientific Publications

No. 5   *A Key to the British Species of Freshwater Cladocera* (3rd Edition 1966) D J Scourfield and J P Harding.

No. 13   *A Key to the British Fresh – and Brackish-Water Gastropods* (4th Edition 1977) T T Macan

No. 16   *A Revised Key to the British Water Bugs (Hemiptera-Heteroptera)* (2nd Edition 1965) T T Macan

No. 17   *A Key to the Adults and Nymphs of the British Stoneflies (Plecoptera)* (3rd Edition 1977) H B N Hynes

No. 18   *A Key to the British Freshwater Cyclopid and Calanoid Copepods* (2nd Edition 18974) J P Harding and W A Smith

No. 20   *A Key to the Nymphs of British Species of Ephemeroptera* (3rd Edition 1979) T T Macan

No. 23   *A Key to the British Species of Freshwater Triclads* (2nd Edition 1978) T B Reynoldson

No. 24   *A Key to the British Species of Simuliidae (Diptera) in the larval, pupal and adult stages* (1968) L Davies

No. 31   *A Key to the larvae, pupae and adults of the British Dixidae (Diptera)* (1975) R H L Disney

No. 32   *A Key to the British Freshwater Crustacea Malacostraca* (1976) T Gledhill, D W Sutcliffe and W D Williams

No. 35   *A Key to the Larvae and Adults of British Freshwater Megaloptera and Neuroptera* (1977) J M Elliott

No. 40   *A Key to the British Freshwater Leeches, with notes on their life cycles and ecology* (1979) J M Elliott and K H Mann

No. 43   *A Key to the Caseless Caddis Larvae of the British Isles, with notes on their ecology* (1981) J M Edington and A G Hildrew

These publications may be obtained direct from The Librarian, Freshwater Biological Association, The Ferry House, Far Sawrey, Ambleside, Cumbria, LA22 OLP.

5 Freshwater fish

Maitland P S (1972) 'A Key to the freshwater fishes of the British Isles' *Freshwater Biological Association Scientific Publications*, No. 27.

Muus B J and Dahlstrom P (1971) *Collins Guide to the Freshwater Fishes of Britain and Europe*, Collins.

6 Land invertebrates

Cameron R A D, Eversham B and Jackson N (1983) 'A field key to the slugs of the British Isles' *Field Studies*, **5**, 807–824.

Chinery M (1972) *A Field Guide to the Insects of Britain and Northern Europe*, Collins.

Cloudsley-Thompson J L and Sankey J (1961) *Land Invertebrates*, Methuen.

Eason E H (1964) *Centipedes of the British Isles*, Warne.

Higgins L G and Riley N D (1970) *A Field Guide to the Butterflies of Britain and Europe*, Collins.

Jones D (1983) *The Country Life Guide to Spiders of Britain and Northern Europe*, Country Life Books.

Joy N H (1932) *A Practical Handbook of British Beetles* (2 vols) reprinted 1976 by E W Classey Ltd.

Kerney M P and Cameron R A D (1979) *A Field Guide to the Land Snails of Britain and North-West Europe*, Collins.

Lewis T and Taylor L R (1967) *Introduction to Experimental Ecology* (keys to insect orders and families), Academic Press.

Linssen E F (1959) *Bettles of the British Isles*, Warne.

Paviour-Smith K and Whittaker J B (1969) *A Key to the Major Groups of British Free-living Terrestrial Invertebrates*, Blackwell.

Reader's Digest Association Ltd (1984) *Field Guide to the Butterflies and other Insects of Britain*, Reader's Digest.

Royal Entomological Society of London *Handbooks for the Identification of British Insects* (available from the Society at 41 Queens Gate, London SW7 5HU)

Sims R W and Gerard B M (1985) *Earthworms* Synopses of the British fauna, No 31, published for the Linnean Society of London by E J Brill.

Southwood T R E and Leston D (1959) *Land and Water Bugs of the British isles*, Warne.

Sutton S L (1972) *Woodlice*, Pergamon Press.

Tilling S M (in prep) 'A key to the major groups of terrestrial invertebrates' *Field Studies*, **6**.

Unwin D M (1981) 'A key to the families of British Diptera' *Field Studies*, **5**, 513–533.

Unwin D M (1984) 'A key to the families of British Coleoptera (and Strepsiptera)' *Field Studies*, **6**, 149–197.

Willmer P (1985) 'Bees, Ants and Wasps, a key to the genera of the British Aculeates *Occasional Publications of the Field Studies Council*, No. 7.

Field Studies Council publications are available from: 'Field Studies', Nettlecombe Court, Williton, Taunton, Somerset TA4 4HT.

Index

Acknowledgements

I would like to acknowledge the help of Jonathan Oldham of the Field Studies Council for providing a number of the photographs and for his project suggestions for moorlands, sand dunes and salt-marshes (Chapter 8); thanks also to David Rees, John Rowan, Peter Rogers, and Nic Paul. I am indebted to the Freshwater Biological Association for permission to use their photographs of freshwater invertebrates (Chapter 5), and to Professor J A Wallwork for supplying the photographs of soil animals (Chapter 4). I would particularly like to thank Dr Ronnie Lawson, John Jones, and Diana Williams for their encouragement during the writing of the text, Julie Morley and Carolyn Warner for typing the manuscript and especially Jonathon Wray of UTP for initiating the project and guiding it through its early stages. Finally, my thanks to Gillian Young, Chris Blake and all the staff involved in the preparation of the typescript for publication at Bell & Hyman.

G M Williams

Both the author and publisher are also grateful to the following individuals and organisations for information and ideas used in the book: Barnaby J Lenon and Paul Cleves, authors of *Techniques and Fieldwork in Geography*, UTP, in particular for Chapter 7; Science Education Software for permission to use the graphs and symbolic sections in Figs 2.9, 2.10 and 6.15 taken from the *Plant Ecology Field Study Techniques* computer program written by Graham Hall; The Field Studies Council; Griffin and George Ltd and Philip Harris Ltd for the photographs and information on equipment; Associated Examining Board, Joint Matriculation Board, Welsh Joint Education Committee and University of London School Examinations Department for permission to reproduce examination questions; Mel Calman for the cartoons, (pp 103, 105, 115, 119, 127) first published in *How to Lie with Statistics*, Huff D, Penguin; Bob Gibbons Photographic Agency; Michael Shoebridge for the line drawings; and Colin Lewis for the cover.

TECHNIQUES
AND FIELDWORK
IN ECOLOGY

GARETH WILLIAMS

Head of Biology,
Poynton County High School,
Cheshire.

Bell & Hyman

For Robin and Lyn

Published by
BELL & HYMAN LIMITED
Denmark House
37/39 Queen Elizabeth Street
LONDON SE1 2QB

British Library Cataloguing in Publication Data

Williams, Gareth M.
    Techniques and fieldwork in ecology.
    1. Ecology—Study and teaching—Field work
    I. Title
    574.5′0723   QH541.2

ISBN 0–7135–2730–7

Typeset by August Filmsetting, Haydock, St. Helens
Printed in Great Britain by
Scotprint Ltd., Musselburgh